SPITBALLERS

SPITBALLERS

The Last Legal Hurlers of the Wet One

Charles F. Faber *and*
Richard B. Faber

McFarland & Company, Inc., Publishers
Jefferson, North Carolina, and London

ALSO BY CHARLES F. FABER AND RICHARD B. FABER
AND FROM MCFARLAND

*The American Presidents
Ranked by Performance* (2000)

ALSO BY CHARLES F. FABER AND FROM MCFARLAND

*Baseball Pioneers:
Ratings of Nineteenth Century Players* (1997)

*Baseball Ratings:
The All-Time Best Players at Each Position* (second edition, 1995)

Frontispiece: According to our rating system,
Red Faber was the greatest of all the grandfathered spitball pitchers
(COURTESY OF NATIONAL BASEBALL HALL OF FAME LIBRARY, COOPERSTOWN)

LIBRARY OF CONGRESS CATALOGUING-IN-PUBLICATION DATA

Faber, Charles F.
Spitballers : the last legal hurlers of the wet one /
Charles F. Faber and Richard B. Faber.
p. cm.
Includes bibliographical references and index.

ISBN 0-7864-2347-1 (softcover : 50# alkaline paper) ∞

1. Baseball players—United States—Biography. 2. Pitching (Baseball)
I. Faber, Richard B., 1932– II. Title.
GV865.A1F29 2006   796.357092'2—dc22   2006003236

British Library cataloguing data are available

©2006 Charles F. Faber and Richard B. Faber. All rights reserved

*No part of this book may be reproduced or transmitted in any form
or by any means, electronic or mechanical, including photocopying
or recording, or by any information storage and retrieval system,
without permission in writing from the publisher.*

On the cover: Burleigh Grimes
(National Baseball Hall of Fame Library, Cooperstown, N.Y.)

Manufactured in the United States of America

*McFarland & Company, Inc., Publishers
Box 611, Jefferson, North Carolina 28640
www.mcfarlandpub.com*

Contents

Acknowledgments vi
Preface 1
Introduction 3

1. Red Faber 17
2. Burleigh Grimes 35
3. Jack Quinn 53
4. Urban Shocker 65
5. Stan Coveleskie 77
6. Bill Doak 90
7. Ray Caldwell 98
8. Clarence Mitchell 111
9. Dutch Leonard 120
10. Ray Fisher 129
11. Dick Rudolph 137
12. Allen Sothoron 145
13. Phil Douglas 151
14. Allan Russell 161
15. Doc Ayers 167
16. Dana Fillingim 174
17. Marvin Goodwin 180

Appendix: Rankings 187
Chapter Notes 193
Bibliography 199
Index 203

Acknowledgments

Writing this book would have been impossible if not for the kind and generous assistance of some very good people. First and foremost, we wish to express our appreciation to the Society for American Baseball Research (SABR), whose online research program made available to us material that we otherwise could not have accessed. Through the organization's newsletter and at its 2004 National Convention in Cincinnati we got in touch with knowledgeable and helpful baseball researchers who willingly contributed their time and talents.

Among persons contributing valuable information, either through interviews or personal correspondence, were Rich Benner, Urban C. Faber II, Tom Hufford, Loma Hurst, John Leidy Jr., Norman Macht, Raymond J. Nemec, John Rice, Steve L. Steinberg, and Evelyn Trinkle. To all we are grateful.

Early drafts of portions of the manuscript were read by Brian E. Cooper, Daniel Faber, John Leidy Jr., James G. Webb, and Zachariah Webb, all of whom made valuable suggestions. Daniel Faber, Laura Kurman, Emma Kurman-Faber, and Jonah Kurman-Faber assisted in selecting photographs to be used in the book.

W.C. Burdick and Bill Francis of the National Baseball Hall of Fame Library in Cooperstown were both exceedingly helpful, Burdick in supplying a large number of photographs from which to choose and Francis by sending clipping files on some of the lesser-known spitball pitchers. We are also grateful to Steve Gietscher of the *Sporting News*, to the librarians and staff members of the Library of Congress and the University of Kentucky Libraries, and especially to the staff of the Interlibrary Loan Department.

Charles F. Faber
Richard B. Faber

Preface

This is a book about 17 baseball players and a pitch they threw called the spitball. They were not the first pitchers to throw the spitter, nor were they the last. They were, however, the last hurlers to throw the pitch legally in the major leagues.

During baseball's Deadball Era (the first two decades of the twentieth century), several major league pitchers included the spitball among the assortment of pitches they used in their efforts to subdue batters. Despite sporadic attempts to ban the pitch, the moist delivery remained legitimate until 1920. In February of that year, the rules committee banned the spitball, effective immediately, with certain exceptions. Each club would be allowed to designate two pitchers currently using the delivery who would be exempt from the rule during the 1920 season only. Before the 1921 season began, the rule was modified to permit the exempted pitchers to use the delivery throughout their careers.

In the Introduction we discuss the pitch, exploring such questions as: What is a spitball? How is it thrown? Why was it so effective? Why was it outlawed in 1920? Were the reasons given for its banning valid? Why was the 1920 rule modified less than a year after its adoption? Who were the exempted pitchers? What is the history of attempts to reinstate the pitch?

The 17 chapters, one for each of the exempted pitchers, contain some biographical information. When appropriate, we provide a discussion of the factors that led him to become a professional ballplayer. There are interesting stories about how some saw pro ball as a way to escape from the drudgery of life in the mines, on the farm, or in the lumber camps. Others drifted into a life in baseball simply because they enjoyed playing the game. Some pitchers have discussed in detail the reasons they included the spitball in their arsenal of pitches, how they threw the pitch, and what moistening agent they found most satisfactory. Others have preferred just to throw the pitch, and not to talk about it. The bulk of each chapter focuses on the pitcher's major league career and his use of the spitball. Although most of our attention is given to key games, we include other incidents that shed light on the game and the particular pitcher's role in it. His greatest accomplishments are summarized and expert assessments of his career are provided. Finally, brief mention is made of his experiences in and out of baseball after his final pitch was thrown from the major league mound.

The chapters are arranged according to the pitcher's rank according to the Faber

System for ranking ballplayers.[1] The system is based on the concept that the fundamental objective of a starting pitcher is to win games for his team. The most effective pitcher is the one who wins frequently and consistently. The more wins the better, but club standings are based on a wins-losses percentage, so the pitcher with the better winning percentage deserves commendation for the consistency of his performance. Winning percentage represents the quality of the performance; total decisions represent the quantity of work done.

One variable remains. It is far more difficult to win for a weak team than for a strong one. As a means of recognizing this fact, the Faber System incorporates into its ratings the Weighted Ratings system devised by Ted C. Oliver.[2] A pitcher's Weighted Rating is determined by the difference in his winning percentage and the team's winning percentage in games wherein the pitcher under consideration is not involved in the decision. Percentages are converted to whole numbers by multiplying by 1,000. The difference is multiplied by the number of decisions charged to the pitcher in question. Quality of work is represented by the difference between the two percentages, and quantity by the number of decisions. Noted baseball researcher Bill James uses an identical method to compute what he calls a pitcher's Above Team statistic, except he does not multiply by 1,000.[3] Thus a Weighted Rating of 8700, for example, would be 8.7 Above Team wins in the other system. We use the Weighted Ratings simply because Oliver's work predates that of James.

The Faber System uses Weighted Ratings along with wins and winning percentage as the measure of a pitcher's performance. The formula is: $R = W + 100p/2 + WR/200$, where R is the Faber System Rating, W is wins, p is winning percentage, and WR is Weighted Rating. One modification in the formula is used. If a pitcher is involved in fewer than 15 decisions, his points for winning percentage are adjusted by applying a multiplier (the percentage his total decisions are of 15). This is to avoid the obvious unfairness of awarding 50 points for a percentage of 1.000 based on one win and no losses, for example.

The Appendix provides additional statistical data on each pitcher's major league career, both year by year and by lifetime totals beyond that which is included in the chapters. We rank the 17 exempted spitballers in relation to the hurlers who were their contemporaries and provide other interesting facts.

Introduction

A spitball is a pitch in which some portion of the baseball has been dampened to make the ball behave in an unorthodox manner when delivered to the batter. The most common wetting agent used is saliva, hence the name spitball.

According to Bill Doak, one of the foremost practitioners of the art, his spitter was thrown with a reverse action from the fastball. He applied a liberal amount of saliva to an area about the size of a half-dollar. Gripping the dry part of the ball tightly with the thumb and outside finger, he threw the ball with exactly the same motion as he threw a fastball. However, because of the wet surface, the ball left the two middle fingers last, giving the ball a reverse spin and causing it to break downward. Whereas the normal fastball spins toward the thrower, the spitball spins away from the hurler. "The spitter," said Doak, "must sink or it's no good. You control the direction of the drop by tilting the top fingers slightly to the left or right. If they remain directly on top when you let the ball go, it will break straight down.... Throwing it with a rigid wrist is absolutely essential. That is why curveball pitchers with long supple wrists never had much success with it"[1]

Not everyone agreed with Doak's description of the spitter's action. For example, Colin Campbell of the *Atlanta Constitution* claimed that the lubricant on the ball allowed the pitcher to release it in such as way that it did not rotate at all.[2] One sportswriter explained the tendency of the spitball to sink by stating its break results from the inequality of air friction on the slippery moistened and rougher unmoistened segments of the ball.[3] The one thing upon which almost everyone did agree was that the spitter tended to fall off the table when it reached the plate, causing batters to top the ball, thus leading to more grounders and fewer fly balls. Fewer fly balls mean fewer home runs. We shall say more about that later.

Pitchers, like other humans, do not have an unlimited supply of saliva with which to doctor the ball. Most of them resorted to chewing some substance to generate the required amount of moisture. For most, the substance of choice was slippery elm, a mucilaginous demulcent, made from the fragrant inner bark of the North American or red elm tree. The bark had been used for centuries by Native Americans and early white settlers of America as a home health remedy to treat coughs and sore throats or to apply externally to relieve burns and rashes. By the late nineteenth century, lozenges made from the bark were widely available in drugstores throughout the country. Red Faber thought slippery elm produced too much saliva and made the ball hard to control. So he used tobacco, but he chewed only when on the field.

Although some pitchers may have given the spitter a trial run in the 1800s, it was not until after 1900 that the spitball became popular. As David Hinckley wrote: "By the turn of the century, pitchers were experimenting with anything that might make a baseball behave differently on its flight to the plate. They found that applying a slippery substance or nicking a ball's surface would change their grip, their release and the ball's behavior. Furthermore, though most pitchers did not doctor the ball, the fact that some of them did made it a psychological weapon for all."[4]

The only two American League hurlers to ever win 40 games in a single season — Jack Chesbro of the New York Highlanders in 1904 and Ed Walsh of the Chicago White Sox in 1908 — were spitballers. Walsh, especially, became famous for the devastating saliva-aided drop pitch with which he retired batters.

For most of the Deadball Era the spitball had thrived without much dispute. From time to time someone would call for its abolition on the grounds that it was unsanitary or that it was making hitting more difficult, but such agitation never got very far with major league rule makers until Babe Ruth's home run exploits changed the nature of the game. Even before Ruth's heyday, however, there was some concern that hitting needed to be enhanced. In 1918, I.E. Sanborn wrote: "Practically all the changes that have been advocated recently in any part of the country have had for their purpose an increase in batting so as to multiply the uncertainties of the game."[5]

Sanborn attributed the action of the American Association in banning the spitball in the spring of 1918 to such a concern. He thought that outlawing the spitter would not achieve the desired result and suggested several other means of increasing hitting.

In the major leagues, Clark Griffith, owner and manager of the Washington Nationals, led the charge for the ban, which was adopted by the joint rules committee of the major leagues on February 9, 1920. The day before the rules committee met, an informal session was held in Chicago, wherein the fate of the spitter and other so-called "freak" deliveries was the sole topic of discussion. Attending the meeting were the four members of the rules committee — Griffith, Bill Veeck of the Chicago Cubs, Barney Dreyfuss of the Pittsburgh Pirates, and Connie Mack of the Philadelphia Athletics — league presidents John Heydler and Ban Johnson, club presidents from three major league clubs, umpires Hank O'Day and Bill Klem, manager Tris Speaker of the Cleveland Indians, and a few baseball writers and others associated with the game.

As adopted, the rule banned not only the spitball, but also other pitches in disfavor. "At no time during the progress of the game shall the pitcher be allowed to apply a foreign substance of any kind to the ball; expectorate either on the ball or his glove; to rub the ball on his glove, person or clothing; or deface the ball in any manner or to deliver what is called the shine ball, spitball, mud ball, or emery ball. For a violation of this rule the pitcher shall be ordered from the game and be barred from participation in any championship contest for ten days."

Although the spitter was lumped with the shine ball, the mud ball, and the emery ball as a freak delivery, the rule makers recognized that it was not quite as "bad" as the others. For the spitball, and for it alone, a period of grace was given. This provision allowed veteran pitchers who had been using the wet delivery a chance to wean it from their systems, while learning to use a legitimate method.

The American League announced that each club was allowed to designate for the 1920 season two pitchers who had been using the delivery in the past and exempt them from the new rule. In the National League, the St. Louis club objected to this limitation and the senior circuit decided that all clubs would be allowed to play every spitball pitcher then on their roster during the 1920 season. Thereafter all use of the spitter was to be banned in both leagues.

Ten American League pitchers and 12 senior circuit twirlers were put on the exempt list for 1920, as follows:

American League

Boston — Allan Russell
Chicago — Eddie Cicotte and Red Faber
Cleveland — Ray Caldwell and Stan Coveleskie
Detroit — Doc Ayers and Dutch Leonard
New York — Jack Quinn
Philadelphia — none
St. Louis — Bert Gallia and Urban Shocker
Washington — none

National League

Boston — Dana Fillingim and Dick Rudolph
Brooklyn — Burleigh Grimes and Clarence Mitchell
Chicago — Claude Hendrix
Cincinnati — Ray Fisher
New York — Phil Douglas
Philadelphia — Brad Hogg and Roy Sanders
Pittsburgh — none
St. Louis — Bill Doak, Marvin Goodwin, and Oscar Tuero

Several spitballers did not make the list. Young Bill Sherdel of the Cardinals said he could win without using the spitter and went on to prove it with a successful major league career. Hal Carlson of the Pirates also survived without the spitter. He had no choice in the matter. Owner Barney Dreyfuss was opposed to the moist delivery on principle and refused to certify any of his hurlers as spitballers. Clark Griffith and Connie Mack were other executives who refused to put any of their pitchers on the list. According to Steve Steinberg, Lee "Spec" Meadows had used the spitball in his early years but was not listed.[6] John Thorn identified Rosy Ryan as another pitcher in this category.[7] Others who occasionally used the spitter, but were not exempted, may have included Ray Keating and Fred Toney.

Why was the spitball banned? Several possible explanations were offered:

1. It is unsanitary.
2. It is hard to control.
3. It is dangerous.
4. It is difficult to field.
5. It is hard on the pitcher's arm.
6. It depresses hitting.

Were these legitimate concerns?

Is the spitter unsanitary? Probably. One prominent person who thought so was John K. Tener, president of the National League, who said, "The spitball is a disgusting, unsanitary delivery not likely to endure more than a few more seasons at most."[8] An article in *Baseball Magazine* admitted that there was sense behind the criticism that the spitball is unsanitary. The article averred that the spitball certainly is not nice from an aesthetic standpoint. However, the piece pointed out that there are a number of crude, unrefined details about professional baseball.[9] However, there is little evidence that more than a few baseball players of the early 1900s were much concerned about sanitation. Many players of that era chewed tobacco and spat indiscriminately on the ground or in the dugout. Improving sanitary conditions on the playing field did not appear to be a major concern of players, owners, or fans. It is unlikely that the pitch was banned for sanitary or esthetic reasons.

Is the spitter difficult to control? Not if thrown by an expert practitioner. During the decade of the 1920s, American League hurlers pitched 109,899 innings and gave up 40,220 walks for an average of 3.29 walks per nine innings. In the same years, National League pitchers yielded 34,242 bases on balls in 110,099 innings, an average of 2.80 walks per nine innings. The walks per nine innings ratios of the top spitball pitchers of the era were as follows: in the American League, Red Faber 2.97, Stan Coveleskie 2.34, Urban Shocker 2.20, and Jack Quinn 1.97. The National League's top twirlers had ratios of 2.79 and 2.75 by Burleigh Grimes and Bill Doak, respectively. It will be noted that all six pitchers had better control than the average hurler in their league. To top them all, Ed Walsh in his great 40-wins season of 1908 walked only 56 men in 66 games. He gave up 56 free passes in 464 innings, an average of 1.28 every nine innings.

Is the spitter dangerous? After the event, some writers tried to link the abolition of the spitball to the death of Ray Chapman. For example, one columnist wrote: "Agitation for the ban on the spitball was generated by the attack on all trick deliveries after the unfortunate death of Ray Chapman, Cleveland shortstop, who was beaned by a submarine ball delivered by Carl Mays, of the Yankees."[10] Such a statement was based on sloppy reporting. It would take very little research to discover that the spitball was banned on February 9, 1920, while Chapman was beaned on August 16, 1920, more than six months later. In fact, the pitch that felled Chapman was a fastball, not a spitball. In the days before the adoption of the batting helmet, there is no doubt that the brushback pitch was dangerous. One spitballer, Burleigh Grimes, was a fierce competitor with a reputation for brushing back hitters. He kept the batsmen from crowding the plate by throwing his high hard one up and in. Despite his reputation, he did not hit an inordinate number of batters—a total of 101 in 19 years. On the other hand, Walter Johnson, the best fastball pitcher of the day, was highly regarded as a gentleman who said he would never deliberately throw at a batter. In his career he plunked 205 batsmen, more than twice as many as Grimes. This refutes the argument about spitballs being dangerous to hitters. Besides this, the spitball was a drop pitch. If it did hit a batter it would likely be on the shin or the ankle, not in the head.

Is the spitter hard to field? The argument was that the wet spot on the ball would make it difficult for fielders to handle and would result in middle infielders making wild throws to first base as the ball soared in an unexpected direction. That contention has some validity. The ball has a wet spot on it when it is delivered by the pitcher. If it is still wet after being hit to an infielder, a wild throw could result. More often, if the batter succeeds in getting a piece of it, the ball rolls or bounces through the dirt and grass to the infielder. By the time the fielder picks it up and makes his throw the wet spot is long gone.

Is the spitter hard on the pitcher's arm? Concern was raised by the fact that the two foremost spitballers of the early part of the century — Jack Chesbro and Ed Walsh — had relatively short careers. Umpire Billy Evans was among those expressing such solicitude. He claimed that he had seen the major league careers of many pitchers end because of the strain throwing the spitball put upon their arms. In 1914 he wrote: "The history of the spitball is that it has ruined many an arm of steel.... Most pitchers when going along successfully through the use of the spitball delivery were blind to the injury it was steadily working on their pitching arm. I know of only one pitcher who got his chance to make good because of a deceptive spitball and yet he had entirely abandoned that style of delivery. The player I refer to is Ray Fisher, a valued member of the pitching staff of the New York team of the American League. At the beginning of his career, Fisher used the spitball almost exclusively, only mixing in a fast one now and then. He was a mighty hard man to beat, because he boasted of a spitter that had a very good break, and his control of it was such that he could keep it at the knee almost constantly. It is a well-known fact that the spitball is not hard to hit when broken high. Only when the ball is kept below the knee are the best results obtained."[11] Evidently Evans thought the strain of keeping the ball low would shorten the pitcher's career.

Even a practitioner of the art, the above-mentioned Ray Fisher, endorsed this view. In a speech to the YMCA Training College, Fisher offered his opinion that the spitball would eventually ruin a pitcher's arm.[12] Of course, Fisher soon changed his mind. He was again (or still) throwing the spitter in 1920.

Although it was widely believed in 1919, the theory that throwing the spitter would shorten a pitcher's career was put to rest by the 1930s. Jack Quinn was nearly 50 when his major league career ended; Red Faber was 45; Burleigh Grimes was 41. Surely the spitter had not hurt their careers. Faber is quoted as saying: "It's because I'm a spitball pitcher that I am able to keep on going. The spitter is the easiest delivery there is upon the arm. If it were not so, how do you account for the success of Jack Quinn.... Ed Walsh did not have to quit because of the spitter. It was overwork that turned the trick."[13]

Faber may have been right about Walsh being overworked. From 1907 through 1912, Big Ed led the major leagues in innings pitched four times. The 464 innings he worked in 1908 are the most posted by any major league hurler since 1893. The other early spitball pitcher with a relatively short career, Jack Chesbro, ranks second in that category with 454 ⅔ stanzas racked up in 1904.

Does the spitter depress hitting? Yes. At long last we come to the real reason the pitch was banned. It was difficult to hit a home run off a spitter. The ball tends to dive as it reaches home plate, and the batter is likely to top it, hitting an infield grounder. By 1920 the fans were enthralled by the home run hitting of Babe Ruth. The owners and other powers-that-be in baseball wanted to see more home runs, thus enticing more paying customers into the ball parks. At the same meeting at which the spitball was banned, other rule changes were proposed to increase the number of home runs. The rule makers proposed a penalty that would virtually eliminate the intentional walk from the game. There was no play in baseball that was more unpopular with the fans than the opposing pitcher intentionally passing a batsman like Ruth. The proposed rule provided that if the catcher got out of his position behind the plate to aid the pitcher in giving an intentional base on balls, the runners on base would all be entitled to an extra base. Another change provided that whenever a ball was hit into the stands in fair territory, but went foul after entering the stands, it counted as a home run. Again a beneficiary of the rule was Ruth, who had repeatedly hit drives into the stands which had gone foul after going over the wall. These rules all had the same purpose — to increase the revenue of club owners by bringing more fans to the parks. President Veeck of the Cubs offered another suggestion to increase hitting. His proposal would have abolished the out by foul fly rule, meaning that foul flies would not result in outs whether caught or not. This proposal proved to be too radical for the other rule makers to adopt, but it would have been a great boon to the sluggers.

In actual practice, did banning the spitball actually increase hitting? As banning the spitball coincided with the end of the Deadball Era, hitting would have increased during the 1920s even had all pitchers been allowed to use the spitter. After 1919, the 17 exempted spitballers gave up almost as many hits per nine innings as did their dry counterparts. However, there was a marked difference in the number of earned runs allowed. The grandfathers had an earned run average of 3.63 compared to an ERA of 4.13 by all other major league pitchers from 1920 through 1934.[14] By 1922, it was obvious that batters needed no more help in multiplying the number and distance of safe hits. Slugging had increased to an extent the rule makers never foresaw, but this was due to a combination of factors, not merely to restricting use of the spitball.

Another factor involved in outlawing the spitter was guilt by association. For several years, some pitchers had been trying to gain an advantage by doctoring the ball. First came the emery ball, made possible by roughening the ball with emery paper. Then some pitchers forced a base of paraffin or oil between the seams of the ball, thereby weighting it at a certain spot, enabling the pitcher to get an unusual break. Some pitchers cut the cover of the ball in such a way that would escape detection unless carefully examined, yet by rubbing the ball opposite the cuts, it was possible to make the ball do tricks. These so-called freak deliveries caused hitting to suffer. Some of them may have been guilty of the charges made against the spitball, i.e., that it is dangerous, hard to control, and difficult to field. Although the spitball was innocent of those charges, the rule makers did not differentiate saliva from other "foreign substances." The solution the moguls saw was to eliminate all trick deliveries, including the spitball.

Linking the spitter with the other freak pitches gave it an unsavory reputation. In the minds of some, spitball pitchers were uncouth villains. Babe Ruth's response to this charge was: "What does it matter if a guy wets the ball? Gosh, Red Faber is the nicest man in the world."[15]

Faber defended the spitter against some of the charges made against it. In a 1922 interview he stated: "They say the spitter is bad for a pitcher's arm. This is not true. I can prove it by my own experience. I never used a spitter in my life until I was obliged to by a kind of necessity because I had nearly ruined my arm by throwing curves. That was when I was in the minor leagues, and I can remember how sore my arm was from curve ball pitching. The spit ball may be a little harder on a pitcher's arm than throwing a straight, fast ball. But certainly it is not half as bad as throwing a curve. The curve causes a continual grind at the elbow and in many cases permanently shortens a pitcher's arm…. A spitter has to be thrown moderately fast and the ball slips away from under the two front fingers of the pitching hand and sails up to the batter rotating very slowly. Then it breaks down and to one side. What is there unnatural about that or hard on the arm? I have been using a spit ball for some years and I have never been able to discover."[16]

He went on to explain how he threw the spitball: "I never wet the ball but merely the ends of the first two fingers of my right hand. The whole theory of the spitball is to let the ball slide away from a smooth surface. Wetting the fingers gives this smooth surface."

As to the charge that the spitball depresses fielding, Faber said: "By the time the ball has traveled through the air, met the bat, and been driven to some infielder it is perfectly dry. No infielder needs to make an error on such a ball."[17]

A cursory review of a few newspapers from the 1920 season uncovered no stories about illegal use of the spitball, but at least one pitcher was ejected for suspected application of a foreign substance to the ball. In a game at the Polo Grounds on June 11, Slim Sallee of the Cincinnati Reds began jamming his left hand into his hip pocket before every pitch. The umpire suspected him of tampering with the ball. After Sallee ignored the umpire's warning to stop doing it, he was ejected from the game.

Before the beginning of the 1920 season, a sportswriter for the *Washington Post* predicted that the spitball pitchers were likely to have a successful season that year. He opined that with the outlawing of the shine ball, the spitballers would have a better ball to moisten. The scribe averred that it was harder to fix the spitter when the ball has been shined than when the saliva is applied to the ordinary surface. Because of the shine ball, some of the better spitball pitchers had been having a harder time than usual in winning consistently, he asserted. Now the spitballers would have the added advantage of being allowed to use the only freak delivery in the game. This, coupled with the fact that they would have a better surface on the ball for the application of saliva, ought to enable them to get better results.[18]

As it turned out, during the 1920 season several of the exempted pitchers had highly successful seasons. Burleigh Grimes, Bill Doak, Stan Coveleskie, Red Faber, and

Urban Shocker all won 20 or more games, while Jack Quinn notched 18 victories and Shufflin' Phil Douglas contributed 14 wins. However, a few of the players on the list of recognized spitball pitchers were marginal players, soon to be gone from the major leagues.

On behalf of the recognized spitball pitchers in the National League, Bill Doak submitted a request to the league that the pitchers be allowed to continue use of the delivery throughout their careers. An intelligent and articulate young man, Doak had spearheaded a season-long campaign to get the rule modified. The effort got under way during spring training and was carried on in a quiet but effective manner all summer. Spitball pitchers got together whenever two teams met and word was passed along that the pitchers should discuss frequently with their club owners the idea of having the rule changed so that all pitchers now in the game could remain until their effectiveness was gone.

One of the more eloquent pleas was one made by Burleigh Grimes, who claimed that it took him 10 to 15 years to develop a big league caliber spitter. "Had I been able to master a curve ball, I never would have worked so hard on the moist fling," he said.[19]

Grimes claimed to have spoken to all of the spitballers pitching in the National League and learned that each one of them said he did not have an effective curve ball in his repertoire. He maintained that a twirler who has depended for any length of time solely on his spitter and fastball cannot get by on the fastball alone. He asserted that the muscles in a pitcher's arm develop in the way the arm is used. According to Grimes, for a fully mature adult to change from the customary delivery is physiologically impossible.[20]

Grimes concluded his plea by saying: "If all spitball pitchers, including myself, are called upon to discard the moist ball next spring, I am sure that in the spring of 1923 there will be a large number of ex-major league pitchers pounding the pavements in seeking an honest living. When a man has given his whole life to developing himself in a particular baseball specialty it is impossible for him to give that specialty up in his prime and yet retain his effectiveness and his drawing power. Nor is it fair to expect such a change."[21]

When asked how many pitchers who used the spitball in 1920 could get along without it, umpire Billy Evans said he doubted if one-third of them would be able to get by with any degree of success without the moist delivery in their arsenals.[22]

Regardless of the accuracy of the assertions by Grimes, many baseball people came to consider it unjust for pitchers who had specialized for years in a certain delivery to be compelled to give up the particular style at which they were most effective. The argument was that while it may be all right to make rules against an objectionable delivery, the rules should become effective at a time when they did not work an injustice to the pitchers currently using the pitch. According to *Baseball Magazine,* even the bitterest enemies of the spitter sympathized with the just protest of these pitchers and joined in the demand that they be allowed to continue the use of their favorite delivery. [23]

Although Doak, Grimes, and other pitchers cast their arguments in terms of fairness to the pitchers who depended on the pitch to earn their livelihood, an additional factor influenced the owners. Gradually, a majority of the moguls became convinced that it was in their own best interests to keep their star pitchers eligible to better compete in the pennant races. After all, the league champions in 1920 each had two spitballers, including stars such as Burleigh Grimes, who won 22 games for the Brooklyn Robins, and Stan Coveleskie, who racked up 24 victories for the Cleveland Indians.

The *Sporting News* summed up this view in these words:

> The total abandonment of all spitball hurling might mean the complete loss of several high-class stars, men who could not change their pitching styles as they change their coats. In other words, if the one-year clause continues former hurlers like Coveleskie of the Indians and Shocker of the Browns and other stars will be completely ruined and cannot be replaced by any talent in sight, managers believe. Teams would thus be weakened and pennant races impaired.... Coveleskie, the greatest pitcher in baseball last season, used the spitter almost entirely instead of just bluffing with it most of the time. Deprived of this asset, the Indians would not have won the world's title and perhaps not the league pennant.[24]

Of course, not everyone agreed that that the one-year clause should be modified. Another writer in the *Sporting News* opined that: "The decision to grant a further lease on life to the spitter is based on selfish interest only and absolutely. The magnates admit that use of the delivery is undesirable.... The ban on spitballers is to be mollified by the selfish attitude of magistrates and managers who happen to have spitball artists on their clubs who can win with the slobbery shoots and fancy they cannot without it. So be it, but if we must endure the spitball a spell longer, then why not permit a little cheating along other lines."[25] That judgment seems overly harsh. Use of the spitball by pitchers legally entitled to use it was not cheating.

On October 26, 1920, six of the eight National League clubs voted to recommend to the new Advisory Board that the exempt pitchers be allowed to use the spitball for the remainder of their careers. Neither of the two clubs opposed to the move — Chicago and Pittsburgh — had a pitcher they wished to put on the exempt list. The American League went along with the idea, and the new rule was adopted by both leagues early in the spring of 1921.

Six pitchers who had been exempted for the 1920 season were not on the list of those permanently exempted. Eddie Cicotte, who had been permitted to use his spitter even though his more famous shine ball was outlawed, was barred from baseball because of his part in the Black Sox scandal. Claude Hendrix of the Chicago Cubs, one of the game's premier pitchers, was accused of betting against his own team and was released by the Cubs, ending his major league career. Gallia, Hogg, Sanders, and Tuero were out of the majors by the end of the 1920 season.

Brad Hogg was the first pitcher to retire from baseball as a result of the ban on the spitball. Asserting that abolition of the pitch after the season's end would leave him only one more year of effectiveness, he announced his retirement in February 1920. Hogg was a successful lawyer in his home state of Georgia and did not wish to sacrifice a part of his law practice to rejoin the Phillies for just one more year. He felt he would be wasting time to return to Philadelphia as he would be out of baseball after the 1920 season anyway.[26]

One pitcher was added to the exempt list. Allen Sothoron of the St. Louis Browns had been excluded in 1920 because of the American League's restriction of only two exemptions per club, but he became one of the 17 pitchers covered by the grandfather clause.[27]

The eight National League grandfathers were as follows:

> Bill Doak — St. Louis Cardinals
> Phil Douglas — New York Giants
> Dana Fillingim — Boston Braves
> Ray Fisher — Cincinnati Reds
> Marv Goodwin — St. Louis Cardinals
> Burleigh Grimes — Brooklyn Robins
> Clarence Mitchell — Brooklyn Robins
> Dick Rudolph — Boston Braves

American League owners went their senior circuit counterparts one up by certifying nine spitballers to the exempt list:

> Doc Ayers — Detroit Tigers
> Ray Caldwell — Cleveland Indians
> Stan Coveleskie — Cleveland Indians
> Red Faber — Chicago White Sox
> Dutch Leonard — Detroit Tigers
> Jack Quinn — New York Yankees
> Allan Russell — Boston Red Sox
> Urban Shocker — St. Louis Browns
> Allen Sothoron — St. Louis Browns

The rule specified that to be eligible the pitcher had to be on a major league roster during the 1920 season. No new players could be added to the list. This rule may have prevented one of the best pitchers of the 1920s from achieving major league stardom. As a 19-year-old rookie, Frank Shellenback had won nine games for the Chicago White Sox in 1918. The next year, Red Faber was back from the navy and Lefty Williams back from the shipyards, so Shellenback was sent down to the minors. He was not on the club roster in 1920; therefore he was ineligible to be grandfathered. The Pacific Coast League put Shellenback on their exempt list, and he went on to become one of the most successful pitchers in the history of that league, winning 295 games while losing 178 in 20 seasons, a .624 winning percentage.

Shirley Povich wrote about Shellenback in his *Washington Post* column of August 8, 1931:

> The best pitcher in the minors is languishing on the Pacific Coast.... Not a single recommendation for his purchase has reached the front office of the big league ball parks. Does this column hear somebody ask why? Echo answers that Shellenback (horrors!) is a spitball pitcher."[28]

Evidently, Shellenback was unable to convince scouts that he could win without using the banned pitch. Apparently some pitchers could make the adjustment, and some could not.

Rob Neyer listed the 10 best spitballers of all time. Shellenback was on the list, as were five grandfathers (Coveleskie, Faber, Quinn, Grimes, and Douglas), three old-timers (Walsh, Chesbro, and Jeff Tesreau), and one more recent pitcher who allegedly threw the pitch illegally (Gaylord Perry.)[29]

How successful were the exempted spitballers in 1921, the first year in which the new rule was in effect? *Baseball Magazine* maintained that

> this clan, though small in numbers, is still great out of all proportion to its membership.... Doak was last year, not only the leading pitcher on the fighting Cardinal Club, but he had positively the best record of any pitcher in the National League. Burleigh Grimes all last season was the backbone of the Brooklyn defense and one of the most effective, all-around slab performers in a baseball uniform. We could hardly call Douglas McGraw's ace, but he was a tremendously effective pitcher as his World's Series record amply proves. Urban Shocker was and is the foundation of the Browns' pitching staff and the corner stone of the Browns' pennant hopes. Coveleskie may be slipping but he has been for several years the leading pitcher on the powerful Cleveland Club. The other pitchers on the list are all at least average, if not better than average in quality.
>
> While Urban Faber was undoubtedly the pitching sensation of 1921 last season Faber was with a club that competed all year with the Athletics for a place in the cellar. Had it not been for Faber's good right arm, the White Sox might well have finished last. Everyone knows what a handicap to a pitcher is a losing club, and yet last season with the White Sox, Faber won more games than any other pitcher in baseball with two exceptions and these exceptions were Carl Mays, with the pennant-winning Yankees behind him and Urban Shocker of the powerful Brown machine. Furthermore, Faber's average in earned runs was the best in either league.[30]

How did other major league pitchers of the 1920s and early 1930s feel about the exempted spitballers being allowed to use a pitch that was banned for all others? Did they think that the grandfather clause gave an unfair advantage to a favored few? In response to a question by Eugene Murdock, Hall of Fame pitcher Waite Hoyt made the following comments: "I didn't think about it and neither did anybody else. If you're writing about it, make a point of that. We didn't think much about the fact that some could continue throwing it while others could never use it. We didn't think about that at all. We didn't think the spitball was any more effective than the curve. It wasn't that effective. Mainly, the spitball pitchers were effective, but there were a lot of spitball pitchers who weren't effective too. We didn't think the spitball was very unusual. We thought our stuff was as good as that."[31]

The last legal spitball pitch in the major leagues was thrown by Burleigh Grimes in 1934. The next edition of the Spalding *Guide* celebrated the demise of what it called the only menace baseball ever had to the general health of its participants. "While no question has been raised as to effectiveness of this style of delivery, there is serious doubt whether it does not carry with it all elements of wild pitch in practically every delivery of ball to a bat. Pitcher may have ever so good control, but there will come dangerous slip which may incapacitate batsman. There is no doubt as to its unsanitary features, which make it almost repulsive. There might be traced to its use the carrying of disease, which is quite enough to condemn it, if there were no other objections to anointing ball freely with secretions of mouth."[32]

Over the years there have been a few attempts to reinstate the spitter. On December 12, 1950, a proposal to legalize the pitch was defeated by a vote of 7 to 1. In 1957, the highly respected columnist Red Smith proposed reinstatement of the spitter. He wrote: "When the pitcher is being subjected to cruel and unusual punishment, the rules ought to be changed to permit him to retaliate against the batter, i.e., to spit in his eye. The suggestion is put forward in all seriousness. If, as some believe, emphasis on hitting has knocked the game out of joint, the rule makers could take a long step toward restoring balance between offense and defense by returning the spitball to respectability."[33] Smith pointed out that misconceptions had grown up in the popular mind about the spitball, partly because of unpleasant associations with the word "spit." Smith continued: "The spitter would do more than arm the pitcher with a weapon which he needs. There is at least some ground for a belief that it would mitigate the plague of sore arms which is an occupational hazard blighting many young lives."[34] Smith's suggestion led to no immediate action.

Another attempt to reinstate the spitter was made in 1961. In October, Ed Short, general manager of the White Sox, wrote a letter to Joe Gallagher, chairman of the Official Playing Rules Committee, in which he petitioned the rules committee to legalize the delivery and to take other appropriate action that would "eliminate the accusation and suspicion leveled on a number of pitchers in recent years.[35]

Short's proposal received support from some powerful baseball figures, among them American League president Joe Cronin, Commissioner Ford C. Frick, and the celebrated baseball executive Branch Rickey.

Cronin told the Associated Press that some pitchers could add three to five years to their careers if allowed to use the pitch. He noted that most spitballers had long careers. "A spitball is not a dangerous pitch and not harmful to the arm," he said. "Burleigh Grimes and Red Faber pitched after they passed 40. When Jack Quinn retired he was 48."[36] Rickey stated that the spitter baffles the hitters at the plate. He maintained that it is easy on the arm and the intelligence. "I could teach any strong-armed young man how to master it in a week," he claimed.[37]

Opposition to the proposal was led by Warren Giles, president of the National League. He claimed, "A look at the records will show that the pitchers of today are not the much maligned individuals they are painted all too often.... It's true that more home runs are being hit today than were hit a few decades ago, but what's so terrible about that? The home run is the most exciting play in baseball, comparable to the long touchdown play in football or the field goal from far out in basketball. It is my firm belief that the long ball, particularly the home run, is what the fans want to see."[38]

Giles's opposition to the spitball was forthright. In his view fans wanted to see home runs, and use of the spitball decreased the number of home runs, thus diminishing attendance. However, some of the opposition to revoking the ban was based on a lack of understanding. For example, Ralph Houk, manager of the New York Yankees, said: "The spitter would increase wildness, fights between batters and pitchers, and the beanball dangers to the hitters."[39] None of these charges had been borne out by previous experience.

On November 26, 1961, the Rules Committee met and voted the proposed reinstatement down by a margin of 8 to 1. In announcing the decision Gallagher said,

"There was very little sentiment for any change."⁴⁰ He did not believe the pitchers needed any help and thought the return of the spitter might swing the balance to the defense. He also said that the committee feared that legalizing the damp pitch might get some pitchers, especially good young hurlers "all fouled up" Experimentation with the spitter might spoil some pitchers. "Cheating by throwing an occasional illegal spitter is not as great a problem as some people think," he asserted. "The umpires report they get complaints on only about two pitchers in each league."⁴¹

The rules provide that an umpire shall immediately eject any hurler who uses an illegal pitch and that the pitcher shall be suspended for 10 days. Apparently there has been great laxity in enforcing this rule. A writer in the *Sporting News* reported that he believed the last major leaguer to draw this penalty was Nelson Potter of the old St. Louis Browns in 1944.⁴²

The only committee member to vote in favor of the change was Cal Hubbard, supervisor of American League umpires. He said he believed the pitchers could use some help, that they had been complaining that all the legislation in recent years favored the batters. He said, "I don't know if the spitter would aid the pitchers much physically, but they'd have the advantage of a psychological weapon."⁴³ Although he doubted that many pitchers could successfully master the damp pitch, Hubbard stated that one of his main reasons for favoring the return of the spitter was to bring an end to the suspicions and accusations that it was being used surreptitiously.

In reporting on the failed proposal, Arthur Daley wrote: "The ridiculous outbreak in home run hitting is destructive of baseball's finely attuned checks and balances. The newest pitch to be invented, the slider, hasn't slowed down the distance pace the slightest bit. But the spitter could. Batters would have to give it the respect it deserves and therefore swing with more caution, less power. The spitball is an excellent pitch. Too bad it lost its bid for a pardon."⁴⁴ Since Daley wrote his article, the home run binge has accelerated. Yet we hear few cries for reauthorization of the spitball. Accusations that certain pitchers throw the spitball and other illegal deliveries continue to be made, but the rule makers pay them little heed.

How many of today's fans share the views of Naiph J. Daher? When there were only three spitballers left in the major leagues (Red Faber, Burleigh Grimes, and Clarence Mitchell), Daher penned this eulogy to the moist delivery: "When the last of the spitball trio has hung up his glove, braced his shoulders to hide the grief that will permeate his soul upon leaving the hurling mound and turn his back upon the major league firing line, the fans of baseball will then know a great void has been created in their most loved of sports."⁴⁵

1

Red Faber

The Chicago White Sox were underdogs in the 1917 World's Series. Regarded as one of the better teams to come out of the senior circuit in several years, John McGraw's New York Giants were still favored to win game six, even though they had lost three of the first five games and were facing the pitcher who had twice defeated them. It was a delightful day for a game, warm and bright with sunshine. The Polo Grounds were packed as the largest crowd of the series jammed the grandstand and filled up the bleachers. The home team fell behind 3–2. McGraw's men attempted to rally, but they were stymied by a pitcher who stood up under fire and emerged as the hero of the series. As one sportswriter put it,

> Out there in the center of the diamond he stood in the seventh with a runner on third, and only one out with a storm of cheers for the Giants breaking over his head. Cool and collected, unshaken and unafraid, when facing a situation where one run would tie the score. His spirit, as his hair, was that of a fighter, and he pulled through unscathed, just as he did in a similar perilous situation in the ninth inning.... Urban Faber this was, called Red by his teammates and admiring Chicago fans.... The victory made his third in the series, and put him in the sun with the greatest twirlers who in the past have been world series heroes.[1]

When the train bearing the victorious team back to Chicago reached the station, an immense throng was assembled to meet their heroes. Faber slipped away and went hunting. Back in Iowa, his father stood on the sidewalk in front of his hotel, passing out cigars to everyone who passed by.[2]

Urban Charles Faber[3] was born on a farm near Cascade, Iowa, a small town on the North Fork of the Maquoketa River, about 25 miles southwest of Dubuque, on September 6, 1888. He was the second child and oldest son of Margaret and Nicholas Faber, a hotel keeper whose ancestors had come from Luxembourg. Around 1910, the family lived in Dubuque for a time, but moved back to Cascade. The lad, nicknamed Red for the color of his hair, enjoyed hunting and fishing and followed these pursuits all his life. When he reached high school age, he first enrolled in Sacred Heart Academy (a college preparatory boarding school in Prairie du Chien, Wisconsin), where he joined the baseball team in 1903. He finished high school at St. Joseph Academy in Dubuque, where he again was a ballplayer. In 1908 and 1909 he pitched for a local amateur club and for St. Joseph College (the forerunner of the present Loras College).

While at St. Joseph he once struck out 24 batters in a nine-inning game against St. Ambrose College.

Red Faber started his professional career with the Dubuque Miners of the Three-I League in 1909. His first appearance came on July 27 of that year against the Springfield Senators in the nightcap of a doubleheader. At the start of the game, Faber got in a jam. Two errors and a sacrifice bunt put Springfield runners on second and third with one out. After Faber struck out the clean-up and number five hitters to get out of the inning unscathed, he coasted to a 12–1 victory. Although he won only one game more than he lost for the weak Dubuque team, the redhead had an impressive earned run average of 1.60.

One account says that Faber's contract was bought by the Pittsburgh Pirates, and Red went with the Corsairs to spring training in 1910. He had managed to save no money from his minor league salary of $100 a month, so he was broke. Needing money for incidentals and tips, he got a $5 advance from Pittsburgh manager Fred Clarke. He nursed this money as long as he could, but eventually it was all gone. When he asked Clarke for another advance, the manager said, "You must be gambling."[4]

Returning to Dubuque in 1910, Faber won 18 games. The highlight of his season was a perfect game pitched against Davenport on August 18. He gave up no hits, no runs, no walks; no batters reached base by any means. Red struck out seven. Only one ball was hit to an outfielder, and there were two infield pop-ups. Faber's pitches had the Paragon batters beating the ball into the ground. The Dubuque infield had 17 assists, including five by the pitcher himself. It was the first perfect game in the history of the minor leagues and only the third up to that time in all of organized baseball. Although this was only a Class B league, the Paragons were no pushovers. At least two members of the team advanced to the major leagues, including Ray Chapman, who was to become the first major leaguer to be killed by a pitch 10 years later, and Bob Coleman, who was both a catcher and a manager in the big leagues. In 1910 Faber pitched 242 innings, had 200 strikeouts, and an ERA of 2.03.

After Faber's perfect game, the Pittsburgh Pirates signed him for 1911. He sat on the bench with the big league club until May 26 when the Pirates sent him to Minneapolis of the American Association. Before he earned any decisions with the Millers, Faber injured his arm in a distance throwing contest. After he recovered, he was sent to the Pueblo club of the Western League on July 12. The injury cost him some velocity on his fastball, which appeared to be a blow to his major league prospects. However, this may have been a blessing in disguise as it led him to develop his spitball, the pitch that would become his ticket to the Hall of Fame. In an interview for *Baseball Magazine*, Faber did not mention the distance throwing contest. Instead, he said: "I never used a spitter in my life until I was obliged to by a kind of necessity because I had nearly ruined my arm throwing curves. That was when I was in the minor leagues, and I can remember how sore my arm was from curved ball pitching."[5]

Opposite: Red Faber won three games for the Chicago White Sox in the 1917 World's Series. Faber spent his entire career with the Sox, winning 254 games for them, more than any other spitballer won for a single club. (PHOTOGRAPH COURTESY OF NATIONAL BASEBALL HALL OF FAME LIBRARY, COOPERSTOWN.)

During the discussion about exempting established spitball pitchers from the ban on the pitch, umpire Billy Evans said: "Of all American League pitchers using the spitball I would say Faber of Chicago and Shocker of St. Louis would be most effective minus the spitball. A good fastball is essential to the success of any pitcher. Faber has a puzzling sidearm fastball, delivered in a peculiar manner. This, coupled with a fairly good curve that he possesses should enable him to be a fairly consistent winner. His change of pace is well nigh perfect, and he knows how to pitch."[6] Of course, Red was grandfathered, and the umpire's theory was never put to the test.

Former major league catcher Ray Hayworth told Eugene Murdock that Faber could break his spitter down or away, making it harder to hit than one that broke down only. Hayworth quoted Ty Cobb as saying one day when Red was pitching against the Tigers in Detroit: "That man is the toughest man I have ever hit against; the most difficult to hit ... because the ball just moves so fast your eye cannot adjust quickly enough to it."[7]

To develop his spitball Faber experimented with things to chew. A spitball pitcher had to chew something in order to create the proper amount of moisture. Most used slippery elm, but Faber said, "Slippery elm doesn't work with me. It's too slippery and I can't control the ball. I have tried chewing gum. But that wasn't quite slippery enough. So I have had to fall back on the good old custom, now much abused, of chewing tobacco. Tobacco juice fills the bill. And I don't chew it because I like it either. In fact, I never chew except when I'm pitching. But it seems to be an indispensable part of my business just like a mason's trowel or a carpenter's hammer."[8]

Many years later Faber and fellow spitballer Burleigh Grimes were among eight baseball "immortals" attending the ceremonies accompanying the opening of Shea Stadium. Grimes asked the redhead what he chewed when he pitched. Red replied, "I chewed gum on one side of my mouth and tobacco on the other side. I never got them mixed either."[9]

Following the 1911 season, Pueblo traded Faber to Des Moines for two players named Belden and Hersche, neither of whom ever made the major leagues. In 1912 and 1913 Faber began his climb to the top, mastering the spitball, and winning 20 or more games each season for the Des Moines Boosters of the Western League. In the Iowa capital, Faber became a local favorite because of talent, his competitive fire, and his modest demeanor.[10] He was a tireless worker, pitching 373 innings to lead the league in 1913. On one hot June day that year he battled Denver for 18 innings until the game was called because of darkness in the nineteenth. The lad from Cascade led the Western League in strikeouts in both 1912 and 1913.

On August 25, 1913, Charles Comiskey purchased Faber's contract for $3,500, a hefty price to pay for a minor leaguer in those days. The future Hall of Famer signed a contract of $1,200 for his rookie season in 1914. Before the 1914 season rolled around, however, the White Sox had a surprise for the recruit. Believing him to be the best prospect in their farm system, but in need of further seasoning, the Sox assigned the redhead to make the Cincinnati to Seattle portion of an around-the-world tour the Pale Hose and John McGraw's New York Giants were planning for the fall and winter. The tour was to start in Cincinnati on October 18, 1913, and end in London on February 26,

1914. The Giants and White Sox were to oppose each other in 35 games as they crossed the country. Before going overseas, Faber was supposed to be sent home.

However, when the tour reached San Francisco, New York's ace pitcher, Christy Mathewson, declined to complete the tour, citing family reasons, but the real reason probably was his fear of seasickness.[11] Matty's departure left the Giants short on pitchers. In a surprising move, the Sox manager — Nixey Callahan — loaned Faber's services to the Giants for the remainder of the trip. So the redhead started the tour pitching against the Giants and ended it pitching for the New Yorkers against his once and future teammates. Ironically, Faber himself became extremely seasick during the voyage. He spent most of the trip in sick bay under care of the ship's doctors. When the teams reached Japan, Faber was still so weak and unsteady that he was scratched from the opening game in Tokyo.[12] The teams played in Tokyo, Hong Kong, Manila, Brisbane, Sydney, Melbourne, Columbo, Cairo, Rome, Nice, Paris, and London. One of Faber's more unusual starts was in Cairo before the grand khadive of Egypt and his harem of 60 wives, all of whom kept their backs to the field during the game. Faber won four games and lost only one, his loss coming in an 11-inning game in London, with King George V in attendance. He won his starts in Hong Kong, Brisbane, Melbourne, and Cairo. Faber's pitching during the tour so impressed McGraw that he tried to acquire the redhead, but Comiskey refused to part with his hot prospect.

Faber's minor league record was as follows:

Year	Team	W	L	Pct.	IP	H	BB	SO	ERA
1909	Dubuque	7	6	.538	114	93	50	82	
1910	Dubuque	18	19	.481	334	239	98	200	
1911	Minneapolis	0	0	—		10	1	1	
	Pueblo	12	8	.600	188	145	39	99	
1912	Des Moines	21	14	.600	304	293	69	190	
1913	Des Moines	20	17	.540	***373***	328	103	265	2.49
5 years		78	64	.549	1319	1108	360	837	

Bold italics indicates he led the league.

League affiliations: Dubuque, Three-I League; Minneapolis, American Association; Pueblo and Des Moines, Western League.

After their return from spring training in California in 1914, the Sox assigned Faber to the second squad, which included a group of youngsters on whom waivers would be asked. Fortunately, Kid Gleason, a White Sox coach and future manager, noticed the mistake and saved the Iowan for the Pale Hose. During his rookie season, Faber broke even in 20 decisions for the Sox and led the American League in saves with four.

The erstwhile Iowa farm boy made his major league debut on April 17, 1914, against the Cleveland Naps. Faber pitched shutout ball for the first four innings, but gave up two runs in the fifth before being removed with one out and runners on base. Although the Sox won the game 6–5, the redhead was not involved in the decision. I.E. Sanborn wrote of Faber's debut in the *Chicago Tribune*: "For four innings Faber gave promise of penciling his name in large letters on the brain cells of the fans. In that time he pitched shutout ball with the aid of a swell shot to the plate by Collins, and things looked as rosy as dawn was ever painted. But the sixth brought trouble for Faber. He began to slip. A pass, a pair of hits, and a wild pitch put two Naps over with nobody out. Callahan let Faber stick until he had erased Hagerman on strikes, then hustled Tex Russell to the rescue."[13]

Sanborn must have suffered a lapse of memory, for about six weeks later he penned this piece for the *Tribune*:

> Because Chicago's celebrated exponents of advanced baseball could not score one run for him in nine innings today, Red Faber, globe trotter, lost a great thirteen inning battle with Detroit's Tigers and began his major league career with a 2 to 1 defeat instead of what ought to have been a brilliant victory. For nine innings of the first American League game in which he was allowed to start Faber held the Tigers to four hits, two of which were measly infield scratches. Not a run could Jennings' men get off him, and seldom could they get a man within scoring distance of the plate. In spite of a tendency to wildness this graduate of Des Moines was so good in the pinches that the Tigers did not even look as if they could score a run off him....
>
> Detroit gave Chicago a run in the eleventh on a muff by Kavenaugh after tagging a runner out at second. That might have been enough, but Sam Crawford tied it up in the home half with a home run. It was not a real home run of which Sam could be proud, but only a freak which was converted from a genuine two bagger into a joke home run by local ground rules. Detroit has some sort of contraption in right field to provide a screened runway for the bleacherites. Crawford's drive hit some part of this which entitled him to a round trip, according to the home made ground rules.... Moriarty opened the last half with a double to left and was sacrificed to third by Stanage. Veach went to bat for Dauss and was passed under sealed orders from the bench. This brought Bush up and he soaked a single to left, scoring Moriarty [with the winning run].[14]

White Sox manager Nixey Callahan filed a protest with American League president Ban Johnson to ascertain if the ground rule by which Crawford was given a home run had been passed on previously. The protest was disallowed and the results stood.

The following year the Sox had a new manager, Clarence "Pants" Rowland, who had first met Faber in Dubuque. As a matter of fact it was Rowland who had encouraged Faber to sign his first minor league contract.[15] Faber may have been surprised when Rowland replaced Callahan as manager, but he ultimately was destined to play under 10 different managers in his 20 years with the Sox — Callahan, Rowland, Gleason, Frank Chance, Johnny Evers, Eddie Collins, Ray Schalk, Lena Blackburne, Donie Bush, and Lew Fonseca. Faber had remarkable control. Rowland said he could never get the redhead to throw four obviously wide ones for an intentional base on balls. "I'll walk him, all right," the pitcher told his manager, "but just by throwing him balls he doesn't like. I don't want anybody to think I'm afraid of any batter." Faber had such excellent control that he could get by with this tactic.[16] Ted Lyons, who pitched 21 seasons in the American League, told a reporter that Faber had the best control of any pitcher he had seen during his years in the circuit. "He could almost always hit the right spot at the right time," the veteran hurler asserted.[17]

In 1915 Faber had a banner sophomore season. On May 12 he went the distance and beat Washington 4–1 while making only 61 pitches in the entire game, an American League record.[18] He had excellent control, walking nobody. The Senators started swinging at the first pitch and seldom connected with enough force to drive it through the infield. Three times in this game he retired the side on three pitches. Evidently he threw his spitter with a sidearm delivery that day. James Cruisenberry wrote in the *Chicago Tribune*: "The crowd gave its attention to the superb and masterful powers of the boy from Cascade, Ia. Faber was going in his best stride and the Washington fellows were just about helpless. His strong side arm soakers swooped across the plate with deadly effect."[19] Until there were two out in the ninth inning he had given up but one scratch single that shortstop Buck Weaver had knocked down with his bare hand but was unable to recover in time to make a play.

On May 21 he won his seventh straight game, beating Carl Mays and the Boston Red Sox 3–2 in a thrilling 17-inning contest. Faber did not pitch the entire 17 innings. He entered the game at the beginning of the eighth inning and pitched brilliantly for 10 rounds, allowing only two hits and walking none. Both hits were made by Forest Cady, a fellow Iowan, who was catching for the Red Sox that day. One was a single in the 10th and the other a two-out triple in the 15th.

Faber and teammate "Death Valley" Jim Scott each won 24 games as the Pale Hose racked up 93 victories in 1915, tying the 1906 Hitless Wonders for the most wins in a season by a White Sox team up to that time. For the first two months of the season the Sox battled the Detroit Tigers for first place, but in June the Boston Red Sox mounted a charge, led by the heroic efforts of "Smoky" Joe Wood. The erstwhile ace had strained his ankle in spring training in 1913. In May he slipped while fielding a bunt and injured his right thumb. When he next tried to pitch he altered his motion somewhat to compensate for the thumb injury and the sore ankle. Something happened to his shoulder or perhaps his rotator cuff, and he was never able to pitch again without a terrific amount of pain in his right shoulder.[20] On June 7, 1915, Wood and Faber hooked up in a pitchers' duel in Beantown. Each pitcher allowed only four hits, as Smoky shut out the White Sox 3–0 in a game that took only 1 hour and 28 minutes to play. That defeat dropped the ChiSox to second place behind Detroit, with Boston coming on strong. On July 19, the same two hurlers matched up again. Wood, pitching in severe pain, with his fastball gone, relying on a changeup, guile, and guts, won 6–2 as the Pale Hose defense collapsed, allowing four unearned runs. This win put the Red Sox in first place, and they went on to capture the pennant.

On July 14 Faber stole three bases in one inning against the Philadelphia Athletics. With the White Sox leading 4–2 in the fourth inning and rain threatening, the White Elephants tried to delay the game, hoping for a rain out before the game could become official. Faber was at bat. In order to keep the weak-hitting Iowan from making a quick out, opposing pitcher Joe Bush purposely hit Faber with a pitch. The redhead, trying to speed up the game, tried to get thrown out while stealing. He stole second, third, and home with the A's making little effort to retire him. As it turned out, the expected rain did not fall, and Faber's steal of home provided the decisive run as the Sox prevailed 6–4.

In 1915 Faber tied for the American League lead in appearances with 50, tied for second in wins with 24, was second in strikeouts with 182, and was fifth in innings pitched, finishing the season just one shy of 300. Although not noted as a great hitter, Faber walked seven times in a row during the 1915 season. He stole home twice.

After the season, Charles Comiskey stocked his hunting preserve with four moose, one of which he named after his brilliant young pitcher, who was one of his favorite players and a sometime guest at the preserve. Faber seemed to have a special place in the Old Roman's heart.[21] In September 1916, Faber's namesake found an open gate and ran away. Soon after that a boy tending his cattle let out a scream. Red Faber (the moose, not the pitcher) was charging him. Luckily, the lad's brother was nearby with a gun and killed the moose before anyone was injured. According to the story, the headlines in the newspaper the next day read "Red Faber Killed in Self-Defense."

In 1916 Faber was again among the league leaders. His .654 winning percentage was fourth highest in the circuit and his earned run average of 2.02 was fifth best. The White Sox again challenged for the American League flag in a see-saw race in which the Sox became the sixth team to take the league lead, if only briefly. The Sox took the lead on a rainout on August 3. Red Faber and Walter Johnson had pitched one scoreless inning each when the deluge came, causing the game to be postponed. When the Red Sox lost to the St. Louis Browns, the Pale Hose backed into first place. The next day a doubleheader was played, with the same two pitchers facing each other in the opener. Faber outpitched the great Washington star 3–2, and the Sox held the lead for a time, even though they dropped the nightcap 8–3. As the season wore on the Red Sox regained the lead. In the final game of the year between the two teams, Faber pitched a masterpiece. He took a no-hitter into the fifth inning, but Tris Speaker sneaked a hit into the gap between short and third for a clean single. The Grey Eagle took second on a sacrifice bunt, stole third, and scored on an outfield fly. Boston connected for no more safeties, and the redhead had a one-hit 3–1 victory. But it was too little, too late. The Red Sox took their second consecutive American League pennant by a margin of two games over the runner-up Chicagoans.

Gentleman though he may have been, Faber was not above teaching rookies to respect their elders. In 1917, Joe Dugan joined the Philadelphia A's. In one of his early games he faced Faber in a game at Chicago. "Here am I," Dugan told a sportswriter, "a little innocent guy from Holy Cross, and the first pitch comes up and hits me in the cap."

As Joe walked to first base, he shouted at Faber, "What's that for?"

"Respect," Faber replied.[22]

In 1917 Faber improved on an already outstanding ERA by lowering his mark to 1.92, fourth best in the league. His win-loss record that year was an unimpressive 16–13, but it should have been much better. Nearly half of the runs scored against him were unearned. Red permitted 93 runs that season, and 40 of them were unearned. While pitching against Detroit in a 3–0 loss on April 29, the big righthander suffered a muscle strain. He did not start another game until June 22. After struggling well into the summer, Big Red regained his dominance, getting stronger and more effective in August. In September, Faber became one of only two American League pitchers to start and win three consecutive games. Walter Johnson is the other. The Big Train's wins were spread out over four days. Faber's three victories came in a two-day span. On September 3 he defeated the Detroit Tigers in both ends of a morning and afternoon doubleheader. The next day he beat the St. Louis Browns.

Faber's accomplishments in the September 3 doubleheader were somewhat tarnished by allegations that the Chicago-Detroit games of September 2 and 3 were fixed. Swede Risberg and Chick Gandil, both of whom had been permanently suspended from organized baseball for their part in the 1919 Black Sox scandal, brought the charges, years later. Baseball commissioner Kenesaw Mountain Landis held hearings and dismissed the allegations on January 12, 1927. Apparently, White Sox players had collected a pot of $870 and presented it to the Detroit pitching staff as a gift for their success in the season series against the Boston Red Sox, Chicago's chief rival for the pennant, but this had occurred after the doubleheaders in question and had no bearing on those games. Landis stated that the affair was reprehensible, but he found no criminal intent. Among those who contributed money were Faber, Schalk, and Collins, none of whom were involved in the 1919 scandal.[23]

The Red Sox had been favored to win their third straight pennant in 1917 and were in the race for a while, but the White Sox eventually pulled away to a commanding lead. On September 21, the Sox went into Boston needing to win only one game in a three-game series to clinch the pennant. Reb Russell was scheduled to start the first game, but before game time Red Faber, who had been ailing, approached manager Pants Rowland and said he was feeling fine and would like to start. Rowland obliged and Faber responded. For six innings Faber pitched a perfect game, allowing nobody to get on base by any means. Meanwhile, spitballer Dutch Leonard was pitching well for the Red Sox, holding the lads from the Windy City to only one run. In the seventh Faber lost his bid for perfection as Harry Hooper tripled and playing manager Jack Barry drove him in with a single to tie the score at 1–1. The teams battled through the scoreless eighth and ninth innings. In the top of the 10th Shano Collins knocked Ray Schalk in with the go-ahead run. With a one-run lead Faber had only to retire the side in the bottom of the 10th to clinch the pennant. Easier said than done. With one out, Duffy Lewis and Larry Gardner hit successive singles. Men on first and third and one out. Everett Scott was due up next, but manager Barry went to his bench and brought in Babe Ruth to pinch hit. The Bambino sloughed a bounder to second baseman Eddie Collins, who snatched it up and flipped it to shortstop Buck Weaver, who fired the ball to first baseman Chick Gandil for the game-ending double play as Lewis was scampering across home plate with what would have been the tying run. Faber had pitched a five-hitter and given up no walks as the White Sox clinched their first pennant since 1906. It was the big righthander's sixth consecutive win. For the first and only time in their history, the White Sox had won 100 games in a season.

A famous American author wrote years later about being a small boy and getting up about four o'clock on a chilly October morning, riding the elevated trains and the 35th Street Trolley to the ticket office on Wentworth Avenue, and standing in line for hours to buy tickets to see his first World's Series game.[24] For the 1917 World's Series, the first in wartime, the White Sox wore new red, white, and blue uniforms. The S on the shirt was red and blue against a white background, and the white stockings were banded with blue and red stripes.

Faber's exploits in the 1917 World's Series are legendary. After Eddie Cicotte bested Slim Sallee in a pitchers' duel to take the first game 2–1, Faber started the second game.

He fell behind 2–0 in the second inning as the McGrawmen scored two runs on three hits and an error. Faber held the Giants scoreless the rest of the way as his team rolled to a 7–2 win. He threw only 99 pitches and shut out the Giants in eight of the nine innings. He also made a spectacular fielding play. When Benny Kauff hit a dribbler down the first base line, Faber shoveled the ball into his glove and then made the putout himself with a lunging dive into first base, touching the base with his glove a split second before the speedy Giant reached the bag.[25] One of the Iowan's most embarrassing moments occurred in this game. In the second inning, with teammate Buck Weaver on first base, Faber hit safely to right field and took second on the throw to third. With the next batter at the plate, Giant pitcher Pol Perritt went into a full windup. Faber took off for third and slid in to find Weaver looking down at him. It is alleged that Weaver asked the bewildered redhead, "What are you doing here?" Faber, who was tagged out to end the inning, replied, "Why I'm just going out to pitch, of course."[26]

Due to travel and rain, there were two open dates before the third game, in which Sox hurler Cicotte pitched well, but lost as Rube Benton pitched a shutout for the National League champions. In game four, Faber was the victim as the Giant hurlers tossed their second consecutive shutout. With the series tied at two games apiece, the White Sox started Reb Russell in the fifth game, the only time in the series that anyone other than Cicotte or Faber started for the Pale Hose. It was a mistake. Russell did not retire a single batter, walking the first batter, then giving up a single and a two-base hit. Cicotte was brought in to relieve. Cicotte pitched six innings, and Lefty Williams pitched the seventh. With the score tied 5–5, Faber came in to finish the game. He blanked the Giants in the eighth and ninth and picked up the win when the Sox scored three runs in the eighth inning. This was the redhead's second win of the series.

With one day's rest, Faber came back to start the sixth game. Neither team scored during the first three innings. In the fourth inning came one of the most famous plays in the history of baseball. Eddie Collins led off that stanza with a grounder to third baseman Heinie Zimmerman. The Great Zim, as he was known, threw the ball past first baseman Walter Holke for a two-base error. "Shoeless" Joe Jackson then hit an easy fly ball to right field, which Dave Robertson dropped, Collins going to third. The next batter, Happy Felsch, hit a grounder back to the box. Pitcher Rube Benton had Collins trapped halfway between third and home. The speedy Collins jockeyed back and forth, buying time for the other base runners to advance as far as possible before he himself was tagged out. Benton threw to Zimmerman. Catcher Bill Rariden came up the third base line to participate in the rundown. Suddenly Collins darted past the catcher and headed for home, with Zimmerman in pursuit behind him. The Great Zim had no chance of catching up with the faster Collins. For years Zimmerman was ridiculed for his bonehead play of chasing Collins across home plate. In reality Zim was not the culprit. If anyone was a bonehead it was first baseman Holke for not covering the plate. "Who was I going to throw the ball to? Klem?" Zim asked his critics. (Bill Klem was the home plate umpire.) The Sox wound up scoring three runs in that inning and added an insurance tally later in the game.

Despite giant boners, the main problem for the Giants was the real hero of the series, Red Faber, "who simply turned the lights out on the McGrawmen, with another gritty triumph."[27] Faber pitched a six-hit, complete game 4–2 victory for the White Sox for his third win of the series and a world's championship for the Chicagoans. After the game was over, John McGraw, ever the sore loser, refused to shake hands with Rowland, snarling "Get away from me, you busher."[28] He did, however, congratulate Faber, whom he had grown to admire during their world tour a few years back.

Pete Palmer and Gary Gillette named Faber as the winner of their 1917 World's Series ex post facto Most Valuable Player Award.[29]

Although the United States entered World War I on April 6, 1917, the war had little impact on baseball that year. The next year was different, however. It was estimated that 200 major league baseball players were eligible for the draft.[30] By opening day of 1918, all teams had at least one player in the armed forces. Married men and those with dependents were exempt. On May 23 the government issued its "work or fight" order, making it mandatory for men to get into essential work by July 1 or face induction. Baseball was declared a nonessential industry. However, Secretary of War Newton Baker allowed the major leagues a two-month extension in order to enable them to complete a shortened season of about 125 games. The clubs played through Labor Day, ending the season one month early. The secretary then granted an additional two-week extension for the two teams that qualified for the World's Series.

Red Faber did not wait until the end of the season to decide to work or fight. On June 7 he enlisted in the Navy. One newspaper described his enlistment thusly: "Urban (Red) Faber of the Chicago White Sox is through with professional baseball until the war ends. The man who pitched the Sox to the world championship enlisted today as a chief yeoman and will report to the detention camp next week. He will be sent through the regular training routine just the same as the most humble rookie and at the conclusion, if he has his way, will be sent out to sea to whiff the Hun."[31] That article turned out to be incorrect in several respects. Nine days later, another newspaper reported that "Red Faber, who will go to the Great Lakes Naval Station Monday pitched his last game for the White Sox today. He is scheduled to be made a chief yeoman within a month and hopes to get a submarine assignment.[32]

Faber did not get his submarine assignment, nor was he treated exactly like any other recruit. He spent the summer of 1918 at Great Lakes, pitching for its baseball team against other service teams and semipro outfits. On at least one occasion the Navy permitted him to pitch for a semipro team, the Logan Squares, against a Garden City team featuring his former White Sox teammate Joe Benz. He hoped to pitch occasionally for the Sox when they were in Chicago for weekend contests, but the Great Lakes brass did not look kindly upon that request. An outbreak of Spanish influenza caused the Great Lakes team to disband in October. Faber began a special course of training for overseas duty. The war ended in November, and the redhead was discharged from the Navy in December. According to the official American League averages, Faber led the league in earned run average with a 1.23 mark for the 1918 season, but as he had pitched in only 11 games for the Sox before joining the Navy, most people considered Walter Johnson at 1.27 as the real leader.

Faber's enlistment was met with approval by White Sox owner Charles Comiskey, as was that of his teammate Eddie Collins, who enlisted in the Marines in August 1918.

However, when Joe Jackson, Lefty Williams, and Byrd Lynn chose to go to work in a shipyard upon receiving their draft notices, the Old Roman was livid. "I don't consider them fit to play on my ball club. I would gladly lose my whole team if the players wished to do their duty for the country, as hundreds of thousands of other young men are doing."[33]

Comiskey's outburst and the cries of "Slacker!" that met the returnees in 1919 may have contributed in a small way to exacerbating the already serious schisms on the club. Faber, Dickie Kerr, and Ray Schalk were members of a clique led by Collins that was considered pro-management and viewed as recipients of favored treatment. With his private school background, degree from an Ivy League college, haughty demeanor, and high salary, Collins was resented by some of his teammates who had come up through the school of hard knocks. (While salary data are difficult to obtain, we know Collins received a multiyear contract in 1915 paying him $15,000 a year, perhaps more than twice the salary of any of his teammates. Jackson and Buck Weaver probably received about $6,000 each, while Williams and Swede Risberg probably made less than $3,000. By 1920, these salaries had been increased somewhat. Richard Lindberg gives these figures, exclusive of bonuses: Schalk, $12,000; Cicotte, $9,075; Jackson, $8,000; Weaver, $7,644; Felsch, $7,400; Faber $6,600; Shano Collins, $4,800; and Risberg, $3,435.)[34]

Collins was not on speaking terms with Chick Gandil, an angry malcontent who was to become a principal figure in the fixing of the 1919 World's Series. Happy Felsch, whose nickname belied his mien, left the team temporarily on July 1, 1918. He was a sixth-grade dropout, son of dirt-poor immigrants, and was often ridiculed by his teammates. Cicotte had been known as a surly troublemaker and an anti-management agitator in Boston before joining the White Sox. The point is that the White Sox were not a bunch of happy campers. Could Faber's patriotism have unwittingly made the situation worse?

In 1919 Faber saw limited service because of an ankle injury, followed by a sore arm and a late season case of influenza. During the season he was about 30 pounds underweight.[35] He appeared in 25 games and had a record of 11 wins and nine losses. He did not pitch at all in the World's Series that fall when eight of his teammates allegedly accepted bribes from gamblers to throw the series to the Cincinnati Reds in the infamous Black Sox scandal. At Cooperstown in 1955, on the occasion of his induction into the Hall of Fame, Ray Schalk, who had been Faber's catcher from 1914 through 1928, said that if Red Faber had been able to pitch in the 1919 World Series, there would have been no Black Sox scandal.[36] James Farrell wrote that it has often been said that had Faber been in good health he might have won the series for the Sox.[37]

After recovering from his sore arm and the flu, Faber came back strong in 1920, winning 21 games. Faber kept his team, which had been favored to repeat, in contention until the final week of the season. On September 23 the White Sox were in second place, one game behind the Indians, when Comiskey suspended the seven Black Sox who were still with the team (Chick Gandil did not play in 1920.) The Sox lost two of their remaining three games and finished in second place, two games behind the champion Cleveland team. The Sox fell to seventh place the next year and never again finished in the first division during the remainder of Faber's pitching career. Faber had the fourth most wins of all American League pitchers in 1920, tied for second in complete games, was fourth in strikeouts, and second in innings pitched.

In 1921 Faber won 25 of the 62 victories the Chicagoans posted, accounting for more than 40 percent of the team's wins. Since 1900, only six other pitchers have been responsible for as many as 40 percent of their team's wins in a season — Steve Carlton, Ed Walsh, Jack Chesbro, Cy Young, Eddie Rommel, and Walter Johnson. Pitching for a decimated team, Faber compiled an amazing record in 1921. He led the American League in complete games, in fewest base runners permitted per nine innings, in opponents' batting average, in opponents' on base percentage, and in earned run average. He ranked third in wins, fifth in winning percentage, and fourth in strikeouts. The 2004 edition of *Baseball Encyclopedia* named Faber as the winner of its ex post facto Cy Young Award in the American League for 1921.[38] He also led all junior circuit hurlers that season in Weighted Rating points as computed by Ted Oliver.[39] Furthermore, he was ranked as the leading American League pitcher of the year in Charles F. Faber's *Baseball Ratings*.[40] John Thorn and John Holway named him their Jim Creighton Award winner as the best AL hurler of the year.[41] In the city series between the Cubs and the White Sox that October, the redhead slipped while fielding a grounder and had to undergo an operation for the removal of the internal semilunar cartilage from his right knee.

Following the successful knee operation, Faber did not miss a beat. Despite having a poor supporting cast behind him, the Iowan won 21 games in 1922, his third consecutive season with more than 20 victories. For the second straight year he led the league in earned run average, complete games, base runners allowed per nine innings, and opponents' on base percentage. He also led innings pitched, had the second most strikeouts, and ranked third in opponents' batting average. He again was named the Jim Creighton Award winner by Thorn and Holway.

Although Faber was only 34 years old in September 1922, he was considered old by baseball standards. W. R. Hoefer wrote the following piece for issue of *Baseball Magazine* published in that month:

> He's an aged bloke, as players go and they'll tell you his fast one is pretty slow. He can't cut loose as he used to do with the same old smoke; but he isn't through. He's lost a bit of his pitching stuff but his poor old wing is live enough to limber up on the hurling hill and win some games for the White Sox still. His speed is less and his years are more and his curve won't zip as it did of yore. But he has control and a wise old head and the batters cuss when they face old "Red." They say he is ancient, his day is past. They don't see how the old guy can last. But when they see him out there in the box they know there's trouble with Gleason's Sox. The pitchers come; the pitchers go. With the added years they fade and blow. They lose their stuff and their arms go dead — but Old Man Time doesn't worry "Red." He still goes out on the hurling hill and grabs his glove and the little pill and grins at the wise ones who say he's through and keeps on copping for Gleason's crew. He may be old in a playing way. He's had his fame and done his day. And it may be time that the old bird blew, but believe me, neighbor, he isn't through. He still gets out in the pitcher's box and wins his games for the Pallid Sox.[42]

Hoefer added the following bit:

Said Urban Faber to Tyrus Cobb,
"I see, old man, you're on the job."

"And YOU'RE not bad, for an old man, neighbor,"
Said Tyrus Cobb to Urban Faber.[43]

Of course, Big Red was still winning games for the White Sox a decade after Hoefer's rhymes were published.

In 1923 Faber slipped to a record of 14 wins and 11 losses—not bad for a pitcher on a seventh-place team, but far below his performance in the previous three years. Even so, he was far better than an average pitcher, besting the league average in the important categories of wins, winning percentage, and earned run average. He held his opponents to the fourth lowest batting average and the third lowest on base percentage of all the American League hurlers.

On April 21, 1924, Faber underwent an operation for the removal of a small piece of bone chipped off the elbow of his pitching arm. That year he had the first losing season of his major league career, but he came back to post winning records in both 1925 and 1926. In 1925 he ranked fourth in the fewest bases on balls given up per nine innings. In 1926 he had the third best Faber System rating of any American League pitcher.

In 1927 a near-tragedy occurred during spring training in New Orleans. On March 7, rain prevented the team from practicing. Late in the afternoon, Johnny Mostil, the star centerfielder of the White Sox, visited Red Faber's hotel room, ostensibly to borrow a deck of cards for a game among the players. He emerged without the cards and went to the room of a close friend and White Sox fan, Pat Prouty, who at the time was visiting elsewhere in the hotel. When Prouty returned to his chamber, he discovered Mostil lying in a pool of blood in the bathtub, with a pocket knife and a razor blade at his side. An ambulance was called and the unconscious player was carried out through a rear exit of the hotel. Lou Comiskey, son of the White Sox owner, did his best to suppress the news. In a suicide attempt, Mostil had attempted to sever the jugular vein in his neck with the razor blade, slashed his ankles almost to the bone, and inflicted deep gashes on both wrists. He had stabbed himself just over the heart with a knife blade. That was the wound that attending physicians thought would probably cause his death.

However, the centerfielder recovered and news of his suicide attempt became public very quickly. At first no explanation for the player's actions could be offered, but the Comiskeys soon settled on a story that Mostil, suffering from bad teeth, high blood pressure, and neuritis, was despondent over his ill health. However, an unsubstantiated rumor gained wide circulation to the effect that Mostil had been having an affair with Red Faber's wife, Irene, and had attempted suicide when Faber found out and threatened to kill him. Johnny recovered in time to play 13 games for the Sox in 1927, a full season in 1928, and a few more games before retiring in 1929. Faber had his worst major league season up to that point winning only four games while losing seven in 1927.

In 1928 Faber resumed his winning ways, compiling a record of 13 wins against nine losses. In 1929 he again won 13 games, while losing an equal number. On May 29 he pitched a one-hit shutout, beating the hard-hitting Detroit Tigers 2–0. A two-out single by Charlie Gehringer in the fourth inning was the only safety allowed by the veteran spitballer. On August 29, the White Sox, in cooperation with several eastern Iowa counties, held a Red Faber Day. In appreciation for his career, the hosts presented Faber with a radio, a travel bag, a diamond ring, and a check for $2,700. Unfortunately, Red lost the ball game to the defending world champion New York Yankees 5–4.

By now it was evident that the aging star's career was winding down. He never again had a winning season. Of course, neither did his team during this portion of Red's tenure. In a game in late July 1930, Faber gave up a two-base hit in the first inning. Then the White Sox infield committed two errors. In disgust, the veteran pitcher stalked off the mound. Manager Donie Bush punished him by leaving him home on the team's road trip to Detroit on the 1st of August. In 1930 Faber made 29 starts and pitched 10 complete games. It was the last season in which the redhead was used primarily as a starter.

During his remaining three seasons, he was used mainly in relief. Faber claimed that if Bush had let him start he would have won 50 more games, putting him over the magic 300 mark.[44] However, the main impediment to his not winning 300 was the caliber of the team for which he was pitching. His longtime battery mate Ray Schalk said the Sox were a lousy team in the 1920s and early 1930s and with better support Red could have won 300 easily. One source wrote that Schalk always insisted that if Faber had pitched for one of the better teams in the league, he would have won upward of 400 games.[45] That may have been a bit of an exaggeration, but there is little doubt that Faber could have racked up many more wins with a good team behind him. John C. Skipper wrote: "His time in the service, coupled with the downslide of the White Sox after the Black Sox scandal, probably prevented Faber from being a 300-game winner. Another factor: He spent six years in the minor leagues, despite winning 20 games in each of his last two minor league seasons."[46] The record shows the redhead won 254 major league games and 78 in the minors for a total of 332 professional regular season victories, excluding World's Series, Chicago City Series, and exhibition wins.

On July 7, 1931, Faber was the winning pitcher in a game containing a statistical oddity. The White Sox and the St. Louis Browns played a 12-inning game in which neither team recorded a strikeout, the longest such occurrence in major league history.[47] Faber picked up the victory in relief of Tommy Thomas when the Sox pushed across two runs in the top of the 12th to pull out a 10–8 win at Sportsman's Park. All told Red won 10 games that year for a mediocre Sox team. The following May, a writer for *Baseball Magazine* conducted a lengthy interview with the aging star and noted, "when Faber discusses pitching, he speaks with authority, for he is one of the undoubted masters of the craft."[48]

In the interview Faber credited his longevity partly to his avoidance of a sore arm. "Many a pitcher has been cut down in his prime because of a sore arm. Most pitchers have spent dismal and unprofitable months in nursing sore arms. Sore arms, rather than batters and their little peculiarities, are really the pitcher's major problem.... There are two factors which are responsible — a pitcher either overexerts himself, or he isn't in proper condition, or both."[49]

Faber recognized that sometimes pitchers were overworked by managers desperate for wins. He pointed out that a pitcher's arm is like a delicate and costly piece of machinery. He suggested that from the cold angle of dollars and cents, club owners should consider pitcher's arms like any other machinery, as something that if misused may become injured beyond repair. He noted that old-timers were fond of talking about the iron man stunts of the good old days. "With all due respect to the old-timers this is a lot of bunk." As for the pitchers of the 1880s, who pitched day after day for days on end, in his view they were not pitching major league baseball.

> They were pitching the best type of baseball that existed at the time.... In a properly pitched big league game now-a-days, every pitched ball is a study. It may win or lose the ball game. A dozen angles have to be considered — the batter, his preferences, the state of the game, the men on bases, if any, the shape of the ball park, the wind, the amount of light, your own outfielders and infielders, and many other things.[50]

In 1932 the Sox set a club record by losing 102 games in a season. With a record of only two wins and 11 losses, Faber had his worst major league season that year.

Faber stuck around for the 1933 season, winning three games while losing four and picking up five unofficial saves. His last start came against the New York Yankees on September 20 at Yankee Stadium. The 45-year-old veteran threw the last legal spitball in the American League in the bottom of the fourth inning. With his team trailing 3–0 the Iowan was lifted for a pinch hitter, Earl Webb, in the top of the fifth, and his major league career was over as far as the regular season was concerned.

However, there was still the city series between the White Sox and their cross-town rivals, the Cubs. On October 5 the wily veteran shut out the Cubs 2–0. Old Red pitched a complete game, held the Cubs to five hits, and gave only two free passes. Only one runner made it as far as third base. In the ninth inning Red retired Babe Herman, Riggs Stephenson, and Charlie Grimm on infield taps to wrap up the victory. It was the 17th time that the crafty spitballer had defeated the Cubs in a city series game. His stellar career ended on a winning note.

On February 17, 1934, Faber announced his retirement. He walked into the office of club president Lou Comiskey and said he would not accept the pay cut the Sox proposed and that he was hanging up his spikes. Three days later, the Oakland Oaks offered the spitballer a contract to pitch in the Pacific Coast League. He turned them down. The Chicago Cubs gave him a tryout. After working out and pitching batting practice, he decided he had had enough.

The famous novelist James T. Farrell wrote a book about his baseball memories, in which Red Faber was the only pitcher to whom he devoted a full chapter biographical sketch: "Why Red Faber? All I know — and it says so in the record books— is that he was a pitching prototype of his generation, now forgotten, when the spitball and the stolen base were as common as today's home run and franchise shift. Faber was a major part of White Sox baseball — pre–World War I and post–Black Sox era."[51]

Faber's major league record was as follows:

Year	Club	W	L	Pct.	IP	H	BB	SO	ERA	WR	PTS
1914	Chi AL	10	9	.526	181	154	64	88	2.68	1482	43
1915	Chi AL	24	14	.632	300	264	99	182	2.55	1406	63

Year	Club	W	L	Pct.	IP	H	BB	SO	ERA	WR	PTS
1916	Chi AL	17	9	.654	205	167	61	87	2.02	1950	60
1917	Chi AL	16	13	.552	248	224	85	84	1.92	-3480	27
1918	Chi AL	4	1	.800	81	70	23	26	1.22	1775	26
1919	Chi AL	11	9	.550	162	185	45	45	3.83	-1820	30
1920	Chi AL	23	13	.639	319	332	88	108	2.99	720	59
1921	Chi AL	25	15	.625	331	293	87	124	***2.48***	***12000***	***116***
1922	Chi AL	21	17	.553	***353***	334	83	148	***2.80***	2660	62
1923	Chi AL	14	11	.560	232	233	62	91	3.41	3350	59
1924	Chi AL	9	11	.450	161	173	58	47	3.85	420	34
1925	Chi AL	12	11	.522	238	266	59	71	3.78	230	39
1926	Chi AL	15	9	.625	185	203	57	65	3.56	2712	60
1927	Chi AL	4	7	.364	111	131	41	39	4.55	-1496	10
1928	Chi AL	13	9	.591	201	223	68	43	3.75	3168	59
1929	Chi AL	13	13	.500	234	241	61	68	3.88	3510	56
1930	Chi AL	8	13	.381	169	188	49	62	4.21	-525	24
1931	Chi AL	10	14	.417	184	210	57	49	3.82	1440	38
1932	Chi AL	2	11	.154	106	123	38	26	3.74	-2431	-3
1933	Chi AL	3	4	.429	86	92	28	18	3.44	-133	12
20 years		254	213	.544	4088	4106	1213	1471	3.15	26938	874

Bold italics indicates led the league.

Faber's World's Series record:

		W	L	Pct.	IP	H	BB	SO	ERA
1917	Chicago AL	3	1	.750	27	21	3	9	2.33

After his major league playing career ended, Faber was not done with baseball. In December 1937 he signed a contract to instruct young players at a baseball school in Hot Springs, Arkansas. In 1946, Ted Lyons was named White Sox manager. One of his first acts a few hours later was to hire Red Faber as a coach. The Sox had difficulty finding a uniform to fit as Faber had added a few pounds to his six-foot, two-inch frame since retiring. He donned an ill-fitting uniform on May 26, 1946, and was back in the major leagues, but for only two seasons. On September 28, 1947, a two-inning old-timers game was held between the New York Yankees and an all-star team for the benefit of the Babe Ruth Foundation. Faber pitched one inning for the all-stars. Lyons was released as White Sox skipper after the 1948 season, and his head coach was soon gone. On White Sox opening day in 1954 Red Faber threw out the first pitch to his former battery mate Ray Schalk. The pair also teamed up for the opening pitch in 1959. Faber drew a big laugh when he pretended to load up the ball.

Among many prominent figures who advocated the election of Faber to the National Baseball Hall of Fame were Pants Rowland, Arch Ward of the *Chicago Tribune*, and John Lardner of *Newsweek*. In the days before selections could be made by the Veterans Committee, the only route to the hall was through election by the Baseball

Writers Association of America. Eligibility for election expired a set number of years after the player's retirement. None of the exempted spitballers had been elected by the 1950s, and time was running out for most of them. Lardner wrote of Faber: "It's curious how the merciful life-giving powers of the spitball continue to work for a man after his arm has stopped working.... The spitter saves the arm, and because it saved Red's arm, it saved him a good five years of eligibility for the Hall of Fame, in which he belongs."[52]

Use of the spitball may have prolonged Faber's career by five years, but neither he nor any of the other spitball grandfathers were ever elected to the hall by the writers. In 1964 Red Faber and Burleigh Grimes were selected by the Veterans Committee and became the first of the exempted spitballers to be named to the National Baseball Hall of Fame. Stan Coveleskie joined them in the Cooperstown shrine five years later. Faber was elected to the Iowa Sports Hall of Fame in 1951 and was inducted into the Loras College Athletic Hall of Fame in 1983. The Faber-Clarke Field at Loras is named in his honor. Jerry Clark named Faber as the top starting pitcher on his all-Iowa team, ahead of such stalwarts as Bob Feller and Dazzy Vance.[53]

During his baseball career, Faber toiled in a quiet, workmanlike manner. He did not exhibit a flamboyant lifestyle. Perhaps that is why one eminent baseball researcher regards him as a "colorless figure."[54] Popular with players and fans alike, humble, and basically an Iowa farmboy throughout his life, he is remembered as a gentleman.[55] Perhaps that is better than being colorful.

Faber continued living in the Chicago area for the rest of his life. For a while he sold real estate in Grayslake, near one of his favorite fishing spots. He also owned and managed a bowling alley in that Chicago suburb from 1933 to 1946. In the days before automatic pin setters, Faber cited a shortage of workers to set the pins manually as the reason for the sale of his alleys on May 1, 1946. He even tried his hand at selling automobiles for a while. Mostly, however, he worked for the Cook County Highway Department on a survey crew and as an inspector. He was employed by the county from 1954 until he retired in 1967, when he was nearly 80 years old.

He married Irene Walsh in 1920. The couple had no children. She preceded him in death in 1942. Five years later, the 59-year-old widower married Frances Knudtzon, a 29-year-old divorcee. The age difference inspired a few wisecracks among Chicago sportswriters. A devout Roman Catholic, elderly Nicholas Faber disapproved of his son's marriage to a divorced woman and refused to speak to Red for some time.[56] Red and Fran's only child, a son named Urban Charles Faber II, was born in 1948.

Red Faber died in Chicago on September 25, 1976, a short time after his 88th birthday. He was survived by his wife Frances and his son, Urban II. He is buried in the Acacia Park Cemetery in the Windy City.

2

Burleigh Grimes

All eyes were on the man on the mound. Stocky and muscular, he had a day's growth of stubble and a scowl on his face. He brought the fingers of his right hand to his mouth and covered them with his gloved hand, so the batter could not see whether he wetted them or not. Then he delivered the pitch, a high hard one, up and in. The batter hit the dirt to avoid being struck by the pitch. Then came an assortment of pitches, another brushback, a fastball on the outside corner, a spitter in the dirt. Somewhere in the sequence of pitches the batter thought he saw a fastball coming right down the middle of the plate. When the ball reached its destination, the bottom fell out of the pitch. The batter swung, topping the ball, causing it to roll harmlessly back to the mound where the hurler picked it up and threw it to first base, easily retiring the batter. This sequence, or something like it, was repeated hundreds of times in the pitcher's career. The brushback was an important part of his arsenal, and he never hesitated to use it. Was it a crucial game in a World Series or a midseason contest between two second division clubs with no bearing on the pennant race? It mattered not. For the man on the mound was Burleigh Grimes, as fierce a competitor as any who ever played the game, a battler who gave it his all every time he toed the rubber.

Burleigh Arland Grimes, oldest child of Ruth Tuttle and Cecil "Nick" Grimes, was born August 18, 1893, in northwestern Wisconsin on his father's dairy farm about halfway between Clear Lake and Emerald, near the Polk-St. Croix County line. Soon after his birth the family moved to Black Brook, near Clear Lake in Polk County. His father died when the lad was quite young, and his mother struggled to support the family. When Burleigh got old enough he went to work in a lumber camp, toiling from 4:30 in the morning until 9 o'clock at night for $1 a day. Later he got a raise to $36 dollars a month. For four winters he worked in that camp. It was hard, dangerous work. Once a heavy load of logs tipped over on him. Fortunately, he lived to tell about it. Years later he related the story to a sportswriter:

> I was driving the sled. There were seven tiers of logs, two footers at the butt, sixteen feet long. The load was fourteen feet wide. There were four horses, and I was guiding them down a steep grade through the snow. We struck a stump and the load pitched forward. The thought flashed through my mind to jump clear of the load, but I hadn't time. The upper logs slid right over me. Every log on the sled pitched off except one. That was the one I had my back braced against. For some unknown reason it caught on something and held. There was just enough

space for me to lie there while the logs pitched and rolled over me. It took a crowd of husky lumber jacks several minutes to dig me out. It was a close shave for me.[1]

When Burleigh was 13, he attended a baseball game in St. Paul and was so impressed by the spitball offerings of Minneapolis Millers pitcher Hank Gehring that he went home and practiced the damp delivery until he mastered the pitch. In 1912 he began his professional career with the Eau Claire Commissioners of the Class D Minnesota-Wisconsin League, but the circuit folded in midseason. He started the 1913 season with the Ottumwa Packers of the Central Association, where he was so effective that the Detroit Tigers purchased his contract for $400. After a week the Tigers shipped him to Chattanooga without his ever having put on a Detroit uniform. He had only moderate success with the Lookouts. In 1914 he was the property of the Birmingham Barons, who loaned him to Richmond in the Class C Virginia League, where he won 23 games. The Barons recalled him on September 12. During the off-season he broke his leg, but he was ready to pitch in 1915 and had a fine season with the Birmingham club. By August 1916 he had a 23–11 record with the Barons when Pittsburgh bought his contract and called him up to the majors. One report asserts that over a six-game stretch in July and August, Grimes five times lost a no-hitter with two outs in the ninth inning.[2] Another account gives a slightly different version of this story: "Burleigh never pitched a no-hit game in the majors, but five times he went into the ninth without having allowed a safety. Once, against the Phillies in 1918, there were two out in the ninth when Fred Luderus connected for the first hit."[3] We cannot confirm the accuracy of either story.

During his four years in the Southern Association, Grimes became known as a kid who would fight at the drop of a hat.

His minor league pitching record:

Year	Club	W	L	Pct.	IP	H	BB	SO	ERA
1912	Eau Claire			Not available					
1913	Ottumwa	6	2	.750	70	46	22	57	
	Chattanooga	6	7	.462	112	110	50	33	
1914	Richmond	23	13	.639	296	260	77	190	
	Birmingham	0	2	—	10	13	11	5	
1915	Birmingham	17	13	.567	296	227	101	158	
1916	Birmingham	20	11	.645	276	214	86	119	
1935	Bloomington	10	5	.667	119	113	32	54	
Total (1912 excluded)		82	53	.607	1179	983	379	616	

League affiliations: Eau Claire, Minnesota-Wisconsin; Ottumwa, Central Association; Chattanooga and Birmingham, Southern Association; Richmond, Virginia League; Bloomington, Three-I League.

By the time he reached the majors, Grimes chewed slippery elm to better load up the ball. He sliced the bark right off the tree, and put the fiber from inside on the ball. However, he said the juice from the wood irritated his sensitive skin, so he refrained from shaving on the mornings of the days he was scheduled to pitch (and perhaps on the day before as well). The dark growth of stubble on his face gave rise to his nickname, Ol' Stubblebeard. It also added to his menacing appearance. The *New York Times* reported that he was a pitcher who frightened the hitters. "When he pitched," the *Times* reporter wrote, "he always had a two day black stubble on his face. He walked with a swagger that infuriated batters, and when he measured a hitter from the mound he would peel back his lips to show yellow teeth in a snarl. He often threw at the batters' heads without the slightest hesitation."[4] Someone once said that Burleigh's idea of an intentional walk was to throw four straight fastballs at the batter's head. He had first earned his reputation as an ornery battler at Chattanooga and his actions throughout his career served to magnify that perception.

Years later Burleigh explained his willingness to brush back hitters as an economic necessity. "When I was a teenager, I decided that the best I could make back home was thirty-five dollars a week driving horses in a lumber camp. Baseball was my answer.... There was only one man standing between me and more money, and that was the guy with the bat. I knew I'd always have to fight that man with the bat as if he were trying to rob me in a dark alley."[5]

On good days his spitter would break six to eight inches, four or five when he was not so effective. Unlike other spitball pitchers, who gripped the ball loosely, Grimes habitually held it tight and on one occasion he broke his thumbnail when he released the ball.[6] Burleigh wet the ball more than most spitballers did. Fielders complained that a sloppy wet ball was hard to handle and could cause a wild throw. Babe Ruth told of the time that Heinie Mueller was playing outfield for the Giants when Grimes was pitching for that club. Heinie had been warned about the sloppy ball and he was taking no chances. When a line drive was hit to him, he deliberately wiped the ball dry on his shirt while the runner scored from third base. Ruth said the blunder cost Mueller his job with the Giants, and the next year Heinie was back in the minors.[7] Actually Mueller was with the Boston Braves the following season, which perhaps was just as bad as being in the minors, given the caliber of team the Braves had at the time.

Grimes made his major league debut with the Pirates on September 10, 1916, and picked up the victory over the Chicago Cubs in relief. In his first major league start four days later, he pitched well but was the victim of some poor fielding by his teammates. Through five innings the rookie held the Brooklyn Robins scoreless on only three hits. In the top of the sixth, with the score tied 0–0, one out, Jake Daubert on first base, and Casey Stengel at the plate, Honus Wagner came to the mound to settle the young pitcher down. "Make him hit it to me, Kid," the great shortstop said. Sure enough, Stengel hit a hard grounder right to short — a made-to-order double play ball. Grimes was proud of himself and figured old Honus would be impressed. Horrors, the ball bounced off Wagner's foot into the outfield. Wagner came over to Grimes with his head down and said. "Those damn big feet of mine have always been in the way."[8] Before the inning was over Daubert had scored on a hit by Zack Wheat, and Stengel tallied when leftfielder Bill Hinchman was unable to catch a fly hit by George Cutshaw, giving Brooklyn a 2–0 lead. The Pirates tied it up in the seventh. With the score tied 2–2 and two out in the ninth, it appeared the game was headed for extra innings. Brooklyn's Ivy Olson was on second base and pitcher Larry Cheney was at the plate. The Pittsburgh management motioned for the outfielders to move way in toward the infield with the weak hitting pitcher at bat. Cheney lifted a high fly to left field that Hinchman could have caught easily had he been playing in his usual position. The ball bounced to the fence and Olson scored the winning run. Once again the Pirate defense had let the rookie pitcher down.

Baseball lore abounds with stories about Burleigh Grimes. Some of these tales are true, others are questionable, and still others are demonstrably untrue. One of the latter ilk refers to the spitballer's rookie season. According to this yarn, Grimes reported to the Pirates for his first big league trial while the club was in Cincinnati. He found his assigned hotel room was occupied by Larry Doyle of the New York Giants, who were just preparing to leave town. Doyle treated the rookie with such kindness that when Grimes first faced Laughing Larry in a game, he grooved one and Doyle hit it out of the park for a home run. As Lee Allen pointed out, Grimes was hardly the type to groove one for anybody, but the clincher was that Allen checked the record books. He found that the first time Grimes faced Doyle was in 1917. Doyle hit six home runs that season, none of them off Grimes.[9]

In 1916 Grimes won two games and lost three for the Pirates. The next season was worse. He lost 13 straight during a 3–16 campaign. By the end of his sophomore year, Grimes had a major league record of five wins and 19 losses. Despite his minor league success, there was some question about whether the burly righthander could survive in the majors. In the midst of the 13-game losing streak, manager Hugo Bezdek passed over Grimes's turn and started someone else in his place. As the Pirates were returning by train to Pittsburgh after the game, Grimes protested to the manager. In his reply Bezdek implied that the pitcher's problem might be that his competitive spirit was not strong enough. Wrong thing to say. As Steve Gelman related the story: "He hardly had the words out of his mouth before Grimes was on him like a wildcat. Up and down the aisle of the Pullman the two battled for the better part of an hour. It wasn't in the Marquis of Queensbury tradition, but strictly lumberjack style. The combatants each had the same fundamental idea — to choke the life out of the other. And neither was above biting when a bite would help. Eventually the other players ... pried them apart."[10]

In January 1918 the Pirates traded their brilliant but erratic young pitching star Al Mamaux to the Brooklyn Dodgers for the popular Casey Stengel and aging second baseman George Cutshaw. Pittsburgh also gave up Burleigh Grimes, described as another pitcher, and Chuck Ward, an infielder, but Mamaux was clearly the headliner in the deal.[11] During the remainder of his major league career, the star Mamaux won a total of 27 games while the throw-in Grimes won 265 in the remainder of his long career in the show.

With Brooklyn, Grimes became an instant success. Reversing his 1917 stats, he won nine in a row at one stretch in 1918. He won 19 and lost only nine for the Dodgers (or the Robins as they were frequently called during Wilbert Robinson's reign as their manager from 1914 through 1931.) Although Grimes and teammate Rube Marquard both enlisted in the Navy during the season, they were assigned to a recruiting station in Chicago and allowed to continue pitching for Brooklyn. In an arrangement that defies explanation, Grimes's naval duties cost him almost no playing time, as he led

National League pitchers in game appearances with 40 in 1918. He tied for third in wins, ranked fifth in winning percentage, fourth in base runners per nine innings, fourth in innings pitched, second in opponents' batting average, third in opponents' on base average, and fifth in ERA.

In 1919 Grimes came out of the Navy and won 10 games, despite having a sore arm. It was in this season that his memorable feud with Frank Frisch began. The Fordham Flash bunted and apparently spiked Grimes on a close play at first base. A verbal battle escalated to fisticuffs and the feud was on. "For the next ten years I aimed at least two balls at Frankie every time I pitched to him," Grimes said. "He was equally tough with me every time we came in contact on the base paths."

"He only gets three shots at me, and then the so-and-so must pitch," Frisch would growl. But once Grimes really crossed up his rival. He threw *four* dusters at Frisch, and the fourth really took the batter by surprise. He dropped to the ground so quickly that he literally fell from under his cap, which drifted slowly to the ground after him. "It was one of the few times in baseball that I was really scared," said Frankie, "and Burleigh just stood there and laughed at me."[12]

In 1920 Grimes pitched the Brooklyn club to the National League pennant. He led the league's pitchers in winning percentage; held opponents to the second lowest batting average and second lowest on-base percentage; tied for second in strikeouts; ranked third in wins, earned run average, and innings pitched; tied for third in complete games; and allowed the fifth fewest base runners per nine innings among all the circuit's hurlers. His Weighted Rating was the best in the league, while the Faber System ranked him as the circuit's second best hurler.

After Cleveland's spitballer Stan Coveleskie defeated Rube Marquard 3–1 in the series opener, both teams started their aces in the second game of the World's Series: 31-game-winner Jim Bagby against 21-game-winner Burleigh Grimes. Both hurlers pitched well, but Grimes was more effective in the clutch and shut out the Indians 3–0. The first two games of the series had each been won by a spitball pitcher. Cleveland started spitballers in the third and fourth games, Ray Caldwell losing the third to Sherry Smith of the Dodgers 2–1, and Coveleskie defeating Leon Cadore in the fourth 5–1.

With the series tied two games each, the Robins started Grimes against Bagby in the fifth contest, one of the most memorable games ever played in World Series history. The first two Cleveland batters led off with singles, and when Grimes fell down while attempting to field Tris Speaker's intended sacrifice, the bases were loaded. Up to the plate stepped Elmer Smith, who hit the first grand slam home run in World Series history. In the fourth inning the Indians hit another historic home run. Jim Bagby hit the first fall classic round-tripper by a pitcher, this one with two runners on base. With the bases loaded in the Brooklyn half of the fifth inning, spitballer Clarence Mitchell, who had entered the game in relief of Grimes, was at the plate and hit a line drive that Bill Wambsganss speared and turned into the first triple play in World Series history. Cleveland won the game 8–1 and the next 1–0 as Duster Mails pitched a masterful three-hit shutout to victimize Sherry Smith. Cleveland now led the best-of-nine series four games to two.

The seventh game was spitballer versus spitballer — Grimes against Coveleskie. Burleigh pitched well, but Stan outdueled him, tossing a five-hit shutout for his third

Although Burleigh Grimes looks relaxed in this photograph, he was one of the fiercest competitors the game has ever known. (PHOTOGRAPH COURTESY OF NATIONAL BASEBALL HALL OF FAME LIBRARY, COOPERSTOWN.)

win of the series and Cleveland's first World Series championship. Grimes blamed his loss on everyone but himself. He told an interviewer that three or four of the team's key players had violated curfew and did not show up in the best of shape to play ball.[13] He also found out later that Pete Kilduff, the Brooklyn second baseman, had been giving his pitches away. Grimes used the spitball as a decoy, faking it on almost every pitch. Kilduff would pick up a little handful of dust and put it in his glove every time the catcher called for a spitball. This was so the ball would not be slippery when it was hit to him and he had to throw it. Burleigh said that wasn't too bright. None of the other fielders thought it was necessary. But Kilduff did it and the Indians knew when the spitter was coming and laid off it because they knew it was his best pitch. Grimes blamed Detroit scout Jack Coombs for giving him bad advice that enabled Elmer Smith to hit the grand slam. As the Dodgers had not scouted the Indians, Grimes relied on Coombs, who told him to give Smith high fastballs. So Burleigh threw a high, hard one and Elmer gained immortality. When he was 90 years old, Grimes still waxed emotional about the 1920 World's Series.[14]

Even though the Dodgers had lost the World's Series, Grimes had fashioned a great season and he expected to be paid accordingly. When his 1921 contract came from Dodgers owner Charles Ebbets, Burleigh sent it back unsigned. Ebbets fired back a letter demanding that the pitcher sign. Grimes wrote back that he would stay home all season rather than pitch for the money that was offered. The owner responded with a telegram: VERY WELL. STAY THERE. The Dodgers went to spring training without Grimes. The day before the season opened, Grimes still had not reported, and no one in the Brooklyn organization had heard from him in months. Manager Wilbert Robinson went to Ebbets and said, "I don't care how you get him. All I say is get him."[15] The owner yielded to Uncle Robbie's plea and agreed to Grimes's terms.

In 1921 the burly spitballer won 22 games, tied for the most by any National League moundsman. He led the league in complete games and in strikeouts. He ranked third in innings pitched and fifth in earned run average. Both the Weighted Ratings and Faber System rankings ranked him as the best pitcher in the senior circuit. Palmer and Gillette honored him with their ex post facto Cy Young Award for 1921, the first of three they were to bestow upon him. Nevertheless, the Robins fell to fifth place in the league standings and were not to win another pennant for two decades. Only once in Burleigh's remaining years with the club did they finish in the first division.

Despite pitching for a poor team, Grimes had a good year by most standards in 1922. He won 17 games and lost 14, but he did not like to lose any. With the Dodgers entering their Daffiness phase, Burleigh was too fierce a competitor to accept lax play behind him. In an August game against the Cincinnati Reds, he was hit hard. Convinced that some of the ground balls hit off his spitter should have been fielded and turned into inning-ending double plays, burly Burleigh boiled over. Disgusted, he threw a pitch right down the middle of the plate to Jake Daubert, who promptly knocked it over the fence to climax a six-run inning. As Grimes stomped to the dugout, Robinson was waiting for him. The two laced into each other verbally. Robbie's biographers wrote that the manager had learned his cuss words with the old Baltimore Orioles, but Grimes invented his own.[16] Ebbets fined Grimes $200 and issued a public reprimand. He instructed the pitcher to apologize to the manager and to refrain from future swearing.

In 1923 Grimes again won 21 games, but his 18 losses were hard for the spitballer to stomach. He led the league in complete games and in innings pitched. He ranked third in strikeouts and tied for fourth in wins. He had difficulty with the Philadelphia Phillies, one of the weaker teams in the league. The Phils were laying off Burleigh's spitter and zeroing in on his fastball and curve. At first Robbie thought the Phils were stealing the signs from catcher Zach Taylor. When the signs were changed, the Phils continued hitting. Robbie sent Hank DeBerry in to catch Grimes, and the spitballer was still not a mystery to the team from the City of Brotherly Love. From the bench and the field, the Dodgers watched the catcher and pitcher carefully to see if they could discover the tip-off. They even suspected a spy with binoculars had been planted in the center field bleachers. At last one of the Dodgers solved the mystery. The spitballer's cap was tight fitting. When Grimes faked the spitter, the peak of his cap never moved. When he actually moistened the ball, however, the peak wiggled slightly. Burleigh got a cap a half size larger and the Phils were no problem from then on.

In 1924 the Dodgers rebounded and found themselves in a pennant race for the first time since their championship year of 1920. With Dazzy Vance coming into his own, the Dazzler and Grimes won 50 games between them. The Daffiness Boys that year were a hard-drinking, hard-fighting, high-living crew, but they combined good baseball with their hijinks. Grimes did not live as high or drink as much as some of the others because he always kept himself in top-notch physical shape. Of course, he fought as hard as anyone and occasionally he shared in their extracurricular fun.

One Sunday night the Dodgers board a midnight train in New York for a trip to Boston to play the Braves. They discovered the Braves, who had played in Philadelphia that day, were on the same train. Grimes and two teammates cut eyeholes in pillowcases, slipped them over their heads, and rushed to the Pullman car where the Braves were sleeping. They looked like Ku Klux Klan members or aliens from another planet as they awakened the Boston players screaming, "Tell us your signs." The frightened Boston catcher revealed the signs, and the Daffy trio retreated to their own car.

But when crunch time came, Burleigh was all business. In September, the Robins were in danger of falling out of the chase for the pennant. One afternoon, when Grimes was scheduled to take the mound against the Chicago Cubs, who had defeated the Brooklyn team the previous day, the sturdy pitcher addressed his teammates in the clubhouse. "This is what I have to say to you fellas. This will be the toughest game you ever played in. Anybody who can't take it can get out now. Is that clear? You'll be thrown at, you'll be knocked down and they'll try to spike you. It's up to you to be ready."[17]

Brooklyn catcher Zach Taylor said it was the most harrowing day he spent in baseball. "I had a hunch what was coming, but I never thought it was going to be that rough. I figured Burleigh might throw at Grantham and at Hartnett because of the homers they had hit the day before, but I wasn't prepared when Grimes cut loose with the first pitch at the first Chicago hitter, a kid named Art Weis, who was just up from the Texas League.... Bam! The first pitch sails past the kid's ears and he's in the dirt.... I felt sorry for him. I didn't dare sympathize with him or Grimes might have come charging at me."[18] Weis was not the only Cub to hit the dirt that afternoon; they all did. Burleigh threw behind them and at their feet. When the opposing pitcher, Grover Alexander, came to the plate, Burleigh's pitch came in right behind Alex's neck. "When Alex got up," Taylor said, "he had the strangest look on his face, like a person who finds himself locked in a room with a madman."[19]

Grimes won the game 5–4. In the fifth inning he made one of the strangest plays ever seen at Ebbets Field. Weis was on third base when one of Burleigh's spitters broke into the dirt in front of home plate and caromed off Taylor's shinguards. Seeing the ball get past the catcher, the speedy Weis headed for home. Grimes was quickly off the mound. The ball rebounded in front of the plate and the spitballer scooped up the ball, dived for the plate, and tagged Weis just before he could score. Thus, Grimes made an unassisted putout on his own wild pitch.

The Dodgers did not win the pennant in 1924 but their second-place finish was the closest they would come for many years. Grimes led the league in innings pitched, tied for the lead in complete games, and was second to his teammate Vance in both wins and strikeouts.

Grimes failed to win as many games as he lost during either of the next two years. The most memorable event of the 1925 season was one that he would have preferred to forget. On September 22 in a 12-inning 3–2 loss to the Chicago Cubs, Grimes pitched well enough but was woeful at the bat. In his first three trips to the plate he brought about seven outs, which matched the record for futility set by Clarence Mitchell in the 1920 World's Series. Burleigh ended the third and sixth innings by hitting into double plays, and outdid that by hitting into a triple play in the eighth. With runners on first and third, Grimes grounded to the shortstop, who tossed to the second baseman, who rifled the ball to the first baseman, who heaved the ball home to catch the runner trying to score from third. That game was not indicative of the Wisconsin native's ability with the bat. The burly one was a good batter and was used occasionally as a pinch hitter. Pinch-hitting one day, Grimes hit a double and moved to third on a ground out. The next batter hit a routine fly to the outfield. Grimes did not tag up and attempt to score. The next batter made the final out of the inning. Robbie raged at the pitcher, "Why didn't you tag up and score on that fly ball?" Heatedly, Grimes answered his manager, "Because I'm not a fast base runner. You should have put in a pinch runner for me. When you asked me to bat, I did and I got a hit. You should have replaced me then." Robbie's biographer wrote that the battle raged on, down the clubhouse steps and into the locker room, each man cursing the other violently.[20]

In 1926 Burleigh won 12 games and lost 13. On September 9 of that year at Baker Bowl in Philadelphia, his teammates came off the bench in an amazing display of pinch-hitting to save the burly one another loss. Grimes had been knocked out of the box in the sixth inning and left the game trailing 5–1. In the seventh inning after Johnny Butler's double, three straight pinch hitters—Zack Wheat, Jack Fournier, and Jerry Standaert—each singled to drive in two runs. The Phillies added another run in the bottom of the inning and went into the ninth leading 6–3. In the top of the final inning Butler led off with a double, and Dick Cox hit a pinch hit, driving in Butler. After Hank DeBerry popped out, Moose Clabaugh collected a pinch-hit double. Then came three hits and two bases on balls, along with a ground out, and Cox came to bat for the second time in the inning. He hit another single, his second pinch-hit of the inning and Brooklyn's sixth pinch-hit of the game. Before the carnage was over, the Dodgers had won the game 12–6, getting Burleigh off the hook. (Under present rules, Cox would be credited with only one pinch-hit, as he would be considered batting for himself the second time around and would no longer be a pinch hitter.)[21]

The Dodger management thought that perhaps, at the age of 33, Burleigh was losing his effectiveness. Besides they were tired of constantly bickering over his salary. In a complicated deal that was consummated on January 9–10, 1927, the New York Giants obtained George Harper and Walter Henline from the Phillies in exchange for Fresco Thompson and Jack Scott. Henline was then traded to Brooklyn for Grimes. Before the Phils would give up Henline they insisted on getting Alex Ferguson from the Buffalo Bisons of the International League. The Phillies sent two players to Buffalo, the Giants agreed to option two players to the Bisons and the Robins agreed to do the same with a pitcher, these players to be named at the conclusion of spring training. Sportswriter James B. Harrison wrote that baseball men were inclined to agree that the Giants got the better of the deal.[22]

Events proved the baseball men were right. The spitballer signed a contract with the Giants for $15,000 a year, considered a rather good salary at the time. Grimes won 19 games, including 14 wins in a row and lost only eight during the 1927 season. He had the third best winning percentage of all National League pitchers and ranked fourth in strikeouts. His Faber System ranking was fourth best in the circuit. He continued to ask and give no quarter. He snapped and snarled at his teammates if they failed to give their best. Once he came to blows with Rogers Hornsby in the clubhouse after a game, charging that the Rajah was bungling things in relaying McGraw's signals from the bench. But Ol' Stubblebeard rubbed McGraw the wrong way. The Little Napoleon's dictatorial methods and the fierce independence of the man from lumberjack country very likely were incompatible. At any rate, the Giants benefited from Burleigh's spitball tosses for only one season.

On February 11, 1928, the Giants traded Grimes to Pittsburgh for Vic Aldridge in a straight player transaction, no cash or convoluted deals with other players involved. The newspapers reported that the Pirates got the better of the deal. Once again the newspapers were right. The trade turned out to be much more lopsided that the scribes had predicted. In the remainder of his major league career, Aldridge was to win only four games while losing seven. On the other hand, Grimes, at the age of 34, still had some of his best years ahead of him.

In 1928 Grimes won 25 games for the Corsairs, tying for the league lead in wins. He also tied for first in complete games pitched, had the second lowest opponents' on base percentage in the circuit, and ranked fourth in strikeouts and in base runners permitted per game. He had the fifth highest strikeout total. His Weighted Rating and Faber System rankings both placed him third in the league. Thorn and Gillette awarded him their ex post facto Cy Young Award.

On July 20, 1929, Grimes fired a fastball toward the plate. Bill Terry lined it back to the mound like a bullet. The smash was too hot to handle, but Grimes instinctively put up his hands. The ball struck the thumb of his pitching hand, then caromed off. Grimes picked up the ball and threw to first, then walked off the field. With 16 victories already under his belt, he had hoped to win 30 that year for the first time in his career. Those hopes were gone; he won only one more game in 1929. He finished the year with a record of 17–7 for a winning percentage of .708, third best in the league, and his earned run average of 3.13 was second best in the NL. He had the fifth lowest opponents' batting average. His Weighted Rating and his Faber System rankings were both third in the National League for the second straight year. He was named by Thorn and Gillette as their ex post facto Cy Young Award winner for the second consecutive year. Thorn and Holway named him their Jim Creighton Award winner as the best National league pitcher of the year, the only grandfathered spitballer ever to receive this award. Even so, it was not as good a year as it would have been had Burleigh avoided Terry's line drive.

In his early years, Burleigh had relied so much on his spitter that Billy Evans feared he would not be nearly so effective if he was not allowed to continue using it after 1920.[23] As years went by he developed a wide repertoire of pitches, all thrown with an almost straight overhand motion. He still faked a spitter on every pitch, of course, and threw a lot of spitters, but Burleigh had a live fastball for most of his career, developed a good curve, and had excellent control. He said, "The spitter, which has always been an ace in the hole for me is supposed to be one reason for my success. No doubt it is. But the spitter has its drawbacks. When I'm pitching, I chew slippery elm all the time. I don't like it, but it's the only thing that I can chew that gives me satisfaction."[24] Most pitchers of that era had three pitches in their arsenal: fastball, curve, and changeup, called a slow ball in those days. The slider was thrown by only a few, among whom Burleigh Grimes was the most successful. Thus, Ol' Stubblebeard had five pitches in his assortment, even though he was starting to lose a little off his fastball by 1929. In addition, he had many years of experience. As he put it, "I haven't as much stuff as I used to have, but I'm a better pitcher. I know the batters. I know myself. I understand better what I can do myself and what the opposition is likely to do. A pitcher is like a good oak log. He needs seasoning. I work hard. I bear down all the time.... I've hurt my arm more than once by exerting it. I've hurt it by throwing a fast ball. I've hurt it several times by throwing a spitter. Any ball will hurt your arm if you put everything you have behind it. But, after all, spitters and fast balls are easy deliveries compared with curve pitching.[25]

Responding to statement that at 36 he was growing old for a ballplayer, Grimes said:

> They call me an old pitcher. Why should I be old? One of these physical culture experts told me that a man reached his prime, in physical strength, at thirty, but declined very little until he was forty or older. That's my schedule.... I weigh 190 pounds, in condition. During the season I lose perhaps ten pounds.... At season's end I'm a little stale, a little tired. So I go to a camp I have up in Wisconsin, where I spend the winter. I tramp miles every day in the snow with my gun. I breathe crisp, frosty air many hours out of the twenty-four. I eat a lot of wholesome, well-cooked food. I go to bed early and sleep like a badger in a burrow. And next season I'm fit for whatever deviltry the batters can invent.[26]

For two years with Pittsburgh, Grimes was arguably the best pitcher in the league, but after the thumb injury he was not quite the same again. Whether it was because of the injury or the effects of advancing age we cannot say. He still had a few good years left, however, even if they did not match his seasons of greatness. Grimes and the Buccaneers were unable to agree on terms for a 1930 contract. The pitcher demanded a two-year contract at $20,000 per year. President Barney Dreyfuss announced that club policy was against giving more than a one-year contract to any player. Grimes replied that unless Dreyfuss gave him the salary he wanted, he would ask to be traded or sold. "If he turns me down I will spend this year hunting and fishing in Wisconsin."[27] On April 9, 1930, the Pirates traded Grimes to the Boston Braves for Percy Jones and an undisclosed amount of cash. The lefthanded Jones won nary a game for Pittsburgh and disappeared from the major league scene. Grimes did not fare well in Beantown. He was hit on the ankle by a line drive as soon as he joined Boston and was placed on the invalid list for a while. He won his first game for the Braves by a 13–4 score over Philadelphia on April 27, but won only two more games for Boston. On June 16 the Braves sent Lord Burleigh to St. Louis in return for hurlers Fred Frankhouse and Bill Sherdel, a former spitball pitcher who had long since given up the moist delivery. This trade worked wonders for Grimes, as he compiled a 13–6 record with the Cardinals, giving him a total of 16 wins for the year.

Best of all, the trade to the Cardinals gave him another shot at the World Series, an opportunity for which he had devoutly wished. As he had told F.C. Lane in his lengthy interview the previous year. "I hope before I hang up my uniform for the last time, that I can pitch at least one more World Series game. I got a taste of the Big Series back there in 1920. But they told me afterwards that the Cleveland coaches tipped off the batters [about when the spitball was coming] when I was in the box. At that, I pitched at least one pretty good game against them, but I didn't cover myself with any glory. Now I'm older and a bit wiser and I think I'd make a better record."[28]

Grimes got his chance for glory in the 1930 World Series. Gabby Street, the Redbird manager, picked Lord Burleigh to pitch the opening game against Philadelphia "because the Athletics don't see much spitball pitching during the season and Faber of the White Sox always gives them trouble."[29] Grantland Rice wrote: "The A's are more concerned about Burleigh Grimes than anyone else. Grimes is a strong money pitcher, and he is a spitball pitcher when few are left."[30]

In the opener Grimes held the hard-hitting White Elephants to only five safeties, but two of their hits were home runs. Al Simmons and Mickey Cochrane each connected for a round-tripper and the Mackmen, behind Lefty Grove, prevailed 5–2. Grimes had another chance in Game 5. This time he matched up with George Earnshaw in one of the great pitching duels of all times. Inning after inning the two fought in a scoreless deadlock. According to John Drebinger, "Grimes tormented the A's unmercifully. Every time Mickey Cochrane came up, Burleigh would stick his thumbs in his ears and wiggle his fingers, admittedly a rather inelegant thing to do to a man whose ears protruded slightly. When Simmons came up he mimicked Al's mannerism of flecking dust from his shirt and trousers. For Foxx he saved the gesture of a man feeling his throat in a moment of great fright. Cochrane was furious, but the more good-natured Foxx gave his comrades the last laugh. In the ninth inning, with Mickey on base, Jimmy blasted a tremendous home run into the left-field bleachers."[31] Grimes lost the game 2–0. In his two series starts, Ol' Stubblebeard had pitched two complete games, giving up five hits in each game, and had two losses to show for it.

Few men ever hated to lose more than Grimes did, yet Drebinger wrote: "Grimes confounded the Athletics by jauntily breezing into their dressing room to make his peace with them."[32]

In 1931 Lord Burleigh won 17 games and lost only seven as he helped the Cardinals win another flag. The Redbirds again faced the mighty Philadelphia Athletics in the World Series. Connie Mack's team of powerful sluggers was favored to win their third straight Fall Classic, something that had not yet been accomplished since the series was inaugurated in 1903. Lefty Grove, the dominant pitcher of the times, defeated the Cards in the first game, but Bill Hallahan evened the series by shutting out the Mackmen 2–0 in the second game. Burleigh was Street's choice to start the third game and he went up against Grove, a 31-game winner who had led the American League in wins, percentage, earned run average, strikeouts, and almost every other pitching category. Grimes was superb. He pitched a two-hit masterpiece, giving up two runs on a home run by Al Simmons, and winning the game 5–2. He even contributed two runs batted in to the cause. Earnshaw came back with a two-hit shutout in the fourth game to even the series at two games apiece. Hallahan won his second game for the Cardinals 5–1, and Grove won his second 8–1 to give each team three victories. The world championship was riding on the seventh game.

In the deciding game of the series, Grimes was again matched up with Earnshaw and turned in one of the gutsiest performances in the history of baseball. During the final weeks of the season, the ex-lumberjack's appendix had become inflamed, but he refused to take time off for an operation. As game seven of the 1931 World Series progressed, the appendix began acting up. He took more and more time between pitches. Ice packs were applied between innings. He was obviously pitching in great pain, but he was pitching brilliantly. He shut out the White Elephants for eight innings. Going into the ninth, the Cardinals had a 4–0 lead. Grimes lost the first batter, Al Simmons, with a base on balls. Then Foxx fouled out, and Bing Miller forced Simmons at second base. Ol' Stubblebeard had to get only one more out to register a five-hit shutout and bring the world's championship to the banks of the Mississippi. Pitching in intense pain and showing it in every gesture, Grimes could not finish the job. A walk and two hits plated two runs and left the tying runs on base. Street brought in Hallahan, and Wild Bill induced Max Bishop to lift a fly to centerfielder Pepper Martin, and the championship belonged to the Cardinals. Grimes shared with Hallahan and Martin the role of star of the series. The veteran spitballer's two wins avenged his unfortunate defeats in the 1920 classic.

Despite Burleigh's heroism he was expendable. The Cardinals were overstocked with pitchers and needed to make room for Dizzy Dean, the sensational young pitcher who had been burning up the Texas League. On December 9 the Birds dealt Grimes to the Chicago Cubs in a straight trade with no cash involved for Hack Wilson and Bud Teachout. According to the Associated Press, in acquiring Grimes the Cubs obtained the one pitcher who had ruined more games for them than any two pitchers in the National League.[33]

Grantland Rice wrote:

> When Burleigh Grimes rounds into form and begins pitching his spitter across the plate with all the fire and pugnacity of a veteran gamester, the Chicagoans will have still more to rave about. Grimes has always been an eyeful. He pleases the new men in the game because he has the stuff, and he's a favorite of the oldsters because he still sees a baseball game as a hard, zest-

ful fight. He's been all over the circuit, but once the game starts he pitches to win, no matter what team he happens to be boosting.[34]

Grimes won his first start for the Cubs 12–5 on May 12, 1932, but never had a winning season in Chicago, posting a 6–11 record in 1932 and a 3–6 mark in a portion of the 1933 season. On July 30, 1933, the veteran spitballer was released by the Wrigleys and signed the next day by the Cardinals. He lost his first start with the Gas House Gang on August 8 as three errors by the Cardinal infield in the seventh inning led to three unearned runs. Hampered by injuries, he pitched in only 14 innings for the Cards that season and was involved in no more decisions.

By the spring of 1934 it was clear that the major league career of one Burleigh Grimes was winding down. But the old spitballer was not yet ready to hang up his spikes. Nor were all clubs ready to give up on him quite yet. The Cardinals gave him his unconditional release on May 15, 1934. Two weeks later he signed with the New York Yankees for his first venture into the American League. The Yankees released him on August 8. Three days later he was signed by the Pittsburgh Pirates for his third tour of duty with the Corsairs. He pitched for the last time in the major leagues in relief of Heinie Meine in a 9–4 loss to the Dodgers at Ebbets Field, a game that was already lost when the Lord of Burleigh took the mound. Grimes was 41 years old when he threw his last pitch in the majors. Available records do not show whether it was or was not a spitball.

His complete major league record was as follows:

Year	Club	W	L	Pct.	IP	H	BB	SO	ERA	WR	PTS
1916	Pit NL	2	3	.400	46	40	10	20	2.35	-115	8
1917	Pit NL	3	16	.158	194	186	70	72	3.53	-3781	-8
1918	Brk NL	19	9	.679	270	210	76	113	2.14	*8148*	*94*
1919	Brk NL	10	11	.476	181	179	60	82	3.47	-420	32
1920	Brk NL	23	11	**.676**	304	271	67	131	2.22	3128	73
1921	Brk NL	*22*	13	.629	302	313	76	*136*	2.83	*5565*	*81*
1922	Brk NL	17	14	.548	259	324	84	99	2.83	2139	55
1923	Brk NL	21	18	.538	*327*	356	100	119	4.76	2340	60
1924	Brk NL	*22*	13	.629	*311*	351	91	135	3.58	1435	58
1925	Brk NL	12	19	.387	247	305	102	73	5.04	-2232	20
1926	Brk NL	12	13	.480	225	238	88	64	3.71	475	38
1927	NY NL	19	8	.704	260	274	87	102	3.54	3583	72
1928	Pit NL	*25*	14	.641	*331*	311	77	97	2.99	4290	78
1929	Pit NL	17	7	.708	233	245	70	62	3.13	3792	71
1930	Bos NL	3	5	.375	49	72	22	15	7.35	-672	*
	StL NL	13	6	.684	152	174	43	58	3.01	1209	52
1931	StL NL	17	9	.654	212	240	65	73	4.07	-52	50
1932	Chi NL	6	11	.353	141	174	50	36	4.78	-4420	2
1933	Chi NL	3	6	.333	70	71	29	12	3.49	-1989	*
	StL NL	0	1	.000	14	15	8	4	5.27	-539	1
1934	StL NL	2	1	.667	8	5	2	1	3.52	141	*

Year	Club	W	L	Pct.	IP	H	BB	SO	ERA	WR	PTS
	NY AL	1	2	.333	18	22	14	5	5.50	-849	*
	Pit NL	1	2	.333	27	36	10	9	7.24	-492	11
19 years		270	212	.560	4180	4412	1295	1512	3.53	21356	848

*Faber System points based on total record.
Bold italics indicates he led or tied for the league lead.

World Series record:

		W	L	Pct.	IP	H	BB	SO	ERA
1920	Brooklyn NL	1	2	.333	19	23	9	4	4.19
1930	St. Louis NL	0	2	.000	17	10	6	13	3.71
1931	St. Louis NL	2	0	1.000	18	9	9	11	2.04
1932	Chicago NL	0	0	—	3	7	2	0	23.63
Total		3	4	.429	57	49	26	23	4.29

After his major league playing career ended, Grimes remained active in baseball for another 35 years.

In 1935, Branch Rickey wanted Grimes to be the playing manager of the Cardinals' farm team at Bloomington, Illinois, in the Three-I League. A problem developed as Rickey and the Bloomington officials wanted Grimes to pitch, using his spitball, as well as manage. John Butler, manager of the Decatur club, withheld his consent to use of the spitball until April 1. As soon as Butler relented, Grimes was appointed manager. As a pitcher, Grimes had a record of 10 wins and five losses. As a manager he led the Bloomers to the league championship

His success in the Class B Three-I League earned Grimes a promotion to the Cardinals' top farm club — Louisville of the Class AA American Association. The Colonels finished seventh in 1936, Burleigh's only year with the club. On October 2, 1936, Grimes was in the Polo Grounds watching the World Series game between the Yankees and Giants when Tony Lazzeri hit a home run with the bases loaded. Ol' Stubblebeard no longer held the distinction of being the only pitcher to yield a World Series grand slam. On that same day, Grimes was approached by officers of the Brooklyn club to see if he would be interested in managing the Dodgers.

Grimes accepted the job. He was back in the major leagues, back in Brooklyn. The Dodgers were no longer the Daffiness Boys of the 1920s, but they had much less natural talent. They had finished in seventh place in 1936 under Casey Stengel, who was fired at the end of the season. They showed little improvement under their new manager, finishing in sixth place in both 1937 and 1938. If they did not win, it was not for lack of trying by the manager. Grimes fought with the umpires, with his coaches, and with his players. The Dodger ownership brought in Babe Ruth, ostensibly as a coach, in reality as a box office attraction. The Bambino entertained the crowds with hitting mammoth home runs in batting practice, but Grimes thought the Babe was derelict in his duties as a first base coach. Tom Meany tells a story about Burleigh's encounter with a young pitcher, who had a great fastball but had not achieved much success with the

Dodgers. Grimes decided the reason for the kid's failures was that he tended to give up on himself whenever he was in a jam. When Burleigh shared his opinion with the hurler, the young man became indignant. He started to say to the 43-year-old manager, "Why, if you weren't such an old man...." He never finished the sentence as Burleigh's fist connected with his mouth.[35] Grimes lasted two years with the Dodgers.

In 1939 Burleigh was back in Double A ball, managing the Montreal Royals of the International League. Another season, another seventh-place finish.

In 1940 Grimes stepped down a few rungs on the ladder of organized baseball, clear down to the Class C Michigan State League, where he took the helm of the Grand Rapids Dodgers. While in this league, his natural combativeness got the best of him on one occasion. The old spitballer apparently spat in the wrong place. On July 31, he became engaged in a shouting match with home plate umpire Robert Williams over a close call. According to Williams, Grimes spat in the umpire's face. Burleigh was ejected from the game and suspended by the league for a full season. After several months of testimony and investigation by the National Association of Professional Baseball Leagues and some intervention by Commissioner Landis, Grimes's penalty was reduced to the remainder of the 1940 season.[36]

The problems in the Michigan State League did not end Grimes's managerial career. From 1942 through 1946 he was back in the International League — with Toronto from 1942 through 1945 and with Rochester in 1945 and 1946. His Maple Leafs won the pennant in 1943. The Leafs finished third in 1944. All of his other International League clubs of the 1940s ended up in the second division. In 1948 he managed the Independence Yankees in the Class D Kansas, Oklahoma, Missouri League for part of the season. In 1953 and 1954 he again managed the Toronto Maple Leafs. This was his third time in the International League, and it met with moderate success, the Leafs posting identical 78–76 records in the two seasons he held the managerial reins.

From 1947 to 1952 Grimes scouted for the New York Yankees. In 1955 he was a coach with the Kansas City Athletics. He scouted for the A's in 1956 and 1957. From 1960 to 1971 he scouted for the Baltimore Orioles, relinquishing this assignment at the age of 77.

Even before Grimes retired from baseball, he spent some of his off-season time farming. He had invested his savings from his baseball salary in farmland, first in Ohio and then in Missouri. Grimes was a hard-nosed negotiator with his baseball employers, which sometimes led to his being traded away, but also led to his making a higher salary than most players of his era. As a rookie, he earned $2,600. By the time of his retirement he was reported to be making $25,000 a year, among the highest salaries in baseball. (In contrast, the more compliant Red Faber probably never earned over $10,000 a year.)

Granny Rice wrote that Grimes had given midwinter interviews at his flourishing farm near New Haven, Missouri, just west of St. Louis in Franklin County, where members of the Corps of Discovery had received land grants after completing the Lewis and Clark expedition. According to Rice, Burleigh's oriental rugs and grand piano were not what one would find in a typical farmhouse parlor.[37] His 230-acre stock farm was operated by six farmhands. For recreation, there were sleek saddle horses, a pony for the children of the farm workers, and a trained horse, Crystal Lady, that could waltz, march and do other circus tricks. Later Grimes raised horse, mules, and prize hogs and farmed 545 rich acres near Trenton, in north-central Missouri, where he lived with his third wife, Inez, in a large ranch-type house with one room devoted to his baseball souvenirs. He built his house facing away from the blacktop road and looking down across the fields to the Thompson Fork of the Grand River below. Although his neighbors were aware of his reputation from his baseball days as a rough and tough character, they found him to be a very nice man, and he was well-liked in the neighborhood.[38] One neighbor said she never heard an unkind word said about him.[39] In the 1940s, the local high school built a new baseball field and named it Burleigh Grimes Field in honor of the old spitballer.[40]

Daniel Ross attributed Burleigh's competitive nature to the hardships he endured in his youth. "Grimes's fierce, win-at-all costs style of play represents the earlier era of baseball when professional players were usually drawn from rural and working class backgrounds and whose desire to win may have had roots in economic necessity.... Success on the ball field represented freedom from economic marginalization for Grimes and players like him. Professional sports were far removed from the official, public creeds of fair play and good sportsmanship, which represent the amateur ideals of the economically privileged. Grimes's reputation suffered because of his unconcealed desire to win in any way possible."[41]

When Grimes returned to northwestern Wisconsin, his hometown honored him by naming an athletic field in his honor and placing a sign at city limits proudly proclaiming Clear Lake to be the home of Burleigh Grimes. Best of all he shares with statesman Gaylord Nelson the distinction of having a special room in the village's historical museum. Among the many items on display in the room is a letter from Richard Nixon on White House stationery informing Grimes that the president had included him on his all-time team.

In 1964, Burleigh Grimes and Red Faber became the first two grandfathered spitballers to be elected to the National Baseball Hall of Fame in Cooperstown, New York. As Faber was the best exempted spitballer in the American League and Grimes the best in the National, it seems altogether fitting that they were the first of their ilk to be enshrined in the hall and that both were inducted in the same year. In contrast to Faber, who pitched every one of his 4,088 major league innings for the same club, Grimes toiled for seven different teams during his 19 years in the show.

Ol' Stubblebeard was married five times. In 1913 he married Florence Ruth van Patten in Memphis. They were divorced in 1930, following a series of court battles. Grimes filed suit for divorce on Christmas Eve 1929 in Canton, Ohio, charging that Florence interfered with his profession by accompanying him to spring training camps in violation of league rules. The judge ordered Grimes to pay temporary alimony of $200 per month until a hearing on the divorce petition was held. After a long trial, the divorce was denied in the spring of 1930. In October, Florence sued Burleigh for divorce, claiming that he was cruel, displayed no affection, and received endearing and passionate letters from other women. This time the divorce was granted. In 1931 Grimes married Laura Virginia (surname unknown). This marriage lasted until 1939. In 1940 he wed Inez Margarete Martin, who died in 1964 after 24 years of wedlock. In 1965 Grimes married Zerita Brickell, widow of his former Pirate teammate Fred Brickell. She died in 1974. On October 17, 1974, the 81-year-old Grimes married 48-year-old Lillian Gosselin Meyer. There were no children from any of these marriages.

On December 6, 1985, at the age of 92, Grimes died at Clear Lake, Wisconsin, after a long struggle with cancer. His survivors included his wife Lillian and a brother. Memorial services were held in St. Barnabas Episcopal Church in Clear Lake. It has been erroneously reported that Grimes left instructions that after his death his ashes should be spread over Wrigley Field in Chicago.[42] Perhaps the writer had Grimes confused with Charlie Grimm. Actually, Grimes is buried in a cemetery in Clear Lake under a stone that includes a small Hall of Fame symbol.[43]

3

Jack Quinn

He won 247 games in his 23 seasons in the major leagues, plus dozens more in the minors and as a semipro in a pitching career that spanned more than 30 years. Yet we do not know for certain when or where he was born, the national origin of his forbears, or even his birth name. We know him as Jack Quinn, and the reference books agree that he was born John Quinn Picus, which very likely was not the case. They also agree that he first saw the light of day in the anthracite coal mining region of Pennsylvania, but they differ on the town or the year of his birth. We checked four editions of the *Baseball Encyclopedia* and no two of them gave the same birth date and birthplace. Jack Quinn's personal life was a mystery and he liked it that way.

Depending upon which source one believes, the pitcher known as Jack Quinn was born on July 5, 1883, or 1884 or 1885. His birthplace was southwest of Wilkes-Barre, but whether it was Janesville, Jeansville, Jeanesville, Hazleton, Mahanoy City, Gorman's, St. Clair, or some other coal mining town, is a matter of dispute. The first two places can probably be ruled out, Janesville being in the wrong part of the state and Jeansville most likely being a misspelling of Jeanesville.

As for his age, it was a popular topic of speculation among baseball writers as Quinn was getting along in years. Many were of the opinion that he was at least three or four years older than the age given in most record books. Quinn did nothing to end the controversy. "I'll tell my age when I quit," he once said. "Nobody's going to know before that."[1] Eventually, the old spitballer did retire, but he reneged on his promise and even then he did not reveal his true age.

He told another interviewer, "I'm not as old as they try to make out.... Some of these newspaper fellows had me forty years old ten years ago. I'd be wearing long white whiskers like Santa Claus if I had kept pace with all the dope that's been written about my age. I'm old enough, and there's no argument on that point. But why confine me to the boneyard before my time?"[2]

Discounting the assertion in his *Sporting News* obituary that Quinn had served in the Spanish-American War, which would make him older,[3] for purposes of this work we shall assume that his date of birth was July 5, 1883. All references to his age at the time of various accomplishments will be based upon that assumption.

John Kieran wrote that Quinn was called a Welshman, a Pole, an Irishman, and an Indian, among other things.[4] Greek, Slovak, and French can be added to the mix.

53

Quinn was sometimes called an Irishman, probably by those who thought Quinn was his real name. Usually he was said to have been of Welsh or Polish extraction, a logical guess since most of the miners in the area were of such lineage, but Picus certainly is not a Welsh name. With tongue in cheek, Kieran reported that the pitcher was actually of Russian ancestry and that the family name was originally Pajkosz[5] He based this on a letter from an old resident of Mahanoy City, who said that his father was a grocer in that town, and in his daily rounds with horse and wagon he delivered groceries to the parents of Jack Quinn, who lived in Gorman's, a tiny hamlet on the outskirts of Mahanoy City. He further stated that Jack was born in Gorman's, that he was of Russian parentage, and that he was christened in the Russian church at Shenandoah, as there was no Russian church in Mahanoy City and no church of any kind in Gorman's. The old-timer said that the family's name was Pajkosz, pronounced Pie-kosh. Lee Allen, the baseball historian, wrote that he was able to find a baptismal certificate showing that our hero was born at Jeansville (sic) on July 5, 1884. He went on to state that Picus is a truncated form of the Polish name Paykos.[6]

In order to surmise why some thought Quinn was Indian, we need to understand that he was a silent man, not given to idle conversation. Kieran tells a story about two Yankee ballplayers being out at a late hour one night, liberally imbibing of the cup that cheers. They observed a third figure, silent and unmoving in the darkness. They debated whether it was Jack Quinn or a cigar store wooden Indian. One of them investigated and reported back, "He didn't say a single word." His companion remarked, "Then it must be Quinn."[7] Because of this incident, some of his teammates began referring to Quinn as a wooden Indian. Perhaps some eavesdropping scribe thought they meant Quinn was of Native American ancestry and the story spread.

Jim Zbick said the family was either Polish, Welsh, or Greek.[8] Zbick did not say why he included Greek in the mix; perhaps he thinks the name Paykos sounds Greek.

According to one Internet site, Jack's parents were Anna Czarick and Michael Picus, who lived in St. Clair, a village about five miles north of Pottsville in Schuykill County, and attended the Immaculate Conception Church on Diener's Hill in St. Clair.[9] That particular Roman Catholic Church catered to persons of Slovak descent. To us Czarick sounds like a Slovak name. So could Quinn be of Slovak descent? Perhaps, but Anna Czarick was probably his stepmother. William C. Kashatus, a foremost authority on ballplayers from the anthracite coalfields, wrote that John Picus was born in Jeanesville, the son of Polish immigrants who ran a boarding house for coal miners.[10] Kashatus is also the source of the information that the boy had a stepmother while still a child.[11]

Quinn signed his legal documents John Picus, but said his real name was something different, but he did not remember exactly what it was. He said his mother died when he was a few weeks old, his father married again to give him a stepmother, then his father died, and his stepmother married again to give him a stepfather, and the stepfather's name was Picus, pronounced Py-kus, but Quinn said he thought it was of French origin and should be spelled Piqeues[12] Whether the old spitballer expected anyone to believe his story, we do not know. Most authorities seem to think he was Polish, and we will go along with that.

At the age of 46, Jack Quinn helped pitch the Philadelphia Athletics to the world's championship. He was the starting pitcher in the World's Series game in which the A's overcame an 8-run deficit to defeat the Chicago Cubs. Quinn continued pitching professional baseball past the age of 50. (PHOTOGRAPH COURTESY OF NATIONAL BASEBALL HALL OF FAME LIBRARY, COOPERSTOWN.)

All of this discussion about Quinn's ethnic origins might seem to be much ado about nothing. But ethnicity was important to John Picus and other sons of immigrant coal miners who settled in the anthracite region in pursuit of the American Dream. Poor working conditions, low wages, and ethnic conflict resulted in tremendous hardships. As Kashatus points out, the miners sought refuge in the churches of their own ethnicity. They established fraternal societies and resided in their own ethnic groups in the small towns that dotted the anthracite region. Baseball was an important part of the assimilation process. Baseball flourished as a church-sponsored form of recreation and entertainment for coal miners and their families.[13]

For the young ballplayers, being raised in poverty and miserable working conditions, baseball offered a way out of the mines, a vehicle for upward mobility. In an era when professional baseball was dominated by Irish, English, and German names, it was not uncommon for sons of Polish immigrants to think their baseball careers might be helped by assuming a different surname. Bolinsky became Boley, Kowalewski became Coveleskie, and Wyshner became Gray. Szymanski became Simmons and Jablonowski became Appleton. Picus became Quinn, not only to avoid ethnic discrimination, but perhaps also to escape the derisive cognomen "Pick Ass."[14]

As a boy young Picus worked as a breaker boy at the mines near Pottsville. Pennsylvania law stipulated that boys had to be at least 12 years of age to work in the coal breakers and 14 to work down in the mines. As the state had no compulsory birth registration, the laws could be circumvented by lying about the child's age. When he was about 12, John Picus became a breaker boy, working in tall, wooden structures where coal was broken and sorted for market. As each coal car emerged from the mine, it was pulled to the top of the breaker by a long steel cable, where the car was tipped and the coal rushed down long chutes. The breaker boys separated the coal from the rock, slate, and other refuse as it streamed down, spewing black clouds of coal dust and smoke. To keep from inhaling the dust, the boys wore handkerchiefs and chewed tobacco in order to keep their mouths moist and prevent the dust from going down their throats.[15]

After a year in the breaker, John joined his father in the mine as a laborer, working an early shift so he could play baseball in the afternoon. Early in life he developed a combative personality, often challenging his stepmother who would not allow him to keep much of the money he earned for fear he would spend it on chewing tobacco.[16] His mining career ended when a fire broke out in the pits, forcing him to escape by fighting his way for more than a mile through suffocating smoke.

For a while, young Picus worked as a blacksmith, which helped develop his muscles, but he regarded it as an unhealthy occupation because it required him to breathe sulphur and charcoal fumes.[17]

So the teenager and an older companion hopped a freight train and headed west, riding the rails as far as Montana sometime in the 1890s. In many cases he had fight to survive. Quinn later recounted that his only possessions at the time were dirty, ragged clothes, a tattered cap, and his two fists.[18] Around the year 1900 he returned to Pennsylvania. On the morning of the Fourth of July (probably in the year 1900) he arrived in the town of Dunbar, where the big event of the day was a baseball game between the semipro teams of Dunbar and Connellsville. While he was watching the pregame practice, a ball rolled toward him and he was instructed to throw it back, which he did with such velocity that the Dunbar manager offered him a job on the spot as a pitcher, promising him $5 for a victory and $2.50 if he lost. He won the game, pocketed the $5, and started a semipro career that lasted seven years, pitching for teams from Pennsylvania towns such as Dunbar, Connellsville, Mt. Pleasant, Berlin, and Washington. He later claimed that he was getting $30 a month for pitching ball when he was 14 years old, but he was probably at least 16 or 17 at the time.

When Quinn started employing the spitball is, like many other aspects of his life, a mystery. In a rare interview in 1930, he explained why he used it: "I didn't take up the spitter because I especially like it although I learned to like it later. My fingers were so short I couldn't get a grip on the ball well enough to throw an effective curve. With a fast ball and a spitter, however, I have developed a control that I think will rank as good as anybody's in this circuit. If you bother to look up the records, you'll find that I give up fewer bases on balls, year after year, in proportion to the amount of work I do, than almost any hurler in the league."[19] We looked it up. Jack was right. In the decade starting in 1920, he twice led the league in fewest bases on balls per game and ranked in the top five, eight times in 10 years. No pitcher led more than twice, and no other ranked in the top five more than five times.

According to Zbick, Quinn did not consider his spitters to be as messy or repulsive as were those of the tobacco juice variety. Jack worked up his saliva with chewing gum, and he applied the juice by slightly touching two fingers to his lips. The "dry spitter" which Quinn delivered broke down sharply, but normally stayed in the strike zone. He kept batters guessing by faking the moist delivery on every pitch he threw, of course. He also used a no-name pitch that was a cousin to the knuckler. He threw it without using the index finger. He also developed an excellent changeup pitch.[20]

In 1903 Quinn pitched for Connellsville in the Pennsylvania State League before returning to semipro ball for a few years. In 1907 he posted a 6–5 record with Macon of the South Atlantic League in part of a season. In that same year he also pitched a few games for Pottsville in the outlaw Atlantic League, using the pseudonym Johnson. In 1908 he had an undefeated season, going 3–0 or 1–0 (sources differ) with the Toledo Mud Hens of the American Association and then winning all of his 14 decisions for Richmond, including a no-hitter in defeating Norfolk 8 to 0 on August 28.

While Quinn was pitching for Richmond in a game against Lynchburg, he was "discovered" by Al Orth and soon thereafter drafted by the New York American League club, known both as the Yankees and as the Highlanders.

Quinn made his major league debut on April 15, 1909, for the Yankees against the Washington Senators. In the first inning he gave up two hits and one run, then settled down and pitched three-hit, scoreless ball the rest of the way. He pitched a complete game, allowing a total of five hits and no bases on balls in a 4–1 victory. Among those in attendance at this game were James S. Sherman, vice president of the United States, and Ban Johnson, president of the American League. The win was the first of many over Washington by Quinn, who dominated that club as none other.

In 1910 Quinn had a banner season, winning 18 games against 12 losses for the

Yankees. He seemed well on his way to becoming a star. However, he slipped in 1911, winning only eight games while losing 10.

Things went from bad to worse for Quinn in 1912. In the seventh inning of a game against Detroit at Hilltop Park on May 11, Hippo Vaughn walked four straight batters, as the crowd yelled its displeasure at the balls called by umpire Silk O'Loughlin. In relief of the beleagurered Hippo, Quinn entered the game with the bases loaded and two out. Facing his first batter, he unleashed a wild pitch, allowing a runner to score from third. Then he buckled down and got out of the inning without further damage by striking out Oscar Stanage. In the next frame Quinn fanned Jean Duboc for his second consecutive strikeout. Next up was Donie Bush. While pitching to Bush, Quinn became so angered at one of O'Loughlin's calls that he threw his glove at the umpire. Silk ejected Quinn from the game. When protests by catcher Gabby Street and manager Harry Wolverton became too vigorous, they too were banished from the field. At this point some rowdy fans began hurling pop bottles from the stands toward the umpire. Two bottles came close to Silk's head and one hit him on the foot. The *New York Times* reported that it was the first time in the history of Hilltop Park that a demonstration of that kind had taken place there.[21] Order was eventually restored to the point where the game could be finished, Detroit won 9–5, and four Pinkerton men helped O'Loughlin to the dressing room as the crowd again hissed and hooted and threw objects at him.

American League president Ban Johnson suspended Quinn indefinitely for throwing his glove at the umpire. The suspension did not last long. Johnson lifted it on May 17. On the next day Quinn started against Cleveland. The suspension had cost him one start at the most. However, he did not pitch effectively thereafter. In late July the Yankees sold his contract to Rochester of the International League. After a short visit to Pottsville, he went through New York City on his way to report to his new club. Having been warned of recent activity by pickpockets in Gotham, the pitcher said he kept a weather eye open, but when he went to pay for his lunch, he discovered that his money — amounting to $125 — was all gone. Nevertheless, he made his way to Rochester in early August and won eight games for the Hustlers before the season ended.

In 1913 Quinn won 19 games for Rochester and was acquired by the Boston Braves near the end of August. He won his first start for the Beantowners on the last day of the month, defeating Brooklyn 6–1. Although Quinn won only four games for the Braves in his short stay with them in 1913, he became the subject of a court battle the following year after he accepted $3,500 to pitch for the Baltimore Terrapins of the upstart Federal League. A suit was brought in the United States District Court in Baltimore by James E. Gaffney, president of the Braves, asking for $25,000 in damages for the loss of Quinn's services. Claiming that Quinn had already agreed to pitch for the Braves in 1914, the Boston club unsuccessfully sued Quinn, Terrapin officials, the Federal League, and its president for conspiracy. Undeterred by the suit, Quinn pitched Baltimore to a 3–2 win over Buffalo in the opening game of the Federal League season before 30,000 ecstatic fans. The *Chicago Tribune* reported it was the largest crowd ever to see a game in Baltimore and the most enthusiastic.[22] The former coal miner went on to post 26 victories that season. The next year, however, saw a reversal of his fortunes. Jack led the league with 22 losses. After the Federal League folded, Quinn was unable to hook up immediately with a major league club and went back to the minors, signing with Vernon of the Pacific Coast League.

The spitballer had three highly successful seasons with Vernon, winning 53 games and posting an ERA of less than 3.00 each year. In 1917 he won 24 games for a last-place club. In 1918 he led the Pacific Coast League with a remarkable 1.48 ERA, the best mark ever posted in that circuit during all its years as a Double A league. He also led the league in complete games with 22 and in strikeouts with 99 in the shortened season of 1918. He won at least 102 games in minor leagues affiliated with the National Association of Professional Baseball Leagues. How many more he won in independent and semi-pro leagues is unknown.

Quinn's minor league record was as follows:

Year	Club	W	L	Pct.	IP	H	BB	SO	ERA
1907	Macon	6	5	.545	109	83	33	60	
1908	Richmond	14	0	**_1.000_**	n.a.	102	20	92	
	Toledo	1	0	1.000	10	n.a.	6	1	
1912	Rochester	8	4	.667	108	94	14	44	
1913	Rochester	19	13	.571	268	261	62	153	
1916	Vernon	16	13	.552	289	291	63	118	2.93
1917	Vernon	24	20	.545	409	415	84	169	2.36
1918	Vernon	13	9	.591	213	167	20	99	**_1.48_**
1934	Hollywood	1	1	.500	17	28	4	3	6.35
1935	Johnstown	0	0	—	2	2	0	0	0.00
Total — 9 years		102	65	.611	1425+	1443+	306	739	

Bold italics indicates he led or tied for league lead.

League affiliations: Macon, South Atlantic; Richmond, Virginia; Toledo, American Association; Rochester, International; Vernon, Pacific Coast; Hollywood, Pacific Coast; Johnstown: Middle Atlantic. He also pitched for Connellsville in the independent Pennsylvania State League, 1903–1905, statistics not available.

After the Pacific Coast League suspended operations on July 14, 1918, because of the war, the National Commission announced that players in leagues which had suspended could join, during the emergency, any club willing to pay them a salary. However, the original holding club was to retain rights to their services. Charles Comiskey signed Quinn to a White Sox contract. Quinn joined the Sox on August 1 and had a 5–1 record for the Sox over the remainder of the 1918 season. Meanwhile, the Vernon club had sold the rights to Quinn's services to the New York Yankees on July 19. After the season was over the New York Yankees lodged a claim for Quinn, and the National Commission had to decide whether the White Sox or the Yankees were entitled to his services. Meeting in December, the commission decided in favor of the Yankees, further strengthening the enmity between Comiskey and Ban Johnson, president of the American League and a member of the commission. Quinn declared he would prefer to remain with the Sox, but saw no chance of reversing the commission's decision, so he signed with the Yankees.[23]

Quinn won 15 games for the New Yorkers in 1919 and improved to an 18–10 record in 1920. In the latter season he gave up the fewest bases on ball per game of any American League pitcher and ranked fourth in opponent's batting average. In assessing the ability of various spitball pitchers to survive if forbidden to use the pitch again, Billy Evans said that Quinn would not find the going easy, but that he had a better chance than some others because he had been working on a curve for two years.[24]

The man himself professed no fear of not being able to survive without the wet one. He was quoted as saying, "I have enough stuff on the ball without mouth juice to stand them guys on their heads."[25]

With his right to continue using the moist delivery secured by the grandfather clause, Quinn nevertheless slipped to an 8–7 record in 1921. That October he got his first World's Series experience, being battered by the Giants as he relieved Bob Shawkey in the third inning of a 13–5 loss. On December 20 Quinn, already considered old for a major league pitcher, was traded along with young pitchers Rip Collins and Bill Piercy and veteran shortstop Roger Peckinpaugh to the Boston Red Sox for shortstop Everett Scott and two top-flight pitchers, "Bullet" Joe Bush and "Sad" Sam Jones.

Quinn pitched well in Boston but could never win more than 13 games per season for the woeful Red Sox teams that owner Harry Frazee had stripped of stars. The spitballer continued to exhibit excellent control, ranking among the top five in the American League in fewest walks per nine innings during his entire stay in the Hub of the Universe. Used both as a starter and in relief, he was second in saves in 1923 and third in 1924.

On July 10, 1925, Quinn was sold to the Philadelphia Athletics for the waiver price. His record for the two clubs was 13–11. He again had the league's second fewest bases on balls per game. In 1926 he won only 10 games, but retained his excellent control, ranking third in walks per game. In 1927 his fortunes improved, as did those of his team. He had a 15–10 record for the second place A's. Quinn's remarkable control and his low-breaking spitball were major assets to the White Elephants' young pitching staff as the A's were on their way to becoming the top American League team from 1929 to 1931. Babe Ruth's ghostwriter wrote that as a bluffer, Jack was in a class by himself. He bluffed the spitter on every pitch, but only threw it about one time in six pitches. He would go through the motions and then cross up the hitter with something entirely different.[26]

In 1928, at the age of 45, Quinn logged perhaps his best major league season. He won 18 games, while losing only seven, for a winning percentage of .750, fifth best in the league. He also ranked fifth in earned run average and, as was his habit, he had the second fewest bases on balls per nine innings. The secret to his success at an advanced age was his year-round conditioning program. During the off-season he did a lot of trap shooting at his lodge in Sunbury, Pennsylvania — an activity that he believed kept his eyes sharp. He also walked a great deal because he believed that a pitcher puts as much strain on his legs as on his arm. For an hour every afternoon he stood in front of a mirror and pantomimed his pitching motion. As he put it, this exercise kept his shoulder and arm muscles oiled up and prevented the stiffness that would otherwise set in after the season.[27]

In 1929 his win-loss record slipped to 11–9, but he still ranked in the top five in fewest walks per game. On October 12, the 46-year-old Methuselah became the oldest man to start a World Series game. Quinn got off to a good start in the game, pitching two-hit, shutout ball through the first three innings. In the fourth stanza he fell behind 2–0 when Kiki Cuyler's single was followed by a home run by Gabby Hartnett. In the sixth, the roof fell in on the ex-miner. The Cubs knocked him out of the box with five successive singles. When the relievers could not check the carnage, five runs were charged to Quinn. The Cubs scored another run in the top of the seventh, and took an 8–0 lead into the home half of the inning. Then the White Elephants exploded with an avalanche of runs never before matched in any inning in the history of the World Series. The home team scored 10 runs in the lucky seventh en route to a 10–8 victory in the greatest comeback ever achieved in the fall classic.

Although Quinn had been used occasionally in relief throughout his major league career, he had been primarily a starter until 1930, when he became mainly a reliever. He tied for second in saves among American League hurlers in 1930. On October 4, 1930, he became the oldest pitcher to finish a World Series game as he pitched the final two innings of the A's loss to the St. Louis Cardinals. Earlier that season, on June 27, he had become the oldest man ever to hit a home run in a major league game. On November 10, Connie Mack released the veteran spitballer to make room for a young righthanded pitcher he was calling up from Portland. The youngster, Hank McDonald, stayed in the majors two years and had a lifetime record of three wins and nine losses.

Quinn's career was not over, however. Portland tried to get permission from the Pacific Coast League to employ the spitballer, but Quinn was more interested in another shot at the majors. An Associated Press reporter tracked him down in a cabin in the Pennsylvania hills, where Jack was following his favorite sport of hunting small game. He told the reporter: "I still think I'm good for another year. I'm going to look around the majors and get another year which will give me a record of real service that any player can be proud of. I've been kicking around the country since I was twelve years old when I started out with a battered suit and two hands and a stout heart, and I guess I can keep going. I've been in baseball so long I hate to give up the game. I don't know what I will do if I don't answer the spring training call."[28]

He got his wish and then some. In January or February 1931 he was signed by the Brooklyn Dodgers as a relief specialist and led the National League in saves in both 1931 and 1932. His 15 saves in 1931 set a new senior circuit single season record, which was tied twice in 1945, but not broken until 1947 when Hugh Casey of the Brooklyn Dodgers saved 18 games. After two good years in Brooklyn, Quinn was released by the Dodgers on April 29, 1933.

It did not take him long to find additional employment. The Cincinnati Reds signed him on May 6. He appeared in 14 games for the Reds, recording one save and one loss. His final appearance came in relief of Larry Benton in a game against the Boston Braves on July 8. Cincinnati had been sailing along with a 7–2 lead going into the seventh inning. With one out the Braves drove Benton from the mound with four straight hits, including a triple by Randy Moore. The ancient spitballer came in from the bullpen with the score now 7–5, Moore on third base, and the potential tying run at the plate. Quinn retired the side with no further damage. However, he was lifted for a pinch hitter, Johnny Moore, in the eighth inning, and Jack's major league career was over. The Reds released him on July 13. At the time, Quinn's 57 saves stood second only to Firpo Marberry's record in all of major league history.

Quinn's major league record was as follows:

Year	Club	W	L	Pct.	IP	H	BB	SO	ERA	WR	PTS.
1909	NY AL	9	5	.643	119	110	24	36	1.97	2366	51
1910	NY AL	18	12	.600	237	214	58	82	2.36	630	51
1911	NY AL	8	10	.444	175	203	41	71	3.76	-1152	24
1912	NY AL	5	7	.517	103	139	23	47	5.79	1152	28
1913	Bos NL	4	3	.571	56	55	7	33	2.40	840	21
1914	Bal FL	26	14	.650	343	335	65	164	2.60	5640	87
1915	Bal FL	9	22	.289	274	291	63	118	3.45	-589	21
1918	Chi AL	5	1	.833	51	38	22	13	2.29	2358	34
1919	NY AL	15	14	.517	264	242	65	97	2.63	-2146	30
1920	NY AL	18	10	.643	253	271	48	101	3.20	896	54
1921	NY AL	8	7	.533	129	158	32	44	3.49	-1785	26
1922	Bos AL	13	16	.443	256	263	59	67	3.48	1856	44
1923	Bos AL	13	17	.433	243	302	53	71	3.89	1200	41
1924	Bos AL	12	13	.480	228	237	51	64	3.20	1350	43
1925	Bos AL	7	8	.467	105	140	26	24	4.37	2625	*
	Phi AL	6	3	.667	100	119	16	19	3.88	846	57
1926	Phi AL	10	11	.476	164	191	36	58	3.40	-1890	25
1927	Phi AL	15	10	.600	207	211	37	43	3.18	250	46
1928	Phi AL	18	7	.720	211	239	34	43	2.90	2375	66
1929	Phi AL	11	9	.550	161	182	39	41	3.88	-3300	22
1930	Phi AL	9	7	.563	90	109	22	28	4.40	-1776	28
1931	Brk NL	5	4	.556	64	65	24	25	2.67	351	24
1932	Brk NL	3	7	.300	87	102	24	28	3.31	-1420	1
1933	Cin NL	0	1	.000	16	20	5	3	4.02	-386	-2
23 years		247	217	.532	3935	4234	859	1329	3.27	23478	760

*Faber System points are based on total record of games pitched for two clubs.

World Series record:

		W	L	Pct.	IP	H	BB	SO	ERA
1921	New York AL	0	1	.000	3	8	2	2	9.82
1929	Philadelphia AL	0	0	—	5	7	2	2	9.00
1930	Philadelphia AL	0	0	—	2	3	0	1	4.50
Total		0	1	.000	10	18	4	5	8.44

After Quinn was released by the Reds, he tried to resume his minor league career. On September 19, 1933, he pitched batting practice for the Los Angeles Angels, but was not offered a contract. The Angels did not want him, but they did not want him pitching for any of their rivals, either. On January 7, 1934, on a motion by Bill Lane, president of the Hollywood club, the directors of the Pacific Coast League voted 4–2 to allow Quinn to pitch in the PCL, using the spitball. The two negative votes were cast by the Angels and the San Francisco Seals. David P. Fleming, president of the Angels, said: "If the Hollywood club signs Quinn, we will protest any game in which he pitches and carry our protest to the National Association of the Minor Leagues and we believe we have a legitimate protest that the ruling body will uphold. The spitball is a nasty delivery and was voted out of organized ball; only pitchers who were registered spitball hurlers at the time it was barred were to be allowed to continue its use as long as they remained in the same league. Quinn was not in the Coast League when the bar was put on…. I am sure that Judge W. H. Branham, president of the National Association, will uphold any protest we may be forced to make."[29]

Fleming overlooked the fact that Quinn had already changed leagues once since the ban was imposed. Originally on the American League list, he switched to the National League in 1931. Allen Sothoron had done the same thing in 1924.

One week after the Pacific Coast League voted to make him eligible, but before he had yet been offered a contract, Quinn had a narrow escape that could have ended his career. He and three other passengers were injured when an automobile driven by his brother-in-law Ross Lambert was struck by a milk truck near Ada, Ohio. Jack was cut about the head and face, but was released from the hospital after receiving first aid. However his wife and her two sisters were hospitalized overnight for the treatment of cuts and bruises. Luckily, the slight injury did not prevent the ancient pitcher from resuming his profession.

Despite the objections by the Angels, the Stars offered Quinn a contract. According to the *Los Angeles Times*, the 52-year-old spitballer signed and returned the contract by mail on February 23 from Hot Springs, Arkansas, where he was getting in shape to join the Stars at their spring training camp in Riverside. He made his first appearance of the season in relief in the second inning of a game against the Oakland Oaks. With three runs already in, two out, and two runners on base, the ancient hurler ended the inning by retiring the first batter he faced. In the third inning Quinn gave up two runs on three hits and was replaced. After three ineffective relief appearances, Quinn got his first win of 1934 on April 23, when he took the mound in the seventh inning of a tied game and pitched three scoreless innings while his teammates scored two runs in the ninth to defeat Seattle 8–6. That was his only win for the Stars. After only six games, one win and one loss, he was released.

In 1935 Quinn became manager of Johnstown of the Mid-Atlantic League and pitched two innings in one game, giving up two hits and no runs in his last appearance at the age of 52 or thereabouts.

For many years, baseball executives and sportswriters had been predicting that Quinn was near the end of his rope. Time after time he proved them wrong. In 1927, more than a decade after the first suggestions surfaced that Jack was on the downhill slope, Clifford Bloodgood speculated in the *Baseball Magazine* about the futures of the seven remaining spitballers. In his opinion, Bill Doak would be the first one to be crossed out. Although he hedged his bets, he thought Quinn and Clarence Mitchell would be stricken from the major league roles before the others.[30]

Of course, Quinn had one of his best seasons in 1928 and lasted several years beyond that. He lasted longer than anyone else except the venerable Red Faber and Burleigh Grimes, who was the youngest of the surviving spitballers.

Why was Quinn able to pitch far beyond the age when most hurlers are forced into retirement? One scribe wrote: "A powerful physique, an iron endurance, an easy delivery, and a placid mind are the four cardinal causes of his prolonged activities in the big show."[31]

Writing in 1930, Frank Young pointed out that Grimes, Faber, and Quinn were exceptions to the rule that there is more wear and tear on a spitball pitcher's arm than on that of an orthodox flinger. We would counter that the rule was never valid. Young wrote that Grimes's case was remarkable in that he bore down on every pitch and apparently finished the games as strongly as he started them. The scribe asserted that "Faber and Quinn are easy-motion pitchers and much of their effectiveness is due to their uncanny control and their smartness, for both know the weaknesses of every American League batter and pitch accordingly. From the stands they do not appear to be working hard, but every ball they throw has something on it. Few are good, but they are usually close enough to the plate to make the batter feel that he cannot take a chance on letting them go by and be called strikes."[32]

Quinn himself attributed his surprising longevity to peace of mind. He told a reporter: "There's only one right way to pitch a ball game. Do your best and let it go at that. Fussing and stewing and fretting is like throwing grit into the machinery."[33]

Few people regard Jack Quinn as a great ballplayer, but he was a very good one for many, many years. Perhaps he never had a great season, but he had more good years than most. He has not been named to the Baseball Hall of Fame but he won as many games as most of the 20th century pitchers enshrined in Cooperstown. Among Hall of Fame notables with fewer victories than the old spitballer are Joe McGinnity, Ed Walsh, Three Finger Brown, Stan Coveleskie, Herb Pennock, Dizzy Dean, Sandy Koufax, Don Drysdale, Juan Marichal, Whitey Ford and many others. John Lardner was disappointed that Quinn was not elected to the hall. He wrote: "I voted for the ageless John Picus Quinn, who pitched his spitball even longer than Faber, if not quite as well."[34]

Quinn married Georgenia Viola Lambert. She died in July 1940, in Dolton, Illinois. They had no children. After his wife's death he moved back to his native Pennsylvania, where he spent his time in a Pottsville bar pitching pennies, talking sports, and drinking to excess.[35] In January 1946, he entered Good Samaritan Hospital in Pottsville, where he died on April 17, after an illness due to a liver infection, perhaps brought on by alcohol abuse. Never one to seek publicity, he had lived in comparative obscurity for nearly a decade. He was buried in Charles Baber Cemetery in Pottsville in the anthracite coal country from which he had sprung.

4

Urban Shocker

Six of his 13 major league seasons were spent with the New York Yankees, including their fabulous 1927 season, yet he never won a World's Series game. During the first half of the decade of the 1920s, he was arguably the best pitcher in baseball, winning 20 or more games four years in a row, and racking up more wins than any other major league pitcher from 1920 to 1924. Yet he never got into a World's Series during those years. In 1926, Urban Shocker finally got his first and only World's Series start. It was the second game of the series, and the spitballer was matched up against ancient Grover Cleveland Alexander of the St. Louis Cardinals. Old Alex pitched a four-hitter, striking out 10 Bronx Bombers and giving up only two runs. Shocker pitched well, but lost 6–2. He was slated to start the seventh game of the series, but was scratched from that assignment when he was bombarded in relief of Bob Shawkey in the sixth game. It appeared that opportunities for that elusive World's Series victory would come the following year. His 1927 record was 18 wins and 6 losses for a winning percentage of .750 (second best in the league), with an earned run average of 2.84 (also second best in the league.) He was expected to start in the fall classic against the Pittsburgh Pirates, but it was not to be. Few people knew that Shocker had an enlarged heart, a dangerous condition that often caused him to sleep sitting up. He refused treatment for his ailment and grew steadily worse during the fall. He asked out of his anticipated start in the 1927 series, pleading exhaustion. Before the 1928 series rolled around, he was dead.

Although he played baseball under the name of Urban James Shocker, his original cognomen was Urbain Jacques Shockcor. He was born September 22, 1890, in Cleveland, Ohio, the fifth child and third son among the eight children of William Shockcor, a machinist, and his wife, Anna, nee Spies, a dressmaker. Most sources erroneously list the year of Urban's birth as 1892.

After moving to Detroit at an early age, Urban began his baseball career as a catcher with semipro teams in Michigan and Canada. He exhibited such speed and accuracy in his throws that he was converted into a pitcher. In 1913 he entered the professional ranks as a pitcher with Windsor of the Class D Border League. He acquired a spitter, which he used infrequently, and a variety of curves. His delivery was aided by a permanent crook in the end joint of his ring finger, suffered when he speared a ball while a catcher. He claimed the crooked finger improved his grip and made him a more effective pitcher. "It hooks over a baseball just right so that I can get a fine break on my slow ball, and that's one of the best balls I throw," he told interviewer F. C. Lane. "I can get a slow ball to drop just like a spitter, and as I occasionally throw a true spitter you will find players all over the league talking about my slow spitter, which isn't a spitter at all, but a slow ball with a freak break."[1] The following year he moved up to the Ottawa Senators of the Canadian League, tying for the league lead with 20 wins. In 1915 he led the league in both wins and strikeouts, leading the New York Yankees to purchase him for $750 late in the season.

He was with the Yankees during spring training in 1916. In an intrasquad game on March 16, while Shocker was pitching to Tim Hendryx, the batter hit a grounder down the first base line. Shocker ran over to cover the bag, and Hendryx spiked him in the foot. The *New York Times* reported that Shocker would be out of commission for several weeks.[2] It took more than a spiking to sideline the tough young pitcher. He was back in uniform on March 21. However, he could not stick with the team, and the Yankees released him to the Toronto Maple Leafs of the International League on May 15. Shocker's record with the Leafs was nothing short of sensational. He won 15 games while losing only three, pitched a 13-inning, no-hit, no-run game, and posted five consecutive shutout victories. He led the league with a winning percentage of .833 and an earned run average of 1.31, which is recognized as the league's all-time best. His string of 54 consecutive scoreless innings is another mark that has never been matched in International League history. The Yankees wanted to call Shocker up in late July, but J. J. McCaffery, owner of the Leafs, stated he would not release him until the International League season was over. However, the Yankees prevailed and Shocker was recalled by the big league team on August 3.

Shocker's minor league record was as follows.

Year	Club	W	L	Pct.	IP	H	BB	SO	ERA
1913	Windsor	6	7	.462	131	114	33	90	
1914	Ottawa	**20**	8	.714	237	191	60	158	
1915	Ottawa	**19**	10	.655	**303**	186	48	**186**	
1916	Toronto	15	3	**.833**	185	115	73	152	1.31
4 years		60	28	.682	856	606	214	586	

Bold italics indicates he led or tied for the league lead.

In his first major league start after being called up from Toronto, Shocker pitched brilliantly, allowing only two hits in eight innings, striking out seven, and giving up no bases on balls. He left the game trailing the Philadelphia Athletics 1–0, the only run having been scored by Charlie Pick, who had reached base on an error by second baseman Joe Gedeon. The *New York Times* reported that Shocker had a moist ball that darted around like a Mexican jumping bean.[3]

In 1917 Shocker won 8 and lost 5 for a sixth-place Highlander team. He and fellow spitballer Ray Caldwell, a notorious drunk, were fined for failing to return to the hotel one night in Boston. As it was his first offense, Shocker was fined only $50, while Caldwell received a more severe penalty.[4] On January 22, 1918, he was traded with Les Nunamaker, Fritz Maisel, Nick Cullop, and Joe Gedeon to the St. Louis Browns for

Urban Shocker of the St. Louis Browns was one of the dominant pitchers of the early 1920s. Heart trouble brought his career to a premature end. He died during the 1928 season. (PHOTOGRAPH COURTESY OF THE NATIONAL BASEBALL HALL OF FAME LIBRARY, COOPERSTOWN.)

Eddie Plank, Del Pratt, and $15,000. It has to be one of the worst deals the Yankees ever made. Hall of Famer Plank retired and never pitched a game for New York, and Shocker went on to have great success in St. Louis, especially against the team that traded him. The *New York Times* came to call him the Great Nemesis.

However, before Shocker could reach stardom, his career was interrupted by World

War I. His draft number came up in March 1918. He won six games for the Browns that spring before reporting for army duty on May 31. Unlike some ballplayers who spent their service time playing ball in the states, Shocker went overseas. After the war ended he sailed from France on April 1, 1919, ready to trade his army uniform for a baseball uniform. He won 13 games and lost 11 for the Browns in 1919.

When the spitball was first banned, a lifetime exemption for current practitioners was not included in the rules. There was much speculation about how spitballers would fare if denied use of the moist delivery. Billy Evans predicted that in the American League the two Urbans—Faber and Shocker—would be the most effective minus the pitch. Shocker's ability plus his gray matter would enable him to weather the storm, the veteran umpire said.[5] Of course, the adoption of the grandfather clause made it unnecessary for Shocker to drop the pitch. According to a story future Hall of Fame Waite Hoyt told Eugene Murdock, Shocker had another trick. He would suck the seams of the ball, wet them, then get tobacco or dirt on them and press them. He was able to raise the seams a little bit this way and he could make the ball "sail like hell."[6]

In 1920 Urban started a string of four consecutive years in which he won 20 or more games, the only American League hurler to accomplish that feat in those years. He allowed the second lowest on base percentage by opponents, third lowest earned run average, tied for third lowest opponents' batting average, had the fourth lowest base runners per nine innings, and ranked fifth in strikeouts. Although he started 28 of the 38 games in which he appeared, he tied for the league lead in saves. He had the league's best Weighted Rating and ranked second in Faber System points.

Shocker's 1921 season compared favorably with the previous year's outstanding record. He tied for the American League lead with 27 wins, was second in winning percentage and in strikeouts, tied for second in complete games, ranked third in innings pitched, had the league's fourth lowest opponents' on base percentage, and ranked fifth in fewest base runners per nine innings. His Weighted Rating was second best in the American League, as was his Faber System rating. His numbers in the two latter categories were good enough to lead the league in almost any other year. However, the phenomenal season posted by Red Faber dropped Shocker to second place in 1921.

While moving some furniture in his St. Louis home on December 28, 1921, Urban fractured his wrist. The injury affected his 1922 pitching performance not at all. He told a St. Louis sportswriter:

> I came down to Mobile a week before the squad, but I did not start training until the first group arrived February 23. In other years, I directed my first attention to getting my body into condition.... This year I began with my arm and virtually spent all my time getting it into condition. I began by throwing the ball around, just tossing it for several days before I even started to throw any distance. I found that 100 throws, just light tosses, hardened my arm and prepared it best for the strain of pitching. I would work until my muscles were good and tired, but I never put any great effort into one pitch. The result was that my arm hardened gradually and there never was a chance to get the arm sore.[7]

In a game at the Polo Grounds on May 23, 1922, Shocker was the unwitting cause of a most unusual play. In the bottom of the sixth inning, Wally Pipp of the Yankees grounded to first baseman George Sisler, who attempted to toss the ball to Shocker. When it became clear that Urban would be late covering the bag, Sisler managed to run toward first base and catch his own throw. Unfortunately for the Browns, however, Pipp beat Sisler to the bag for a base hit.[8]

Mel Allen told about another unusual event involving Shocker, but he did not say when it allegedly occurred. He reported that umpire George Hillenbrand said that once Shocker cut 13 stitches on a ball with a razor blade. A Cleveland batter hit it for what appeared to be a home run, but the cover fell off the ball in flight and it dropped for an easy out.[9]

In 1922 the Browns had their only chance at an American League pennant during Shocker's years with the club. The team did not live up to the high expectations their fans held for them. The *Sporting News* reported: "The fans are demanding that the Browns get a little sand and iron in their systems, take a leaf out of Urban Shocker's life and play the sort of never say die ball that hard boiled bird does, and if they don't they might as well stop counting their World Series money — Shocker can't do it all; everybody from the manager down has to help."[10] Shocker got off to a great start that season, posting 12 wins against only five losses by early June. During the remainder of the season he went 12 and 12, winding up with a 24–17 record. Shocker ran into some problems while pitching against his former team. The New York Yankees, whom he had dominated for several years after the trade, defeated him four times in a row. In one of these defeats Shocker lost more than the game. He lost control of himself. In the third inning of a game on June 10, he hit Frank "Home Run" Baker in the right side of the back with a pitch. Fearing that he had broken ribs, Baker went to a hospital for x-rays, which turned out negative and Baker was released from the hospital later the same day. Meanwhile, back at Sportsman's Park the third inning continued. Shocker, pitching to his mound opponent Carl Mays, tossed three pitches close to the batter's head. Words were exchanged. Accounts differ on who taunted whom. Mays rushed toward the mound, but was restrained by his manager, Miller Huggins, and umpire Billy Evans. Mays then drew a base on balls. The next man up was Yankee centerfielder and lead-off man Whitey Witt. He ducked a close one, which started another rumpus. Police and umpires interfered before any blows were struck. Shocker was allowed to finish the inning, but gave up four straight hits to start the fourth inning and was removed from the game at that point.

Six days after the rumpus at Sportsman's, the Browns announced that Shocker would be sidelined because of a broken blood vessel in his right leg. He had been injured at Chicago on the Browns' last road trip, but had gamely insisted on taking his regular turn in the pitching rotation until the team physician ordered him to take some time off. Shocker was hospitalized for nearly two weeks. He left the hospital on June 29 and made his next start two days later. A tough customer was Urban Shocker.

Despite losing two weeks from his injury, Shocker had another banner year in 1922. He led the league in strikeouts and allowed the fewest bases on balls per game, only the fourth man in major league history to accomplish that feat. Christy Mathewson, Walter Johnson, and Grover Cleveland Alexander had done it before Shocker, and only Robin Roberts has done it since.[11] He ranked second in complete games, base runners per nine innings, innings pitched, and opponents' on base percentage. He was third in wins and had the fifth best earned run average in the American League.

Shocker's teammate on the 1922 Browns, Frank Ellerbe, said Shocker had the best control of the spitball of anybody he ever saw. Ellerbe was quoted as saying: "He was a little wild, not wild with his pitching, but a little wild in his living. When he wasn't pitching someday maybe he might not show up, suppose to get four days rest. But he'd come back in the clubhouse and say, 'Give me one today, boys, one run and I'll beat 'em.'"[12]

Roger Godin quoted another player related to Urban's off-the-field activities: "I think he flew pretty high every once in a while.... Urban Shocker used to be pretty well faced all the time. I don't know what it was from, but it would flush up real red."[13]

The spitballer continued his excellent pitching during the 1923 season, again winning 20 games. His superb control again helped him lead the league in allowing the fewest bases on balls per game, as well as leading in fewest base runners per nine innings, and lowest on base percentage by opponents. He had the third most complete games in the American League, tied for third in wins, and ranked fourth in winning percentage. He had the second best Weighted Rating in the circuit and ranked third in Faber System points. All of this despite being suspended near the end of the season.

The suspension and accompanying fine led to developments that could have cost Commissioner Kenesaw Mountain Landis his job and changed forever the structure of baseball as it existed in the 1920s. It happened because Shocker wanted to take his second wife, Irene,[14] with him on the Browns' last road trip east during the 1923 season. The Browns had a rule that wives were not allowed on road trips. When Urban refused to go without Irene, he was fined $1,000 on September 13 and suspended from the team for 10 days. When the Browns returned to St. Louis, they lifted the suspension, but declined to rescind the fine, whereupon Shocker refused to put on his uniform and appealed to Landis to be released from the reserve clause binding him to the Browns. Shocker claimed that the rule was not only unfair, but that it also deprived him of personal liberty, and asked to be declared a free agent.

Given Shocker's reputation for off-the-field exploits, one might have expected that the Browns would have welcomed Irene Shocker's accompanying her husband. However, to the club it was a matter of player insubordination. It became a classic liberal versus conservative confrontation—a matter of principle on both sides: personal liberty against property rights; civil disobedience against the rule of law.

As Irving Vaughan of the *Chicago Tribune* pointed out: "The case is more than a mere dispute between player and club. It involves points that threaten the whole structure of organized baseball, and Landis realizes this."[15]

Writers for the pro-management *Sporting News* were vehement in their denunciation of the pitcher:

> If the rules are not to be observed in baseball, the magnates might as well shut their gates.... Such a rule is well established, justified by long experience, and for the general good of a team on the road, and there was neither reason or sense why one player should have rebelled against it, unless he was obsessed with the notion that he was absolutely indispensable to the team, and therefore able to defy any rule not to his liking.[16]

In the view of the *Sporting News* there was no room for civil disobedience in baseball. Right or wrong, the rules must be upheld. In another article published in the "Baseball Bible," the scribe wrote: "If Landis should rule in favor of Shocker, it would seem that he automatically voids all rules which clubs make and upon which rests the structure of this game's morale and its discipline."[17]

As baseball's winter meetings opened in December 1923, there were many reports that the American League, led by President Ban Johnson, threatened to withdraw from the existing major league agreement under which Landis was appointed commissioner if the judge ruled in favor of Shocker. However, Landis threw down the gauntlet, threatening to resign if the owners were dissatisfied with his administration of the commissionership. Thereupon, the owners gave a vote of confidence to Landis, and the commissioner's job was safe for the time being. Landis postponed the hearing on Shocker's case until late January, well after the winter meetings were over.

On January 18, Shocker withdrew his case against the Browns. Both sides saved face as Shocker agreed to pay the fine, and the Browns reportedly gave him a substantial raise in salary, more than enough to cover the cost of the fine.[18] Landis remained commissioner, the two leagues did not get a divorce, and free agency was delayed for decades.

Shocker's string of 20-win seasons came to an end in 1924, when he settled for 16 triumphs, but those 16 were enough to bring his total for the first half of the 1920s up to 107, more than any other pitcher in the major leagues. His pinpoint control remained with him in 1924, as he ranked third in the American League in bases on balls per game. He ranked fifth in the league in strikeouts. One of the high points of his season came on September 6, when he pitched and won both ends of a doubleheader against the Chicago White Sox.

In the opener Shocker was matched against fellow spitballer Red Faber, pitching on his 36th birthday. The teams were locked in a scoreless pitching duel until the sixth inning, when the Browns scored three runs on some sloppy fielding by the Pale Hose. Shocker went the distance for a 6–2 win. The second game was no contest. The Browns got five straight hits to open the game against Hollis Thurston and continued the assault against reliever Ted Blankenship. Shocker cruised to another 6–2 complete game win. On December 17, 1924, Shocker was traded to the New York Yankees for three pitchers—Joe Bush, Milt Gaston, and Joe Giard, who among them were to have two winning seasons with the Browns. The Yankees had recouped some of their losses from the 1918 deal.

On the day the deal was announced, a newspaperman asked Miller Huggins, the Yankees manager, if he had changed his mind about Shocker. Hug replied in the negative: all along he had known that Shocker was a good pitcher. "Then why did you get rid of him in 1918?" the writer persisted. The manager replied:

> There were a lot of things I had to find out, even about my own players. So I poked around and found out as much as I could about them before the training season started. One of the things I was told was that I would do well to get rid of Shocker as quickly as possible because he was a trouble-maker.... I later discovered that my informant had done Shocker a very grave injustice. Urban never has made trouble for anybody.[19]

A more accurate response might have been that Huggins had learned that Shocker's on-the-field performance more than compensated for his off-the-field antics.

Escape from St. Louis meant that Shocker would finally have a chance to get into a World's Series. But it was not to be in 1925. Babe Ruth had a serious illness before the start of the season, was fined $5,000 soon after he returned for serious breach of conduct, and played in fewer than 100 games. The Yankees fell to seventh place in the standings. Unbeknownst to anyone, Shocker started suffering the effects of a heart ailment. Nevertheless, Shocker won 12 games and was again among the league leaders in fewest bases on balls per game, ranking third in the American League in that category.

Both the Yankees and their spitball pitcher made remarkable comebacks in 1926. The Yanks won the pennant, thanks in no small way to the 19 wins posted by Shocker. Urban ranked third in the American League in wins and winning percentage and fifth in innings pitched and opponents' lowest on base percentage. At long last Shocker had the opportunity to pitch in a World's Series.

Shocker got his first World's Series start in the second game of the 1926, on October 3 against the venerable Grover Cleveland Alexander. Old Pete was at his best. He had great control of his fast one and the fadeaway. He kept them on the outside, hitting the corners, and had the Yankees where he wanted them almost all the time. Wilbert Robinson (or his ghostwriter) reported that "Urban was doing good pitching too. He was mixing them up, giving them everything he had—slow balls, spitters, curves and fast ones—and he was keeping them inside, holding them low and making them hit them on the handle, every time except one."[20] The one exception was a high fastball that Billy Southworth hit out of the park for a two-run homer. That blow turned a 2–2 tie into an eventual 6–2 Cardinals win as Alex retired the last 21 Yankees in succession.

Shocker still had hopes for another start. With the Yankees leading the series three games to two, manager Miller Huggins debated with himself all morning before deciding whom to start in the sixth contest. Would it be Bob Shawkey or Urban Shocker who would face Pete Alexander this time? Finally, Hug gave the nod to Shawkey, holding Shocker in reserve for the seventh game, should such prove necessary. In the seventh inning with the Yankees trailing 5–1 and two men on base, Huggins brought in Shocker from the bullpen. Urban was furious. He thought he deserved to start the sixth game, but when that did not happen, he thought the seventh game would surely be his. He was greeted with a two-run single and gave up a home run and a double before retiring the side, as the Cardinals rolled to a 10–2 win. Did Shocker's anger at his perceived mistreatment get the better of his pitching? As most baseball fans know, the Cardinals went on to win the World's Series, as Jesse Haines defeated Waite Hoyt 3–2, and Alexander gained immortality by lumbering in from the bullpen in the seventh inning and striking out Tony Lazzeri with the bases loaded.

In 1927 the Yankees had a team that many regard as the best squad ever in baseball history. Led by Ruth, Gehrig, and a murderer's row of batsmen and carried by a great pitching staff, Huggins's men won 110 games that season. Urban Shocker made his contribution to the team's success. He had an 18–6 record and a .750 winning percentage, second best in the league. His bases on balls per game also ranked second and his earned run average was the third lowest in the circuit. Babe Ruth was a great admirer of the spitballer, whom he called "Rubber Belly."[21] The Bambino's ghostwriter wrote: "Shocker is a mighty smart hombre out there on the mound, believe me. Time was when he used to have a good assortment of stuff too—but now, as he gets older, he's losing a lot of the swift. And his hook doesn't break any more, it just bends a little. But Shocker has got two things that most pitchers lack. He has control—and he's got a lot of knowledge up there under that old baseball cap of his. And the two get him over many a rough, tough spot, believe me."[22]

Fans thought that Shocker would have another chance at a World's Series victory. He had kept the secret of his illness from virtually everyone, but his health was deteriorating rapidly as series time approached. In concert with the custom of the times, Huggins did not announce his starting rotation before the series against the Pittsburgh Pirates began. The *New York Times* speculated that the Yankees would rely on Hoyt, Herb Pennock, Wilcy Moore, and Shocker. "On paper," a reporter wrote, "the Yank's best bet would appear to be Urban Shocker, who tosses a spitball. The Pirates have shown no fondness for spitballers."[23] Frank H. Young of the Washington Post wrote that Huggins told him that he was figuring on using Hoyt, Pennock, Shocker, and George Pipgras as starters.[24] Irving Vaughan wrote in the Chicago *Tribune* that Huggins would probably start Hoyt or Pennock in the first game. However, he wrote, "The Yanks have another excellent possibility in Urban Shocker, the veteran spitballer. If nothing occurs to disturb Shocker's easily disturbed nature the Pirates should find him tough to hit. No team hits a spitball pitcher hard these days because the batters see so few of them."[25]

However, it was not to be. Shocker never revealed the reason he was unable to pitch. John Drebinger wrote: "The swift elimination of the Pirates prevented the appearance of either Dutch Ruether or Urban Shocker on the mound for the Yankees. Both veterans were primed to give their best if called upon, but neither got a chance."[26] Drebinger may have been covering up for the pitcher, but more likely he did not know about Shocker's illness. Clifford Bloodgood certainly did not know about Urban's health problems. Writing in June 1927 he declined to predict which of the spit ball pitchers would last longest in the majors, but thought Grimes and Shocker should have a better chance than the others.[27]

Shock contracted heart disease, probably around 1925, but only a few of his closest friends knew it. By Christmastime of 1927, he was a very sick man. Weighing only 115 pounds, he was fighting for his life. Shocker knew he would never again take a regular turn on the mound. According to Leo Trachtenberg, Shocker had a legitimate, longstanding grievance against the Yankees and he wanted it resolved.[28] So he returned his unsigned 1928 contract and waited.

On February 16, 1928, Shocker announced his retirement from baseball in order to devote his time to his radio business in St. Louis. He said he was not a holdout and that there was no friction between him and the Yankees. Shocker obviously knew that his health would not permit him to regain his former effectiveness: "The end of my career will come eventually, so why not resign while I can leave a good record behind me. I feel that my work with the Yankees during the last two seasons is the best selling record I have."[29]

A few days after announcing his retirement, Shocker turned up in Okmulgee, Oklahoma, with plans to enter an aviation school. He reiterated his statement that he had permanently retired from baseball. However, he apparently reconsidered that decision and applied for reinstatement. Commissioner Landis reinstated him on April 7, and Shocker signed a one-year contract with the Yankees for $15,000 on April 24. He said he would work into shape and get ready to pitch. On May 8, a piece in the *New York Times* noted that Urban had lost a lot of waistline, but made no comment about his health. While pitching batting practice one day at Comiskey Park, he collapsed. At his and the club's request, the reporters who saw him pass out did not write about it.[30] It soon became obvious to both Shocker and the club that he could not regain his pitching effectiveness.

The spitballer appeared in only one game for the Yankees in 1928. On May 30 he relieved Al Shealy in the eighth inning with the Yankees trailing Washington 3–0. Although he gave up three hits in pitching two innings, the Senators were unable to score against him. This was to be his last appearance in a major league baseball game. The club gave him his unconditional release on July 8. There was still no mention in the newspapers of his health problems.

Why had the Yankees given Shocker a contract for $15,000 and why had Shocker accepted it, knowing he would never pitch a full season again? Bill Corum of the *New York Journal-American* explained. When Miller Huggins, manager of the Yankees obtained Shocker from the St. Louis Browns in 1925, he had promised the pitcher $1,500 for moving expenses. When the front office refused to authorize the payment, Hug offered to pay it out of his own pocket, but Shocker refused to accept it. "I wanted it from the club," Shocker told Corum, "It took me nearly four years, but I got it. My July 1 check squares the promise."[31]

Shocker's major league record is as follows:

Year	Club	W	L	Pct.	IP	H	BB	SO	ERA	WR	PTS
1916	NY AL	4	3	.571	82	67	32	43	2.62	378	19
1917	NY AL	8	5	.615	145	124	46	68	2.61	2535	48
1918	StL AL	6	5	.545	95	69	40	33	1.81	847	30
1919	StL AL	13	11	.542	211	193	55	86	2.69	1728	49
1920	StL AL	20	10	.667	246	224	70	107	2.71	***6360***	85
1921	StL AL	***27***	12	.692	327	345	86	132	3.55	8658	105
1922	StL AL	24	17	.585	348	365	57	***149***	2.97	-1025	48
1923	StL AL	20	12	.625	277	292	49	109	3.41	5600	79
1924	StL AL	16	13	.552	246	270	52	88	4.20	2349	56
1925	NY AL	12	12	.500	244	278	58	74	3.65	1488	44
1926	NY AL	19	11	.633	258	272	71	59	3.36	1560	59
1927	NY AL	18	6	.750	200	207	41	35	2.84	1032	61
1928	NY AL	0	0	—	2	3	0	0	0.00	0	0
13 years		187	117	.615	2682	2700	657	983	3.17	31510	683

Bold italics indicates he led or tied for the league lead.

World's Series record:

		W	L	PCT	IP	H	BB	SO	ERA
1926	New York AL	0	1	.000	8	12	0	3	5.87

After his release from the Yankees, Shocker went to Denver for his health. He pitched in a semipro tournament and was expected to be an outstanding attraction in Denver. However, he made only one start — on August 6 against a team from Cheyenne, which knocked him out of the box. He contracted pneumonia shortly thereafter and was admitted to St. Luke's Hospital on August 13. Physicians believed he was on the road to recovery, but he suffered a relapse on September 8. The next morning he insisted on seeing a newspaper to find out who was pitching for the Yankees that day. When he saw the paper, he said, "I'll be better today. I'll be able to enjoy those two victories the Yanks are going to win." He died 40 minutes later, at 7:10 a.m. on September 9, 1928. His widow said he died of a broken heart, caused by his inability to get into the thick of the American League pennant race and help his beloved Yankees.[32]

Only after his death was it revealed that he had suffered for years from a heart disease that made it impossible for him to sleep lying down. The autopsy revealed an enlarged heart half again as large as a normal one. As his physical skills deteriorated he compensated by intelligence, guile, and craftiness. In a time before advance scouts were common and before computerized reports on the performance of hitters were dreamed of, Shocker studied the tendencies of each batter. He purchased newspapers of the cities where his team was to play next and pored over the box scores and sportswriter's accounts of recent games. "He notices which men on the opposing lineup are hitting and which ones are in a slump. He notes how they go against opposing pitchers — and being a veteran and well acquainted with the styles and types of the various pitchers, he can get a pretty good line on what sort of pitching they are hitting."[33] In *The Ballplayers* he was described as "an intense, unsmiling fellow, a studious pitcher widely admired for his profound knowledge of hitters.... A serious professional, he was known as an excellent fielder and capable hitter, perhaps too serious to have a nickname."[34] Sid Keener wrote that Shocker was one of the smartest pitchers who ever carried a glove.[35]

Although Shocker had a record superior to some pitchers who have been enshrined in the Baseball Hall of Fame, he has not yet been admitted to the hall. His lifetime winning percentage of .615 was well above the median (.591) recorded by pitchers in the shrine. Bill James wrote: "The best pitcher on the 1927 Yankees, in terms of either peak value or career value, was Urban Shocker.... However, two other starters on the team, Herb Pennock and Waite Hoyt, are in the Hall of Fame."[36] On the fiftieth anniversary of the St. Louis chapter of the Baseball Writers of America, an all-star team was announced, honoring the all-time best players for teams that represented the Gateway to the West. Four pitchers were named: Jesse Haines, Grover Cleveland Alexander, and Dizzy Dean of the Cardinals, and Urban Shocker of the Browns. All but Shocker are in the Hall of Fame.

In 1958, *Sport* magazine compiled its all-time, all-star team of St. Louis Browns and Baltimore Orioles, including players from the great Oriole clubs of the 1890s. Two pitchers were selected — one right-handed and one left-handed. The right-hander chosen was Urban Shocker.

Shocker's funeral was held at All Saints' Church in St. Louis on September 15, 1928, with nearly 1,000 persons, including the entire New York Yankees ball club, in attendance. The active pallbearers were all Yankees players—Gene Robertson, Waite Hoyt, Lou Gehrig, Earl Combs, Mike Gazella, and Miles Thomas. The remainder of the team acted as honorary pallbearers. Shocker was buried in Calvary Cemetery in St. Louis. His wife, Irene, and other members of the family lie next to him.

5

Stan Coveleskie

In 1920, for the first time in their history, the Cleveland Indians played in and won a World Series. It was a powerful aggregation, this Cleveland team. Led by player-manager Tris Speaker the Indians hit .303 as a team, led the league in runs scored, and had the second best earned run average in the junior circuit. Usually regarded as the game's best fielding centerfielder, Speaker hit .388 and drove in 107 runs. Third baseman Larry Gardner, who had been Speaker's teammate on world champion Red Sox teams, hit .310, had 118 RBI, and led the league's fielders at the hot corner in putouts, assists, total chances, and fielding percentage. Right fielder Elmer Smith hit .316, with 103 runs batted in, and became the first man in baseball history to hit a home run with the bases loaded in a World Series. Joe Sewell, purchased from New Orleans following the tragic death of Ray Chapman, hit .321 and was on his way to a Hall of Fame career. Left fielder Charlie Jamieson and catcher Steve O'Neill both hit over .300, and first baseman Doc Johnston came close at .292. Second baseman Bill Wambsganss became the only man to ever make an unassisted triple play in the World Series. Pitcher Jim Bagby led the league with 31 wins, the only major league pitcher to reach that total in the 1920s. He also became the first hurler ever to hit a home run in a World Series. Spitballer Ray Caldwell was the comeback player of the year with 20 victories, including a no-hitter. Rookie Duster Mails made his first start on September 1 and was undefeated in seven decisions. Among all of these stars, who would emerge as the hero of the World Series? None of the above. It was Stan Coveleskie, who started and won three games, pitching a complete game each time and allowing only 15 hits, two bases on balls, and two runs in 27 innings. He won the opener 3–1, the fourth game 5–1 and clinched the world's championship by shutting out the Dodgers in the seventh game 3–0. He became the only pitcher between Red Faber in 1917 and Harry Brecheen in 1946 to win three games in one fall classic.

Born Stanislaus Kowalewski at Shamokin, Pennsylvania, on July 13, 1889, he spelled his name Coveleskie throughout his playing career. Most recent publications have dropped the final e from the name. Stan claimed they were all in error, including his Hall of Fame plaque. He signed his name with an "ie" ending.[1] Newspaper accounts written during his playing days almost invariably used that spelling. Why later writers use a different spelling is a mystery. Stanley's parents were both Polish immigrants. His father was an unskilled coal miner, which meant under Pennsylvania laws he was not certified to handle explosives. Stan was the youngest of five brothers, all of whom were ballplayers. His oldest brother was Jacob, a pitcher, who was killed in the Philippines during the Spanish-American War. The second son, Frank, played with an outlaw league in Pennsylvania until rheumatism ended his career. Next was John, an infielder who played several years in the minors and tried out with the Athletics but failed to make the team. Fourth was Harry, a lefthanded pitcher called the "Giant Killer" for his success against John McGraw's team. He had a successful big league career, winning 81 games over a nine-year span, with the Phillies, Cincinnati, and Detroit, and posting three consecutive 20-plus-win seasons for the Tigers.

When Stan was 12 years old he was working in the mines from seven in the morning to seven at night. For the 72-hour week he was paid $3.75, which amounts to a little more than five cents an hour. This left him little time for playing baseball. During much of the year he went to the work in the dark and came home in the dark. He once said he never knew the sun came up any day except Sunday, which is an exaggeration, of course. Every summer evening after he got home he threw stones at tin cans. He would put a tin can on a log or a fence post or tie it to a tree. Standing 40 or 50 feet away, he threw stone after stone at tin cans. He got so good at it that he claimed he could hit his target blindfolded.

When he was 16 or 18 (accounts differ) he was throwing along the sidelines with a friend before the start of a Sunday afternoon semipro game in Shamokin. Bunker Hills, the local semipro team, needed a pitcher and recruited Stan. "I guess those fellows just picked me up and asked me to play because of my accuracy," Coveleskie told William C. Kashatus. "Pitched only five games for them and then signed with Lancaster of the Tri-State League. Left the mines forever to play pro ball."[2] Coveleskie's memory does not jibe with data gathered from official records by Raymond J. Nemec.[3] These data show Stan as appearing in 12 games for Shamokin of the Atlantic League in 1908 and compiling a record of six wins and two losses. Of course, official records as kept in the early 1900s were frequently wrong. Peter Filichia does not include the Atlantic League among the leagues in organized baseball in 1908.[4]

The teenager spent three or four years with the Lancaster Red Roses of the Class B Tri-State League. In 1909 he led the league with 23 victories. For young Stanley the move to Lancaster was a major change in his life. "It was the first time I ever rode on a train," he recalled. "Had to get a new suit of clothes to go off to the big city, but was too bashful to buy it. So Mom and Dad went to town, picked one out for me, and brought it home to fit it on me. When I got to Lancaster I was too shy to eat in the hotel with the rest of the team. I'd go to a hot-dog stand and eat by myself instead."[5] In 1912 he pitched for Atlantic City and led the league in strikeouts. Late in the 1912 season he had a trial with the Philadelphia Athletics, making his big league debut on September 10. In his first start he pitched a three-hitter. Overall he won two and lost one; nevertheless, Connie Mack, who had a stable full of star pitchers, sent him to the Spokane Indians of the Northwestern League, where he pitched for two years. In 1914 he led the Class B league in strikeouts, earning a promotion to Portland of the Class AA Pacific Coast League.

According to Kashatus, by the time Coveleskie got to Portland he already had a good assortment of pitches and was developing a new one — the pitch for which he is best known — the spitter. "I saw a few pitchers throwing the spitball during my years in Lancaster and started working on that pitch," he said. "I could make it do practically anything I want it to do. At Portland, the spitter became one of my best pitches."[6]

Coveleskie told another writer a slightly different story:

> I guess that year with Portland —1915— was the turning point. I was twenty-five years old, was in my seventh year in the minors, and was starting to wonder if I'd ever make it to the Big Leagues. I had good control, a good curve, a good fast ball, and a good slow ball. But evidently that wasn't enough. One day I was watching one of the Portland pitchers throwing spitballs. "By gosh," I said to myself, "I'm going to try to throw that." I started working on the spitter, and before long I had that thing down pat. Had never thrown it before in my life. But before that season was over it was my main pitch, and the next year I was up with the Cleveland Indians. That pitch — the spitball — kept me up there for 13 years and won me over 200 games.[7]

Covey claimed he had as good control over his spitball as over his other pitches. He said he could make it break any of three ways— down, out, or down and out. Depending on his wrist action he always knew which way it would break. He explained how he threw the spitter: "For the spitball, what you do is wet these two first fingers. I used alum, had it in my mouth. Sometimes it would pucker your mouth some, get gummy. I'd go to my mouth on *every* pitch. Not every pitch would be a spitball. Sometimes I'd go maybe two or three innings without throwing one. But I'd always have them looking for it."[8]

In another interview Stan said that he used the spitter fully half of the time. "The rest of the balls I throw are generally fast ones with some curves and a few slow balls. I don't deny that I depend mostly on the spit ball."[9]

In the same interview Covey defended the use of the spitball.

> Those who pan the spit ball ought to criticize a few pitchers who misuse it. The spit ball is all right and properly handled is no more to be condemned than any other delivery. Some pitchers, mostly young fellows without any control, try to fall back on the spit ball for the ability they lack, and misuse the spit ball because they didn't know how to handle it. They are wild and the spit ball in the hands of a fellow without any sense of direction is a dangerous thing. Then they wet the spit ball altogether too much, so that it bothers the infielders. They make the spitball unpopular not only with batters on the other clubs but also with their own fielders. This isn't the fault of the spit ball, but it is the fault of those who misuse it. I never find it necessary to wet more than a small spot on the ball. By the time the fielder gets his hands on it he wouldn't know it was a spitter. And there is no excuse for being wild in throwing the spit ball. I find I can control it better than any other ball.[10]

His minor league record was as follows:

Year	Club	W	L	Pct.	IP	H	BB	SO	ERA
1909	Lancaster	**23**	11	.676	272	225	68	78	
1910	Lancaster	15	8	.652	n.a.	n.a.	n.a.	n.a.	
1911	Lancaster	15	19	.441	272	288	65	154	
1912	Atlantic City	20	13	.606	302	250	84	**199**	
1913	Spokane	17	20	.459	316	300	95	197	

Year	Club	W	L	Pct.	IP	H	BB	SO	ERA
1914	Spokane	20	15	.571	314	269	99	***214***	
1915	Portland	17	17	.500	293	279	82	171	2.67
Total — 7 years		127	103	.529	1769+	1611+	493+	1013+	

Bold italics indicates he led or tied for the league lead.

League affiliations: Lancaster and Atlantic City, Tri-State; Spokane, Northwestern; Portland, Pacific Coast League.

In 1916 the Cleveland Indians purchased Coveleskie's contract from Portland. During spring training at New Orleans, Covey was having trouble making the team. His spitball failed to break sharply, so it was not very effective. The only man who seemed to have faith in him was Jack McAllister, a Cleveland coach. Afraid that he was not going to make the grade, Stan confided his doubts to McAllister, who commented that perhaps the pitcher was gripping the ball too tightly. According to George Moriarty, then an umpire and later manager of the Detroit Tigers, "That was the solution. The next day he applied the saliva and shot the pellet from deft fingers. It broke in wicked fashion as a real spitter should. The same day added confidence came to Coveleskie when his spitter struck the catcher on the kneecap during a warm-up."[11]

So Covey made the team. He won 15 games for the Indians that year, the first of 11 consecutive seasons in which he achieved double-digit wins. Stan's brother Harry "The Giant Killer" Coveleskie was already a big league star who won 20 games each season for the Detroit Tigers from 1914 through 1917. When the Tigers made their first visit to Cleveland in 1916, arrangements were made for the brothers to face each other. When it came time to start the game, Harry refused to start against his kid brother, saying he did not want to try to defeat Stanley in his first appearance after returning to the big leagues.[12] So Stan faced George Cunningham instead and pitched great ball until the 12th inning, when Detroit broke through and handed the spitballer a 3–1 loss. While they were both in the American League, the brothers refused to pitch against each other, believing that whoever won some fans would think the loser had not given an honest effort.[13] In Detroit on September 4, the brothers appeared in the same game for the only time in their major league careers, but they did not pitch against each other. Stan started for the Indians but was knocked out of the box and was not in the game when Harry relieved for the Tigers later in the contest.[14]

The former coal miner really came into his own in 1917, posting 19 wins, with a sparkling 1.81 earned run average, the lowest ERA recorded by a Cleveland pitcher until Luis Tiant turned in a 1.60 mark in 1968. He held opponents to the lowest batting average of any American League hurler that season, and had the second lowest on base percentage by opponents. He allowed the second fewest base runners per nine innings, ranked third in earned run average, fourth in strikeouts, and fifth in number of innings pitched. Thorn and Holway called him their Jim Creighton Award winner, signifying that he was, in their opinion, the league's best hurler that season.

By 1918 Covey was becoming widely recognized as one of the best pitchers in the American League. He notched 22 victories, the first of four straight seasons in which he won 20 or more games. His win total was the second highest and his ERA the second lowest in the league. He ranked third in the junior circuit in winning percentage and in innings pitched, held his opponents to the fourth lowest on base percentage, and ranked fifth in complete games pitched. His Weighted Rating was the fifth best in the league.

In 1919 he had the second highest number of wins in the league, tied for third in game appearances, and tied for fourth in winning percentage. He ranked fifth in complete games, strikeouts, bases on balls allowed per game, and innings pitched. Like most starting pitchers of his day, Stanley occasionally relieved between starts. In 1919 he tied for fourth among AL hurlers in saves.

In 1920 Covey led the American League in four categories: strikeouts, base runners permitted per nine innings, opponents' batting average, and opponents' on base percentage. He gave up the second fewest bases on balls per game and posted the second best earned run average. He ranked third in wins and innings pitched and tied for fourth in complete games. Again Thorn and Holway gave him their Jim Creighton Award.

Although Stan had a great regular season, it was his performance in the 1920 World's Series that guaranteed his baseball immortality. In the first game of the series Coveleskie was called upon to face the National League champion Brooklyn Dodgers (or Robins as they were frequently called), who were favored to take the series crown. It was a cold October day in Flatbush, and the fans came in overcoats and furs. The *New York Times* reported: "A stolid-faced young Polander, Stanley Coveleskie, made a baseball dance before the eyes of the Brooklyn batsmen at Ebbets Field yesterday afternoon in the opening game of the 1920 world's series, and when the Cleveland pitching conjurer had finished his afternoon's task the confident Dodgers were beaten by a score of 3 to 1."[15]

Covey gave up only five hits and one walk, but had only a two-run lead going into the last of the ninth inning. The *Times* reporter described the final half-stanza thusly: "The teeth of the crowd were chattering now and the shadows of the grandstand were stretching far out over the diamond. Coveleskie was the same placid, unruffled individual that he had been throughout the game. The man hasn't any nerves. He was just as unconcerned as if he had been tossing them up for batting practice. The big Bohemian, Konetchy, was at the bat. Covey opened up his bag of tricks once more, flashed the hopping ball over the platter and Brooklyn's ambitions to capture the opening game died as Koney fanned."[16]

The Dodgers were not done, though. Burleigh Grimes shut out the Indians in Game 2 by a score of 3–0, and Sherry Smith put the Robins ahead in the series with a 2–1 win in Game 3.

The first three games had all been played in Brooklyn. Then the scene shifted to Cleveland, where the next four were contested. Coveleskie again drew the starting assignment for the Indians, and again he delivered. His teammates jumped on the Brooklyn pitchers in the first inning and all Covey had to do was protect the lead. And protect it he did, giving up only five hits and one run in a 5–1 Cleveland win. The *Times* reported: "They call Covey the accomplished Pole here, but this afternoon he was a greased Pole to the Brooklyn batters. His smooth saliva tosses slipped harmlessly off Dodger bats, and in the pinches he worked with accomplished finesse."[17]

As impressed as he was with Covey's pitching, the reporter was even more impressed with the Cleveland fans. He described

> a scene of excitement at League Park which matched any carnival of joy ever seen at a world's series game. It was the greatest gathering which has ever witnessed a ball game here. The new bleacher and field boxes were crowded and the stands were filled. Outside the park the fans were draped dangerously around telegraph poles and trees, and the housetops were crowded. Outside were thousands of disappointed men and youths who couldn't get in.... The cheering was deafening, and horns, cowbells and auto sirens, together with the frenzied shouts and yells, made a din.... Basking in the warmth of the Indian Summer sun, Cleveland's partisans got as much enjoyment out of this afternoon's triumph over Brooklyn as any gathering of humans ever got out of a sporting spectacle.[18]

Cleveland pulled ahead in the series as Jim Bagby defeated Burleigh Grimes 8–1 in game 5, the one in which Elmer Smith hit his grand slam and Bill Wambsganss made his unassisted triple play. The Indians increased their lead when Duster Mails outdueled Sherry Smith 1–0 in game 6, the only contest in the entire series in which a spitball pitcher was not involved in the decision. Cleveland now led 4 games to 2, but under the 1920 format it took five wins to clinch the championship.

The two contenders called upon their ace spitballers for game 7 — Coveleskie for the Indians and Grimes for Brooklyn. For the third time in the series, Stan was the man, shutting out his opponents 3–0. The Associated Press dubbed him the Demon Pole:

> The shut-out victory was chiefly engineered by Stanley Coveleskie, the spitball hurler of the local team. Backed by an air-tight defense on the part of his team-mates at the critical moments, the Shamokin, Pa., coal miner let the Robins down with only five hits. Only two Brooklyn players reached second base and only five of the invaders were left on bases. Coveleskie's feat in winning three of the five games necessary to clinch the championship for Cleveland will go down as one of the outstanding features of world's series history.... It is doubtful that a more masterly exhibition of pitching has been flashed before the fans since 1905, when Christy Mathewson, then at the zenith of his career with the New York Giants, shut out the Philadelphia Athletics in three games.[19]

The *Washington Post* echoed the AP praise: "Coveleskie pitched himself into the world's series hall of fame by throwing back the Dodgers three successive times, and also equaled some of the greatest pitching feats in history. Only one man — Christy Mathewson — has surpassed the Clevelander's work in the biggest games in baseball.... Coveleskie pitched three games, allowed two runs, fifteen hits, walked only two men, and what is most remarkable of all, threw the sphere plateward for an average of only 87 times each game."[20]

After the series was over, Wilbert Robinson, manager of the losing team, said: "We were beaten because the Indians outhit us and because they have in Stanley Coveleskie one of the greatest pitchers in the game; a superpitcher whenever superpitching is necessary to win."[21]

Palmer and Gillette awarded Stan their 1920 World's Series ex post facto Most Valuable Player Award.[22]

Following his World's Series triumphs, Coveleskie's neighbors in Shamokin, Penn-

Stan Coveleskie won three games for the Cleveland Indians in the 1920 World's Series, the only pitcher to accomplish that feat between Red Faber in 1917 and Harry Brecheen in 1946. (PHOTOGRAPH COURTESY OF NATIONAL BASEBALL HALL OF FAME LIBRARY, COOPERSTOWN.)

sylvania, wanted to give him a hero's welcome home. After all, as the *Chicago Tribune* pointed out, his name had been on the tongue of more persons in the length and breadth of the nation than either Warren Harding or James Cox, candidates in the upcoming presidential election. But Covey slipped unnoticed into town. Once they knew he was home, a group of boosters immediately arranged a parade and a banquet in his honor. Virtually every inhabitant of the coal mining town lined the sidewalks as the parade passed. An improvised banquet hall in a silk mill was decorated and the room was packed to the limit. When it came time for him to speak, the smiling, modest Coveleskie convinced everyone that he enjoyed pitching best. After offering his sincere thanks, he sat down with nothing more to say. A townsman rose to the occasion and in a smart address extolled Stanley as a ballplayer, a citizen, and an American. Then he presented him with a big diamond ring.[23]

At the peak of his success, Covey's big league future was in danger. The one-year exemption for continued use of the spitball expired at the end of the 1920 season. According to Billy Evans, Coveleskie was one of the greatest spitball pitchers of all time, ranking close to Ed Walsh, who when at his best was without a peer. However, Covey had always been a spitball pitcher, pure and simple. He had devoted practically all of his time to the development of a peculiar assortment of spitballs to the exclusion of everything else. The umpire said Covey's fastball was straight as a string and he never threw curves. He would find it difficult to revamp his style in a short period, and Evans feared Stanley would find the going rough without the moist delivery.[24]

After his fabulous 1920 season in which he hit 54 home runs, more than twice as many as any man had hit before, Babe Ruth was the talk of the baseball world. Naturally, the Babe reveled in the attention. As his New Year's resolution for 1921, he resolved to hit 75 dingers. Covey was not impressed.

> Babe doesn't look any bigger to me than any other batter in the American League. He got only one home run off me last season and that was when we were traveling far ahead of his train in a game. I cased a straight one right into the heart of the pad and I don't think they've found the ball yet. But Babe never scares me.... I think I am just a little bit better than he is and will continue to think so until he biffs one. If I don't break that New Year's resolution of his, it won't be my fault. I am going to try to make that long, lank willow of his look like a perforated toothpick and the ball look like a BB shot. You will understand I said "try" and if I don't succeed it won't be my fault.[25]

Although a fierce competitor, Coveleskie was usually a quiet person. But he did like his fun. In 1921 the Indians did their spring training in Dallas. One day the manager, Tris Speaker, took the squad to his hometown, Hubbard, for a barbecue on a lake. Coveleskie found a rowboat and invited Joe Sewell to take a ride with him. About a quarter of a mile from shore, Covey asked Sewell if he could swim. When Joe replied in the negative, Stan suggested this would be a good time to learn, heaved the shortstop overboard, and rowed back to shore. Sewell struggled in the water, nearly drowning before a rescue party reached him. Covey made no apologies. It was just his idea of good, clean fun.[26] In 1921 Covey finished fourth or in a tie for fourth in four categories: wins, winning percentage, complete games, and innings pitched.

Some years the Indians did their spring training in Lakeland, Florida. According to Harry Grayson, Stan had a mania for fishing. He and his roommate did not once bathe in their hotel room. They kept the bathtub full of minnows for bait. Covey always rose at six in the morning and went to the happy fishing grounds.[27]

In 1922 Stan won "only" 17 games, the first time he had fallen below the 20-win standard since 1917.

In 1923 and 1924 he recorded the only losing seasons in his 14-year major league career, falling just one win short of the break-even mark each year. Nevertheless, he led the American League in earned run average in 1923. Several of his losses could be blamed on lack of run support from his teammates. He ranked second in fewest bases on balls per game and fifth in base runners per nine innings. For the third time Thorn and Holway selected him as the recipient of their Jim Creighton Award, an unusual honor for a pitcher with a losing record. He missed a few games because of illness during the 1923 season. Covey's control was legendary. He once pitched seven and one-third innings before throwing a single pitch that was called a ball. Everything else was either a strike, fouled off, or put into play.

In one game in 1923, Covey's teammates lavished more run support upon him than he needed. Had they spread those runs around to other games Stan's won-lost record would have looked better. On July 7 the Indians faced the hapless Boston Red Sox (who had sold or traded away all of their stars) in a game at League Park. Covey was sailing along with an 11–2 lead in the sixth inning when things fell apart for the Crimson Hose. With Lefty O'Doul on the mound for Boston, the Tribe loaded the bases with two out. Joe Sewell hit a fly ball to right field. If Ira Flagstead had caught the ball, the side would have been retired and Lefty would have escaped with no runs scoring. But the right fielder dropped the ball, and the slaughter was on. The Indians scored 13 runs in the inning, all of them at the expense of O'Doul, who was not relieved during the frame. The Indians won the game 27–3. Joe Dittmar recounted some of the American League records that were set or tied in that game: 16 batters faced in one inning (tied record); 13 runs allowed in one inning (new record); 13 unearned runs in one inning (new record); 13 runs scored in an inning after two were out (new record); 27 runs scored by one team in a game (new record, later broken); Cleveland scored in every inning in which they batted (tied record.)[28]

Arthur Daley of the *New York Times* wrote about the time, probably in 1923, that Coveleskie faced Harry Heilmann of the Detroit Tigers, a .400 hitter. The bases were filled with two out. Steve O'Neill, the Cleveland catcher walked to the mound. "Covey," he said, "don't shake off my signs. We'll get this guy out if you throw what I tell you to throw."[29]

According to the story, Heilmann braced at the plate, waiting for the spitter that just had to come. Covey masked his face with his glove, the ritual that all spitball pitchers followed. In came a fastball. Heilmann took it for strike one. He was sure the next one would be a spitter, Covey's best pitch. O'Neill signaled for another fastball. Harry took it for strike two. Absolutely certain now that Covey would come through with his Sunday pitch, Heilmann stood unmoving at the plate as another fastball zipped past him. "You dirty so-and-so," said Heilmann admiringly to O'Neill.

Cleveland manager Tris Speaker, reflecting upon the two consecutive losing seasons that Coveleskie had endured in 1923 and 1924, opined that the spitballer at the age of 35 was getting too old to be successful in the major leagues. On December 12, 1924, he engineered one of the most lopsided trades in the history of baseball. The Indians traded Covey to the Washington Senators in a straight player transaction with no cash involved for pitcher Byron Speece and a minor league outfielder Carr Smith. After the deal was made Speece won a total of three games in the remainder of his big league career, and Smith never even played in another major league game. The *Washington Post* reported that if Stan could win 15 games in the coming season, he would satisfy his new bosses.[30] As it turned out, he did far better than that.

At 5′ 11″ and 166 pounds or thereabout, Coveleskie was not particularly large for an athlete. Nevertheless, sportswriter Frank H. Young liked to refer to him as the Big Pole. Young reported that the Big Pole had written a letter to the Senators' president, Clark Griffith, expressing elation at being given an opportunity to play with the world champions and assuring Griff that Washington's confidence in him had not been misplaced. Covey went on to say that he intended getting in A-1 condition and giving the Washington club all that he had.[31] A few days later, Young quoted a letter he had received from the Big Pole: "During the off-season I have been fishing and hunting every day and keeping myself in good condition. I am very much pleased with my trade. I know it will help me a great deal, as the climate is much warmer in Washington than it is in Cleveland."[32]

In 1925 Coveleskie made a spectacular comeback. He split his first two decisions, then won 13 in a row. By July 27 he had a record of 14 wins and one loss. He went six and four the rest of the season. In leading Washington to the pennant, he won 20 games while losing only five for a percentage of .800, the best in the league. He also led the circuit with a 2.84 ERA. He ranked third in base runners allowed per nine innings and in opponents' on-base percentage. He tied for the third most wins in the circuit and had the fourth lowest opponents' batting average. His Weighted Ratings was second best in the American League. Palmer and Gillette named him their Ex Post Facto Cy Young Award winner in the junior circuit.

On the Sunday before the 1925 World's Series started, Covey contracted a spasmodic muscular affliction. A headline in the Washington *Post* read "Stan Coveleskie on Shelf with Strained Back."[33] It was not known whether he would be able to play in the championship series. However, he did start the second game and pitched very well indeed, battling the Pittsburgh Pirates to a 1–1 standstill through seven innings. In the bottom of the eighth, shortstop Roger Peckinpaugh committed two errors before Kiki Cuyler hit a home run to give the Pirates a 3–1 lead and an eventual 3–2 win. Covey deserved a better fate.

Coveleskie came back in game five and held the Pirates to a 2–2 tie through six innings. In the seventh the Pirates knocked him out of the box and went on to a 6–3 victory. Ultimately, the Corsairs took the series four games to three.

Covey could never again scale the heights he had reached in 1925. In 1926 his record fell to 14–11. On August 26 of that year, he had the distinction of being the winning pitcher in the second game of a unique doubleheader. It was the only time in major league history when all four starting pitchers in a doubleheader were future Hall of Famers.[34] Walter Johnson defeated Red Faber in the first game 9–3, and Coveleskie shut out Ted Lyons and the Sox 1–0 in a 10-inning thriller in the nightcap. During the 1926 season, Covey gave up only one home run in 245 innings pitched. During his entire career, he allowed a total of 67 home runs, an average of one every 46 innings. For hurlers who pitched a significant part of their careers after 1920, that is second best to only Eppa Rixey. Of course, Covey had the advantage of pitching the 1925–27 seasons in Washington's spacious Griffith Stadium. However, he had spent the majority of his career pitching in Cleveland's League Park, a pitcher's nightmare, with a right-field fence only 290 feet away. As John Thorn and John Holway wrote, apparently it did not make any difference. Covey kept the ball in the park wherever he pitched.[35]

In 1927 he had the honor of starting the first game of the season in a match played before a crowd of about 30,000 persons, including President and Mrs. Calvin Coolidge. Stanley and his mates defeated the Red Sox 6–2. It was the first time in many years that Walter Johnson had not pitched the season opener for the Senators. Covey won only one more game in the remainder of the season. On May 9 he made his third start of the campaign, but had to leave the game early because his muscles were not functioning properly. A reporter wrote in the *Washington Post* that indications were that Covey's days as a successful big league pitcher were numbered. A lack of power seemed to be the problem. He was starting his workouts only a short distance from the catcher and gradually working back to the regular pitching distance. The reporter repeated the canard that spitball pitching is harder on a pitcher's arm than ordinary flinging.[36] Perhaps the reporter should be excused for making that mistake in 1927, but evidence to refute the charge was already accumulating. At the time Covey was in his 20th season in professional baseball and Jack Quinn had been around longer than that.

Later in the month of May, Covey underwent two dental operations, believing that the removal of some pus sacs which had been poisoning his system would enable him to regain his pitching form. Immediate improvement was noted until his arm muscles tightened up on June 1. At his request, the club sent him to Youngstown, Ohio, to receive treatments from Bonesetter Reese, a famous muscle specialist of the time. The doctor found two dislocated ligaments and worked them back into place. One of the culprits had tightened up the pitcher's arm at the elbow, and the other had interfered with the proper working of the shoulder muscles. The veteran spitballer returned to Washington on June 4, full of hope that he would soon be in condition and ready to resume his turn on the mound. Unfortunately for Covey, the Senators did not give him much time to try to recover his pitching form. On June 14, only two weeks after his return from Youngstown, the club gave him his unconditional release.

Coveleskie left immediately for his home in Shamokin for a three-week fishing trip, which he believed would get him into tip-top physical shape. Then he planned to start a come-back attempt by getting his arm in shape. "I'll be back in the big leagues long before the season ends," he informed sportswriter Frank H. Young.[37] He was right. The New York Yankees signed his to a major league contract on July 9 and he joined the Bombers immediately. However, his arm failed to come around as quickly as he and the club hoped, so he did not pitch. Covey was counted out again. In December, the old-timer wrote to Ed Barrow, the Yankee's business manager, that the arm was feeling pretty good again and he still had a fine assorted supply of saliva on hand.[38]

So Covey went to spring training with the Yankees in 1928, pitched well, and received a one-year contract. He made his first start of the season on May 7, pitched into the seventh inning, and was credited with a 4–2 win over fellow veteran spitballer Red Faber and the Chicago White Sox. In his syndicated column that summer, George

Moriarty wrote: "Coveleskie, as a member of the Yankees, still shows much of the craft that brought him fame a dozen years ago. He does it all with his spitter, as his curve was never very effective and he is too smart to put much dependence on his fastball."[39]

For the Yankees in 1928 Covey won five games while losing only one, but the club released him in August and his major league career was finally over. His last major league appearance came on July 28, when he relieved Al Shealy in the fourth inning of a game against the Cleveland Indians. The Yankees were behind 4–2 when Stanley entered the game. He pitched well for a few innings but gave up one run in the seventh and four more in the eighth. He surrendered 11 safeties in the five innings he worked.

His major league record:

Year	Club	W	L	Pct.	IP	H	BB	SO	ERA	WR	PTS
1912	Phi AL	2	1	.667	21	18	4	9	3.43	228	10
1916	Cle AL	15	13	.536	232	247	58	76	3.41	1232	48
1917	Cle AL	19	14	.576	298	202	94	133	1.81	198	50
1918	Cle AL	22	13	.629	311	261	76	87	1.82	2625	64
1919	Cle AL	24	12	.667	196	286	60	118	2.61	3060	72
1920	Cle AL	24	14	.632	315	284	65	***133***	2.49	-190	55
1921	Cle AL	23	13	.639	316	341	84	99	3.37	1332	62
1922	Cle AL	17	14	.548	277	292	64	98	3.32	1612	52
1923	Cle AL	13	14	.481	228	251	42	54	***2.76***	-1782	28
1924	Cle AL	15	16	.484	240	286	73	58	4.04	1798	48
1925	Was AL	20	5	***.800***	241	230	73	58	***2.84***	4925	***85***
1926	Was AL	14	11	.560	245	272	81	50	3.12	600	45
1927	Was AL	2	1	.667	14	13	8	7	3.14	351	11
1928	NY AL	5	1	.833	58	72	20	5	5.74	1104	28
Total — 14 years		215	142	.602	3082	3056	802	981	2.89	17093	658

Bold italics indicates he led the league.

World's Series record:

		W	L	Pct.	IP	H	BB	SO	ERA
1920	Cleveland AL	3	0	1.000	27	15	2	8	0.67
1925	Washington AL	0	2	.000	14	16	5	3	3.77
Total		3	2	.600	41	31	7	11	1.74

At the time of his retirement, Stan and his brother Harry, with 296 victories between them, held the record for the most major league wins by a pair of brothers. That record has since been topped by the Niekro brothers (Joe and Phil) and the Perry brothers (Gaylord and Jim.) In 1969 Stanley was elected to the National Baseball Hall of Fame, joining fellow spitball grandfathers Red Faber and Burleigh Grimes in the Cooperstown shrine. In 1976 he became the fourth baseball player named to the Polish-American Hall of Fame on the campus of the Orchard Lake schools near Detroit. He followed Ted Kluszewski, Stan Musial, and Al Simmons into that shrine. Both halls omit the final e from the name Coveleskie.

Unlike Jack Quinn, his fellow spitballer from the Pennsylvania anthracite fields, Covey was a worrier. He has often been quoted as saying: "I enjoyed playing ball, but it's a tough racket. There's always someone sitting on the bench just itching to get in there in your place. Thinks he can do better. Wants your job in the worst way: back to the coal mines for you, pal! The pressure never lets up. Doesn't matter what you did yesterday. That's history. It's tomorrow that counts. So you worry all the time. Lord, baseball is a worrying thing."

On March 3, 1929, he signed with the South Bend Indians, a semipro team. Several sources said that Stan and his wife, Frances, moved to South Bend in 1929. However, the 1930 United States Census for Coal Township, Northumberland County, Pennsylvania, showed Stanley and Frances Coveleskie and their sons, William, age 15, and Jack, age 10, among the residents of that coal mining area. Stan was identified as the proprietor of a gasoline station. His mother-in-law, the widowed Anna Shivetts, a native of Poland, lived with the family. (His first wife had died in Shamokin on May 28, 1920.)

After the family moved to South Bend, Stan played semipro baseball until 1935. He owned and operated a service station in the city's west end. The media guide of the South Bend Silver Hawks reported that younger baseball fans gathered at the station and Covey devoted hours of free pitching lessons to them. In the afternoons, games were played behind the garage. Through his work with the youth baseball organization, Covey encouraged the youngsters to work hard, to develop their talents, and to keep baseball alive.[40] In appreciation, the community named its baseball field after him. The South Bend Silver Hawks of the Midwest League play their games in the Stanley Coveleski Regional Stadium, as do local high school teams. The stadium hosts high school regional tournament games and musical events, such as the concert featuring Bob Dylan amd Willie Nelson in August 2004.

After a long illness, Stan died at his home in South Bend on March 20, 1984, at the age of 94. Survivors included his wife, Frances, and his son William. He was buried in the St. Joseph's Roman Catholic Cemetery in South Bend.

Bill Doak

On June 4, 1964, Sandy Koufax became the first and only man to pitch three no-hit games in the National League during the 20th century. Except for some fielding lapses, Bill Doak might have achieved this feat many years earlier.

On August 10, 1920, Doak and his St. Louis Cardinals had a 3–0 lead against the Phillies in the seventh inning. Doak walked the lead-off batter, Bevo LeBourveau, who advanced to second on a groundout. The next batter, Cy Williams, hit a grounder between first and second base. The first baseman, Jack Fournier, dove for the ball, but missed it. However, second baseman Rogers Hornsby came up with the ball, but had no one to throw it to as Doak had neglected to cover first base. Williams was credited with a base hit, the only one given up by Doak.

On May 11, 1922, Dave Bancroft led off the game for the New York Giants by bunting down the first base line. Neither Fournier nor Doak was there to field the ball. Doak held the Giants hitless the rest of the game. On July 13, 1922, Doak had his third chance for a no-hitter. Again it was the Phillies who furnished the opposition. With the Cardinals leading 1–0 in the seventh inning, Curt Walker led off with a ground ball between first and second. Doak apparently thought Hornsby would field it. However, Fournier got to the ball, but had no one to throw it to as Doak stayed on the mound. Walker was credited with the only hit the Phillies made in the game. For the third time in three years, Doak had lost a no-hitter through his own fielding inadequacy.

Why these failures? Stephen Boren wrote, perhaps in jest, that Doak was a slow learner.[1] Steve Steinberg wrote that Doak was called Lumbago Bill because he was hampered by back problems throughout his career and suggested that might be the reason he was so slow leaving the mound.[2] Whatever the reason, Doak was always a mediocre fielder. But he was quite a pitcher!

William Leopold Doak was born on January 28, 1891, in Pittsburgh, the son of Bertha R. and William E. Doak. The only son and the older of the two children in the family, the boy was named for his father and for his maternal grandfather, Leopold Shattenbrand. Both the Doak and the Shattenbrand families were of German ancestry. The elder Doak, a civil engineer, wanted his son to become a mining engineer, but Bill chose a different career path.

After playing semipro ball in Pittsburgh in 1909, Doak started his career in professional baseball with the Wheeling Stogies of the Class B Central League in 1910. He pitched for the Stogies again in 1911, having a successful season each year. He started the 1912 season with Columbus in the Class AA American Association, but soon returned to the Central League, this time with the Akron Rubbermen. He received a brief tryout with the Cincinnati Reds. Starting a game for the Reds on September 1, he lasted only two innings during which he gave up four hits, walked one, and was charged with two runs, only one of which was earned. After that one appearance, he was released and returned to Akron.

Doak pitched well for Akron in 1913, compiling a 12–6 record by midsummer. In the middle of July the St. Louis Cardinals purchased his contract for $500.

His minor league record:

Year	Club	W	L	Pct.	IP	H	BB	SO
1910	Wheeling	11	20	.355	309	272	71	98
1911	Wheeling	15	17	.469	283	275	78	120
1912	Columbus	0	2	.000	22	22	14	8
	Akron	10	5	.667	138	129	50	57
1913	Akron	12	6	.667	159	124	30	98
Total — 4 years		48	50	.490	911	822	243	381

League Affiliations: Wheeling, Central League; Columbus, American Association; Akron (1912), Central League; Akron (1913), Interstate League.

In 1913 Bill pitched reasonably well for the Cards, but had some tough luck and won only two games during the remainder of the season while losing eight. Over six feet tall but weighing only 165 pounds, Doak was rather frail-looking and put so much effort into each pitch that manager Miller Huggins suggested he take up the spitball, which requires less exertion.[3]

Bill became an enthusiastic devotee of the spitball which, combined with the requisite speed, he believed to be the pitcher's greatest weapon. In 1914 he told an interviewer that he had only just begun to learn the possibilities of the whirling mystery of the diamond. "The spitball is the most tantalizing problem of the pitcher," he said. "Some day, a man may come out of obscurity with genius enough to comprehend its why and wherefore. That man will be the greatest pitcher the world has ever seen. He will be practically invincible."[4]

Doak studied the wet delivery assiduously, but he never became invincible. However, he became one of its foremost exponents and advocates. In an article in the March 1928 issue of *Baseball* Magazine John J. Ward quoted Doak as saying,

> It makes me smile when I remember what they used to say about the spitter in the old days and how it would wreck a pitcher's elbow and shoulder. Really it's the easiest ball in the world to pitch, far easier than the curve, less trying to the arm than the fast ball, which is supposed to be the most natural of all deliveries. For the spitter is thrown with the same arm motion as the fast ball, only you don't have to put as much stuff on it to fool the batter. If I were obliged to depend on sheer speed, I'd have to burn up a lot more energy. I pitch some curves, but not many. The spitter and curve seldom mix in a pitcher's repertoire. The fast ball and the spitter are natural allies.[5]

See the Introduction of this work for Doak's explication of the pitch and an account of his successful campaign to get the antispitball rule modified so designated pitchers could continue using it after the 1920 season. According to Billy Evans, Doak probably would not have been nearly so successful had he not been able to use the spitter.[6] He not only knew how to throw the spitter, but he also knew when it was useless, such as on a wet field or in a light drizzle. Years later he related to John Drebinger a story about a time Spittin' Bill was pitching for the Cardinals with a two-run lead in the fifth inning when a light rain began to fall. He told the manager, Branch Rickey, that he had better warm up a pitcher in a hurry. Rickey said, "You're doing fine. Stay in there." Doak quickly lost the lead and the Cardinals lost the ball game. When it was over Rickey asked Bill whether he had had a premonition of impending disaster. Doak replied, "Mr. Rickey, when it rains and that ball is wet all over a spitball pitcher just doesn't have any spitball."[7]

In 1914 Spittin' Bill, as he was called, had a banner season. He won 19 games while losing only six. He led the league in earned run average, had the second best winning percentage, the third lowest batting average by opponents, and ranked fifth in fewest base runners allowed per nine innings and in lowest on base percentage by opponents. Doak ranked fifth in the league in Weighted Ratings and tied for fourth in Faber System points. He led the Cardinals to a third-place finish, their best record up until that time.

C.P. Stack, a writer for *Baseball Magazine,* allowed himself to be carried away by Doak's 1914 performance:

> Mathewson, the historic Mathewson, the idol of American fandom; the pitcher supreme, is seeing his pinnacle threatened by still another rival. Whisper it softly. It is a youngster of twenty-three.... So unexpectedly, so quietly, one might almost say so stealthily, has been the meteor-like rise of this newest star pitcher, that the full significance of his advent is only just beginning to be appreciated.... And yet this is the young man, who, in a span of less than five months, is giving the peerless Mathewson one of the hardest fights of the veteran's career, and what is even more startling, has actually elbowed his way past the record of the redoubtable one in the percentage of the season's games won.[8]

The scribe should have known that five months does not a career make. Doak had a great season in 1914, but few people today would compare Bill Doak to the legendary Christy Mathewson.

In 1915 the Cardinals slipped back into their accustomed place in the second division and Doak fell with them to a 16–18 record. In 1916 the Birds finished in a tie for last place in the National League. Doak's 12–8 mark for a percentage of .600 with this team of losers was good enough for fourth place in the circuit's Weighted Ratings. This was followed by three losing seasons, as Spittin' Bill toiled for mostly mediocre Cardinals teams.

On September 18, 1917, Doak pitched two complete games and won both ends of a doubleheader, a feat that has been matched by only half a dozen pitchers in subsequent major league seasons. Spittin' Bill shut out Brooklyn 2–0 on a two-hitter in the opener and came back to win the nightcap 12–4. The wins brought Doak's total for the season to 15, earning him an $800 bonus. He finished the season with 16 wins and 20 losses. Although he pitched well in 1918, he could win only eight games for the last place Cardinals.

One afternoon in 1919, Doak paid a visit to the Rawlings Sporting Goods Company in St. Louis and made a suggestion which ultimately brought him more fame and money than he ever earned on the pitcher's mound. Up until this time, baseball gloves had been used only to protect the hand from the impact of the horsehide. But Doak needed help with his fielding. With Doak's assistance the company developed a glove with a multithong web laced between the first finger and the thumb, thus creating for the first time a natural pocket. The glove now became a true fielding aid. Marketed as the "Bill Doak" model, the glove became so popular that Rawlings produced it until 1953. Bill earned as much as $25,000 a year in royalties.

In 1920 Doak had his one and only 20-win season. Winning 20 games while losing 12 for a winning percentage of .625 for a second-division club earned him the second highest Weighted Rating of any National League hurler. According to Faber System ratings he was the third best pitcher in the league that year. Jack Fournier, who was Doak's teammate on the Cardinals and later on the Dodgers, told about one of Spittin' Bill's pre-game routines: "Doak would regard himself steadily in a mirror for a considerable time before going to the dugout on his day to work, meanwhile assuring himself that he was the greatest pitcher in the world and practically impossible to beat."[9]

Although he won only 15 games in 1921, that season was one of Bill's best. He led the league not only in winning percentage with a .714 mark, but also in earned run average. He ranked fifth in the league in fewest bases on balls per game and held opponents to the fifth lowest batting average. He had the third best Weighted Rating in the senior circuit. During the ensuing winter, he revealed that he had suffered from an injured ligament in his pitching arm throughout the entire season. In February he informed the Cardinals that the trouble had been corrected and his arm was in splendid condition. He explained that he did not mention his ailment during the season because he knew ballplayers received no sympathy.[10]

If his arm was in better condition in 1922 than in the previous year, his record did not show it. He lost more games than he won in both 1922 and 1923. He was used sparingly by the Cardinals in 1924, pitching but 24 innings before he was traded on June 13 to the Brooklyn Dodgers for another right-handed pitcher, Leo Dickerman. It seems that almost every time a club traded away one of the exempted spitballers, that club got the worst of the deal. Dickerman won seven games for St. Louis in 1924 and just four in 1925, his final season in the major leagues. Meanwhile, Doak had a sensational second half of the year for the Robins. He won 10 consecutive games as he, Burleigh Grimes, and Dazzy Vance very nearly pitched the Flatbush team to a pennant. In an amazing streak, Brooklyn came from far back in the race by winning 29 out of 35 games in one stretch, including 15 in a row. During the run, Doak and Vance won seven games each, and Grimes won six. On September 27, Bill's streak of consecutive wins came an end as the Boston Braves defeated Brooklyn 3–2 and eliminated the Dodgers from the race.

If the Flatbush faithful expected Doak to help the Robins take the crown in 1925, and they surely did, they were sadly disappointed. Spittin' Bill expected to be rewarded for his previous year's heroics with a hefty pay raise. When Brooklyn's offer did not meet his expectations, Doak became a holdout. In those days, the reserve clause was a standard part of every baseball player's contract. If a player refused to sign a contract with a club owner that had him on its reserve list, he could not sign with any other club in organized baseball. His only alternative was not to play baseball at all, but to go back to the farm or the mines or to get a job laying bricks or digging ditches.

Doak found his alternative in the buying and selling of real estate. The Florida land boom was in full blast in 1925. A *New York Times* reporter wrote: "The boom now booming in Florida is something between fantasy and farce, miracle and merry-go-round.... The astounding thing about the impossible tales you hear, the improbable advertisements you read, is that so many of them turn out to be true."[11] The population of Miami and its environs grew at an amazing rate. Swamps were drained and thriving communities sprang up.

Bill Doak voluntarily retired from baseball and opened a real estate office in Florida. When the Dodgers became convinced that Doak was serious about quitting baseball, they upped his salary offer to $15,000. A letter was written, signed by manager Wilbert Robinson and every member of the team, asking him to come back. However, Doak said he could not be swayed by sentiment, as he was well established in another occupation now. His business was going well until a natural disaster brought the Florida land boom to a screeching halt. On September 18, 1926, a fearful hurricane struck the Miami area and followed a deadly path across the state to the gulf and into Alabama and Mississippi. In east Florida alone 374 people were killed, 4,000 were injured, and 30,000 were left homeless. Property damage in the two communities of Miami and Hollywood was estimated at over $100 million. Doak closed his real estate office and applied for reinstatement in baseball.

On December 16, 1926, Commissioner Landis granted reinstatement and shifted Doak's name from the voluntarily retired to the active list of the Brooklyn club. He held out for a time, but eventually signed a contract on March 14, 1927. In spring training Bill convinced Robinson that his spitter was as effective as ever. In the regular season he won 11 while losing eight, not bad for a hurler with a sixth-place club. However, it was his last good year. In June 1927, *Baseball Magazine* published an article by Clifford Bloodgood in which the author wrote: "For the last two years he has been out of the game entirely seeking his Utopia in Florida real estate. Any pitcher has a hard time to come back after a long lay off. A pitcher who has sweated through 13 years and 2529 innings will have an exceptionally difficult task to resume Major League efficiency. Were we bold enough to eliminate any of the seven [remaining spitball pitchers], Doak in our opinion would be one of the first to be crossed out."[12] Actually, the scribe was fairly close to the mark. Only Stan Coveleskie and Urban Shocker, suffering from a fatal disease unknown to the writer, hung up their spikes before Spittin' Bill.

On March 16, 1928, the town of Bradenton celebrated William Doak day. The *New York Times* reported:

> There was a parade in which more than a hundred cars made their way through the streets, while more than half a dozen bands rent the air. Out at the ball park ... Bill went out and pitched a couple of innings, although if the truth must be told, William did not show quite

Although an outstanding spitball pitcher, Bill Doak is best known as the inventor of the modern baseball glove. (PHOTOGRAPH COURTESY OF NATIONAL BASEBALL HALL OF FAME LIBRARY, COOPERSTOWN.)

so well on the mound as did his confreres. The Sox scored their only two runs off him, but then, when a man starts out an assignment with a floral horseshoe dangling around his neck one must not be too critical!"[13]

The Robins defeated the Boston Red Sox in the exhibition game 7–2.

During the season Doak managed only three victories while again suffering eight losses, pitching mainly in relief. On October 4, 1928, the Robins unconditionally released the veteran spitballer. Doak announced that he would return to the real estate business at Bradenton, Florida.

As it turned out, Spittin' Bill was not yet quite through with baseball. The St. Louis Cardinals signed him to a contract on March 22, 1929. He appeared in only three games for the Cards, posting a 1–2 record before ending his major league career.

His major league record:

Year	Club	W	L	Pct.	IP	H	BB	SO	ERA	WR	PTS
1912	Cin NL	0	0	—	2	4	1	0	4.50	0	0
1913	StL NL	2	8	.200	93	79	39	51	3.10	-1500	2
1914	StL NL	19	6	.760	256	193	87	118	***1.72***	6800	92
1915	StL NL	16	18	.471	276	263	85	124	2.64	0	40
1916	StL NL	12	8	.600	192	177	55	82	2.63	4780	66
1917	StL NL	16	20	.444	281	257	85	111	3.10	-4536	15
1918	StL NL	9	15	.375	211	191	60	74	2.43	-600	25
1919	StL NL	13	14	.481	203	182	55	69	3.11	2916	52
1920	StL NL	20	12	.625	270	256	80	90	2.53	5568	79
1921	StL NL	15	6	.714	209	224	37	83	***2.59***	3549	59
1922	StL NL	11	13	.458	180	222	69	73	5.54	-2640	21
1923	StL NL	8	13	.381	185	199	69	53	3.26	-3297	11
1924	StL NL	2	1	.667	22	25	14	7	3.27	750	*
	Brk NL	11	5	.684	149	130	35	32	3.07	1552	59
1927	Brk NL	11	8	.579	145	153	40	32	3.48	3344	57
1928	Brk NL	3	8	.273	99	104	35	12	3.26	-2706	-1
1929	StL NL	1	2	.333	9	17	5	3	12.00	-552	1
Total — 16 years		169	157	.518	2783	2676	851	1014	2.98	13428	577

*Records from two clubs are combined to provide Faber System points.
Bold italics indicates he led the league in that category.

Doak retired to Bradenton and operated a confectionary shop for several years, known as Bill Doak's Sweet Shop. He also became the club professional at a local golf course. According to Westbrook Pegler, the American Association ruled that Doak was not eligible to throw the spitter in that league, so Doak's hopes of returning to organized ball ended in 1931.[14]

However, Bill remained involved in baseball, coaching Bradenton High School to the state baseball championship one year. Always busy, he was active in the Boys Club and sponsored and coached midget baseball and American Legion teams.

As a golf pro, Doak's best student may very well have been his son Bobby. In his first major golf competition at the age of 15, Bobby won the Florida amateur golf championship, the youngest golfer ever to win that title. Shortly thereafter the youngster won the state high school championship. The lad credited his father for his success: "Dad perfected my swing and gave me many pointers. But, more important, he taught me to keep plugging when things were not going so well."[15]

In summarizing Doak's career, Steinberg wrote that he was solid but unspectacular, relying on good control and an effective slow drop (curveball) to go with his signature spitball. He noted that Doak was a slow and deliberate worker, who used a huge red handkerchief to wipe his brow a few times each game.[16] Was that for showmanship? Spittin' Bill still ranks second in career shutouts for the St. Louis Cardinals, behind only Bob Gibson. Steinberg quoted the *Sporting News* as calling Doak the only strictly moral man on the Cards, perhaps because he taught a Sunday school class before going to the ballpark.[17]

Bill Doak died in Bradenton on November 26, 1954, apparently of a heart attack, at the age of 63. He was survived by his widow, the former Jessie Porter; his mother, Mrs. William E. Doak; a daughter, Mrs. J.O. Smith; two sons, William E. Doak and Robert J. Doak; and a sister, Mrs. Hazel Shook.

7

Ray Caldwell

He was washed up; just a bad boy of the diamond on the road to oblivion. Broke, forgotten, and without a job — that was Caldwell in August of the baseball season of 1919. Then one day, he showed up in Cleveland and begged manager Tris Speaker for another chance. The Cleveland manager had a sentimental moment and he picked up this unwanted pitcher for nothing! Not long after, Cleveland came to New York to face the pennant-bound New York Yankees. Ray pleaded for a chance to pitch against his former teammates, the club that had branded him washed up. So out on the mound went Ray Caldwell, and he pitched a game that made history. For the ex-bad boy of the diamond hurled a no-hit, no-run game to become one of the elite of baseball.[1]

A great story, told in 1949 by one of America's favorite sportscasters, Bill Stern. The problem is that much of it is not true. Caldwell was by no means forgotten. He had won 18 games in 1914, 19 games in 1915, a dozen games in 1917. When Boston released him on August 5, 1919, he had a record of seven wins and four losses. He was hardly washed up. The Red Sox were just fed up with his heavy drinking. According to the *Cleveland Indians Encyclopedia*, Speaker "jumped at the chance to sign" Caldwell two weeks after Boston released him.[2] Nor were the Yankees pennant bound in late August 1919. They finished in third place, seven and one-half games behind the White Sox. The New Yorkers had not mounted a serious challenge since July.

Stern could have told a better story, one that was true. On August 24, 1919, Caldwell started his first game for Cleveland since his signing by the Indians five days earlier. He was on the mound in Philadelphia, leading the Athletics 2 to 1 with two out in the ninth inning when an electrical storm approached. There was a blinding flash; a bolt of lightning struck Caldwell, knocking him unconscious for five minutes. When catcher Steve O'Neill saw what happened he took off his mask and threw it as far as he could, not wanting to attract any more lightning bolts. When he came to, Caldwell insisted on finishing the game. He struck out Joe Dugan for the final out to wrap up the victory. He later said that he never saw the lightning; he just felt it.

Raymond Benjamin Caldwell was born April 26, 1888, in Corydon, Pennsylvania, of Scotch-Irish forebears.[3] As a youth, Ray worked for seven years as a telegrapher, occasionally playing a little semipro baseball on the side in places like Bath or Kane, Pennsylvania. Before reaching the majors, Caldwell, usually known as Slim but sometimes nicknamed Rube, spent only part of one season in the minors. In 1910 he started his professional career with McKeesport of the Class C Ohio-Pennsylvania League. After his major league career was over, however, he spent many more years in the minors.

Caldwell became a major leaguer through the persistence of Arthur Irwin, a former shortstop who was scouting for the New York Highlanders in 1910. Having heard that the young man was pitching brilliantly for McKeesport, Irwin went to Pennsylvania to have a look at the Slim one. He arrived at the ballpark to find that Caldwell had pitched the day before. Irwin followed the club until Caldwell was due to pitch again. On the appointed day, Slim was knocked out of the box early. This did not appear auspicious, but there was something in the lanky hurler's action and bearing that told Irwin not to give up. The scout trailed the team for another five days and was rewarded by watching Caldwell pitch a 14-inning shutout in a 1–0 win. That night Irwin gave him a New York contract.[4]

A tall, gangling 22 year old, Caldwell was purchased by the New York Highlanders for $1,500 — an enormous figure for baseball players in that era. His principal pitch was a spitball that hooked and weaved as well as any in the American League at that time. He made his major league debut late in a game on September 9, 1910, in Washington with the Highlanders behind 1–0. He replaced another rookie spitball pitcher who had been called up in midseason, Ray Fisher. The *New York Times* devoted two sentences to Slim's first appearance in the big leagues: "Stallings sent in Laporte to bat for Fisher in the visitors' eighth, and when the last half of this chapter opened Caldwell, who had joined the New Yorks here from McKeesport, was on the job. Some flinger, this Caldwell person."[5] In his one inning of work, Ray gave up no runs, no hits, walked one, and struck out one. Later in the month, Caldwell won his first major league decision and finished the season with a mark of one win and no losses. He spent the winter in Tidioute, on the Allegheny River in northwestern Pennsylvania

In 1911 Slim was one of only two Yankees rookies invited to Hot Springs, Virginia, for what the *New York Times* described as two weeks of "out-door jollification"[6] before assembling for regular spring training at Athens, Georgia. At Hot Springs, team members enjoyed hot baths, tramped the mountains, played golf, and worked in the gymnasium. No baseballs or bats were taken, for regular work on the diamond did not start until the entire squad assembled in Georgia two weeks later. During the season, Caldwell broke even with a 14–14 mark.

The following year, he dropped to an 8–16 record, which is not as bad as it appears because the cellar-dwelling Yankees turned in the worst record in their entire history with 50 wins and 102 losses. Caldwell pitched three shutouts in 1912; the rest of the Yankee staff was shut out of the shutout column. However, the season did not go nearly so well as expected. The *New York Times* reported: "At the beginning of the 1912 season it was generally expected that Caldwell would prove a sensation because of his great speed and sharp breaking curves, but he threw out his arm in a game at Cleveland and since that time he has pitched only two or three good games."[7] In 1912 Caldwell also incurred the first of what would be many fines and suspensions. Ray was suspended indefinitely and fined $250 for failing to show up when the team arrived in Washington during a road trip. A fine of $250 is miniscule according to present-day standards, but in 1912 it represented a significant percentage of a player's annual salary. The *Washington*

Ray Caldwell was blessed with exceptional baseball talent but cursed by an addiction to alcohol that prevented him from reaching his potential as a major league great. (PHOTOGRAPH COURTESY OF LIBRARY OF CONGRESS, LC-USZ-115199.)

Post reported that New York manager Harry Wolverton naturally was sore over Slim's nonappearance. "He needs pitchers, and ... the erring slinger is generally regarded as one of the best men in the league when right, and is also a hitter of ability, and not a bad outfielder."[8]

Early in the 1913 season, Caldwell pitched infrequently, owing to arm trouble. In June, new manager Frank Chance of the Yankees asked for waivers on him, with the intent to return him to the minors. However, not all clubs agreed to waivers, so the Highlanders kept him on their roster. By the end of July, Ray had recovered full use of his pitching arm. The *New York Times* reported: "Ray Caldwell, a discard pitcher, who has been tucked away in the right field so that he wouldn't be noticed, was rejuvenated yesterday and requested by Mr. Chance to try to pitch. Ray was all satin and a yard wide.... There was a mystery and a deception about his pitching that left the Chicagos pop-eyed with amazement."[9]

Caldwell finished the season with nine wins and eight losses. He held opponents to the fifth lowest batting average in the American League. Once again his off-the-field activities made the newspapers. His former teammate, pitcher Jim "Hippo" Vaughn, complained to the national commission that Slim refused to repay a loan of $16, which he alleged was borrowed from him by Caldwell in the spring of 1912. The governing body of baseball held that Caldwell had made no defense after a copy of the petition had been forwarded to him, and declared Caldwell ineligible to play unless the debt was settled with five days of the finding.[10] We cannot imagine a baseball star of the present being declared ineligible because of a $16 debt!

Before the 1914 season got underway, Caldwell incurred the wrath of his manager by breaking training rules. Chance gave the tall spitballer a good talking-to and fined him $50. According to the *New York Times:* "From the way the New York leader talked he will not stand for Caldwell's nonsense much longer. That was mostly the big hurler's trouble last season, and unless he takes a brace he will go the way of the majority of ball players who find that they would like to train as some people do on Broadway."[11] Caldwell promised that it would never happen again. Evidently the talking-to did not do much good for within a week Ray had broken training rules again. He was not in his room for bed check and did not return all night. This time Chance fined him $100 and announced: "Caldwell has not far to go in big league baseball if he thinks he can train here like some people do on the Great White Way. This is the second time he has violated rules on this trip, and I think it will be the last. I have stood for enough as far as Caldwell is concerned.... If he intends to play that kind of game with me he is going to suffer for it."[12]

Alcoholism was not widely recognized as a disease in those days. The *Encyclopædia Britannica,* the best English-language encyclopedia of the time, did not even have an entry on alcoholism. Under the entry for drunkenness, the reference stated: "Drunkenness as a habit (as in the form of chronic alcoholism) is one of the most degrading forms of vice which can result from the enfeeblement of the moral principle by self-indulgence."[13] According to the conventional wisdom of the day, Caldwell was not sick; he was either immoral or weak-willed.

When the 1914 regular season got underway, the tall twirler was on his best behavior, and his spitball was working as never before. He pitched 29 consecutive innings before the first run was scored off him. Every start he made resulted in a complete game until August 23. His record of 18 wins and nine losses for a mediocre Yankees team that finished in last place earned him the highest Weighted Rating in the league. He allowed the second fewest base runners per nine innings, held opponents to the second lowest batting average and on-base percentage, and ranked fourth in both winning percentage and earned run average. His Faber System rating was tied for fourth best in the American League.

At the end of the 1914 season, Caldwell signed a contract to play for Buffalo in the new Federal League. However, the national commission ruled that under the reserve clause he was bound to the Yankees. Ban Johnson, president of the American League, tried to broker a deal wherein Caldwell would be traded to the Philadelphia Athletics in return for outfielder Rube Oldring and catcher Jack Lapp. Although Ray had never submitted to the discipline rules of the New York club, Johnson thought Caldwell was a "wonderful" pitcher and was anxious to keep him in the American League and put him under Connie Mack's care.[14]

The deal with the Mackmen did not materialize, and Caldwell stayed with the Highlanders for four more years. Grantland Rice, one of the foremost sportswriters of the era, looked forward to the 1915 season: "Ray Caldwell has made up his mind to give the game his best work this season, and if the tall and stately telegrapher carries out this intention Walter Johnson will have a rival worthy of his best work.... With the tall Yank in condition, a Johnson-Caldwell battle will acquire as much class as the bygone duels between Mathewson and Brown."[15]

Caldwell did not match the Big Train's performance in 1915, but neither did anyone else. Ray had a very good year, winning 19 games and losing 16 for a second-division team. His record suffered because he received some of the most miserable support ever given a pitcher. At one time he pitched for 52 consecutive innings wherein his teammates failed to score a single run for him. He avoided suspensions and ranked fourth in the American League in the number of innings pitched. The lean and lanky pitcher again tied for fourth in the Faber System rankings. He was ejected from one game for throwing his glove high in the air in objecting to an umpire's decision. The derring-do of Ty Cobb in the moments leading up to this decision inspired some colorful writing by a *New York Times* scribe.

> Ty Cobb is loose again on a base-stealing spree. He romps to first on a single. Slim Caldwell pitches to Nunamaker, and the ball nestles in his big mitt. Cobb a few feet off first, suddenly bolts into action and races to second. Nunamaker, amazed at the Georgian's daring, stands dumfounded. He throws the ball to Dan Boone just as the Southern Flyer jumps into second base. The steel spikes flash in the waning sun and Cobb is lost in a cloud of dust. Nunamaker's nervous toss rolls into centre field and the Georgia Gem bounds to his feet and tears to third. He's as safe as the Bank of England. Cobb's sarcastic smile angers the hoodwinked opponents. Now the speed-crazed comet dashes up and down the third-base line, trying to rattle Caldwell. Will Cobb have the nerve to try to steal home? You said it; he will. Caldwell doesn't think so. No one thinks so, but Cobb. The Yanks' lanky pitcher hurls the ball at the batsman like a rifle ball. As the ball left his hand Cobb bounded over the ground like a startled deer. At the plate crouched Nunamaker. He was so surprised that he didn't know his own name. Cobb dashed through the air toward the scoring pan. His lithe body swerved away from Nunamaker's reach and clouds of dirt kicked up by his spikes blinded the eyes of Nunamaker, Caldwell, and Silk O'Loughlin. The umpire ruled that the catcher didn't touch Cobb. He also ruled that Cobb hadn't touched the plate. While the Yankee players were protesting Cobb sneaked around the bunch and touched the plate.
>
> A smart young feller, this same Cobb. The bold piracy of Captain Kidd was like taking ice-cream cones from children compared with that. Caldwell threw his glove high in the air

in derision at O'Loughlin's decision. Naturally Caldwell and Nunamaker were in a very disturbed state of mind. So is a man when a dip relieves him of his watch-chain and wallet. Cobb pulled the wool over their eyes like a sharper unloading mining stock on a Rube. Caldwell was put out of the game for being mad because Cobb had outwitted him.[16]

A few days after the glove-throwing incident (June 10), Caldwell hit a pinch-hit home run in the last of the ninth inning. The very next day (June 11), he hit a three-run pinch-hit homer in the seventh. Nobody else in the American League repeated the feat of two consecutive pinch-hit home runs until 1943. The next day (June 12), Ray hit another three-run homer, but this was not a pinch hit. He was the starting pitcher that day, and the dinger came in his second time at bat, thus giving him three home runs in his last four times at bat. Not bad for a pitcher, nor for any other player as a matter of fact.

In 1916 Caldwell had a poor year. Part of his difficulty was the lack of support from his teammates, causing him to lose several well-pitched games. He also suffered an injury and endured another suspension. John J. Ward, in an article published in *Baseball Magazine* that September, wrote that Ray Caldwell was one of the greatest pitchers in the American League. He maintained that was the opinion of almost all players in the circuit. Ward claimed that Caldwell was equally great as a batter and fielder. But with all his great gifts the pitcher had not won the success he deserved largely through the failure of his teammates to support his fine work. "In fact," Ward wrote, "Caldwell might well be named the hard-luck pitcher of the league. His best work has almost invariably been marred by defective support to a degree far beyond that to which a pitcher should be liable."[17]

Ward was effusive in his praise of Caldwell. He quoted a rival pitcher as saying, "He has one of the best curves in the business, and his fast ball is peach. His control is great and, above all, he has a head on his shoulders. He is a natural ball player if there ever was one and he might be the best all-round pitcher in the American League."[18] The writer went on to state: "Throughout the circuit there is a unanimous opinion among American League players that Caldwell is a great pitcher. He possesses remarkable speed, a fine curve, good control and a keen, active baseball brain. He is at all times a wise, as well as an able pitcher, and these qualifications are rarely so evenly balanced. In addition, Caldwell, unlike most pitchers, is a great all-round player as well as a brilliant twirler. He had a natural batting eye and is a clever fielder. So it happens that Caldwell, a pitcher, is the pinch hitter of his club, a role which he shares with Babe Ruth alone among modern twirlers."[19]

Curiously, Ward did not mention Caldwell's spitball. Perhaps he was not using it much in 1916. Although some sources say it was his mainstay as early as 1910, others say it was a late addition to his arsenal of pitches. After the 1920 season, Billy Evans said that banning the spitball would make little difference to Caldwell, as he used the spitball only in a pinch.[20]

Ward's point about Slim's pinch-hitting was well taken. During his career he had 36 pinch safeties in 154 attempts.

On July 18, 1916, he was pitching in a relief stint against the Detroit Tigers when opposing pitcher Wee Willie Mitchell hit a low liner which caught Ray on the right kneecap. He was so badly hurt he could not reach for the ball. After the knee had been examined he limped off the field. However, he was pitching again a few days later.

On July 29, Caldwell lost another game due to lack of support from his team. The Browns defeated him 3–1 in a game in St. Louis. After the game, Caldwell was involved in another off-the-field incident, which led to a 15-day suspension. When he failed to report to club headquarters at the end of the 15 days, the suspension was made indefinite. Ray disappeared from the scene for months.

According to Stanley T. Milliken of the *Washington Post*, there was a rumor going around in November that the Cleveland Indians were likely to acquire the services of Caldwell from the Yankees. Milliken thought Ray would be of value to any club, provided he took care of himself. His behavior with the Yankees during the last year put him in a bad light with his employers, the scribe wrote, and he would most likely appear elsewhere the next year.[21] Three weeks later, the *Post* retracted the trade rumors, saying that the Yankees would not talk of any trade or sale of the big pitcher, who ranked with the stars of the profession when he tended strictly to business. The article stated that Caldwell was working under one of the highest figured contracts in baseball, and it had another year to run. (His contract was for $8,000 per annum.) "He can realize every cent on the document, and the Yanks are ready and willing to pay it if Caldwell reports and delivers his best. Caldwell has told friends that he is sorry about his 1916 failure, and is anxious to do his best for the Yanks."[22] This despite the fact that the New York club had heard nothing from Caldwell since December.

On the last day of the calendar year, Milliken reported that he had received a letter from Panama informing him that Caldwell was pitching for the Colon club. Playing under the name of Collins, Ray was playing every day. The scribe opined that this activity would not enhance Slim's slim chance of getting into the good graces of the New York management next season. Milliken wrote that "Caldwell is one of the greatest pitchers in the game today, provided he follows the straight and narrow path, but he is inclined to do otherwise. No ball player gets any benefit out of playing winter baseball, but some are foolish enough to attempt it and then wonder why they cannot hold their own when the big grind comes."[23]

Caldwell was expected to join the Yankees for spring training on February 24, 1917, but he did not show up. Milliken was indignant: "Caldwell is an example of a great pitcher going to ruin by his failure to take care of himself. The disciplining of Caldwell has got to be quite a hobby among baseball managers, and as yet no leader has been able to get a good decision. After his fall from grace last summer this wonderful pitcher came to the owners of the Yankees and asked for one more chance. It has been granted him, and it is now up to Caldwell to show his appreciation of what was really a great kindness. Caldwell's presence on the Yankee roster means a chance for the pennant. His failure to report may mean that he will be out of baseball for good."[24]

Eventually he did report and pitched well for the Yankees in the early part of the season. He stayed out of trouble until June. After a loss to the Red Sox on June 28, Caldwell did not return to the team's hotel in Boston that night, nor did he put in an appearance at Fenway Park the next afternoon. Manager "Wild Bill" Donovan fined him

$100 and suspended him without pay for the next 10 days. On July 10, Lucy Dick of St. Louis accused Caldwell of taking from her a diamond ring valued at $150 while he was visiting her on June 30. Slim was arrested, charged with larceny, and released on bond. He quickly returned the ring to the lady, and the charges were dropped.

On this same day, the Browns declined an offer by the Yankees to trade Caldwell to them for second baseman Del Pratt. The very next day, Caldwell pitched nine and two-thirds innings of scoreless relief in a 17-inning battle against the Browns. Three spitball pitchers figured prominently in this game. Ray Fisher started for the Highlanders and allowed only one run in six and two-thirds innings. Al Sothoron pitched the final nine innings for St. Louis and was the winning pitcher.

In retrospect, Milliken's suggestion that with Caldwell the Yankees had a chance for the 1917 pennant seems overly optimistic. Slim won 13 games that season, and the Yanks finished in sixth place. In the shortened 1918 season, the spitballer won nine games while losing eight. As a married man with a seven-year-old son, he was unlikely to be drafted. Nevertheless, he took a position with a shipbuilding concern in Weehawken, New Jersey. The manner in which he began the job would have seemed strange for anybody but Caldwell. He did not show up for the Yankees games on August 17, having someone telephone the manager with the message that Ray was too sick to report. However, it was reported that he pitched a game for shipbuilders that day and played centerfield for them the next. On August 19 he was back in uniform for the Yankees, pitching the full nine innings of a 4–1 loss to fellow spitballer Jack Quinn and the Chicago White Sox.[25] Then it was back to the dry dock company for the next few months.

On December 18, 1918, the Yankees and the Boston Red Sox consummated what the newspapers called the most important baseball trade in years. Pitchers Ernie Shore and Dutch Leonard, together with outfielder Duffy Lewis, were traded to the Yankees in return for Ray Caldwell, pitcher Slim Love, catcher Al Walters, outfielder Frank Gilhooey, and an undisclosed amount of cash. Yankee officials predicted this deal would prove to be the best trade made by the New York club since it joined the American League. Of course, they were to make an even better deal with the Red Sox a little more than one year later. The *New York Times* noted that the players traded away by the Yankees were hard-luck players. "Caldwell, in particular ... had the reputation of losing more games by a single run than any other pitcher in the league. He had an in-and-out career with the Yanks, and it is believed that he will do better in his new surroundings."[26]

A writer in the February 1919 issue of *Baseball Magazine* wrote: "Ask any American League batter the half dozen toughest pitching propositions he faces in a season and nine out of ten of them will include Caldwell's name in the list. Not only is he rated a pitcher with great natural gifts in speed and control, but he is universally considered one of those wise players who uses his head."[27]

Caldwell did not pitch badly for Boston in 1919, winning seven out of 11 decisions. However, the Red Sox management lost patience with his drinking and gave him his unconditional release on August 4. For Cleveland he won five games and lost only one during the rest of the season, his victories including the memorable game in which he was struck by lightning and the one in which he pitched a no-hitter against the Yankees.

According to one publication, the Indians inserted a clause in Caldwell's 1920 contract which specified that after every game he pitched, Slim was required to get drunk. The next day he was not to report to the clubhouse. The following day he would run laps, and the day after that he would throw batting practice. He would pitch a game the next day and begin the cycle all over again.[28]

If that story is true, the contract was a good idea, for Caldwell won 20 games in 1920, the only time he did in his major league career. Behind good hitting and sterling pitching from Jim Bagby, Stan Coveleskie, and Caldwell the Indians won their first American League pennant. Slim played a major role in clinching the flag for the Tribe. On August 30 he defeated the Yankees 3–2 in a pitching duel with Bob Shawkey. Two days later, Caldwell won his 20th game of the season, defeating Detroit 10–3 and clinching at least a tie for the pennant. Bagby wrapped it up the next day.

Ray started the third game of the World's Series for Cleveland, but was allowed to face only five batters. He started the game by walking Ivy Olson, who advanced to second base on a sacrifice by Jimmy Johnston. Tommy Griffith rolled an easy bounder to Joe Sewell at shortstop, which the rookie fumbled. Cleanup hitter Zach Wheat hit a clean single to left field, scoring Olson. Hi Myers then looped a little hit over the first baseman's head, and Griffith scored the second run of the game. Manager Tris Speaker rushed in from centerfield to the mound. With reluctance, Slim gave the ball to the manager, who signaled for a reliever to come in and pitch. The *New York Times* reported that "Caldwell was a sorry figure as he walked to the bench. The greatest chance of his baseball career had come and he had failed. He had made a commendable come-back this season and was a more settled, serious citizen than he used to be when he was causing Wild Bill Donovan to sit up nights worrying about him. He wanted a chance to start one of these games to mark the climax of his rejuvenation and the sudden uprising of the Robins against him must have been a terrible shock."[29]

With the wisdom of hindsight, the Monday morning quarterbacks figured that Speaker had made a mistake when he picked Caldwell to pitch. As the *Times* put it, the baseball sharps made the following case: "Ray has ever been erratic, not only with the Indians, but with the Yankees. He has affected a spitball during these later days of his baseball career and has tried to make it do the work that his blinding speed used to accomplish. It is difficult to teach an old dog new tricks. While Slim has done good work for Cleveland this season, there is always an uncertainty about his work which does not inspire confidence."[30]

To which we might reply, Caldwell was a 20-game winner that season. It would seem very strange not to start him in the World's Series, since his pitching was a major reason for the Tribe getting to the fall classic. We might add that his performance in game three was not so terribly bad. He walked one man, gave up one solid hit, and one bloop single. Had Sewell not booted Griffith's bouncer, Slim might have escaped the first inning with little damage done.

After 1920 Caldwell never had another successful season in the major leagues. He broke even in 12 decisions with the Indians in 1921, being used mainly in relief. On

September 5 the Indians suspended him indefinitely for breaking training. Ray wrote Speaker a note, asking forgiveness and offering to work the rest of the season without pay. The manager lifted the suspension two days later, a move that paid immediate dividends. On the very day Ray was reinstated he entered the game in a crucial situation. Cleveland was leading Detroit 5–4 in the ninth inning, but the Tigers had two men on base with only one out, and there were two balls on Detroit batsman Lu Blue, a .300 hitter. The Grey Eagle summoned Caldwell from the bullpen and Ray issued two more balls to Blue, filling the bases. Then Ray fanned Johnny Bassler for the second out, bases still loaded. Bert Cole came in to pinch-hit for Herm Merritt. Caldwell struck him out; game over. With two successive strikeouts, Ray had saved the game for the Indians.

Ray had at least one more chance to be a hero. On September 25, with the Indians and the Yankees engaged in a hectic struggle for the American League pennant, Speaker elected to start Caldwell in a crucial game against the New Yorkers. With obvious glee, a *Times* reporter described the scene:

> Across the shirt fronts of the Cleveland Indians is emblazoned in glaring bold face the fact that they are the world's champions. At the Polo Grounds yesterday it would have been well if the Indians had worn sweaters over those chest plates. With the tidings of last October's success flashing into view every time a Clevelander made a move the Yankees handed Tris Speaker's men the soundest trouncing that any major league club has been forced to absorb this season.... The final count on the newest of Indians' massacres was 21 to 7, a set of figures more like football than baseball.... More than 38,000 fans jammed their way into the Polo Grounds to see the two pennant contenders battle.... At 1 o'clock, two hours before the game began, the big grand stand was sold out, and the parade into the bleachers got underway. Never before was the big stand closed so early. Shortly after 2 o'clock the bleacher gates were closed, and those who tried to pry their way in after that hour were out of luck.... Ray Caldwell, for years a Polo Grounder, opened for the visitors and was clubbed to the clubhouse before two innings had ended. Four hits, two of which were doubles and another a fluke triple, buried Ray under four runs before Speaker extracted the slim flinger.[31]

At the end of the season, Speaker said he planned to reorganize his pitching staff and gave the veteran spitballer his unconditional release on October 25, 1921.

Caldwell's major league record:

Year	Club	W	L	Pct.	IP	H	BB	SO	ERA	WR	PTS
1910	NY AL	1	0	1.000	19	19	9	17	3.72	420	6
1911	NY AL	14	14	.500	255	240	79	145	3.35	0	39
1912	NY AL	8	16	.333	183	196	67	95	4.47	168	26
1913	NY AL	9	8	.529	164	131	60	87	2.41	2890	51
1914	NY AL	18	9	.667	213	153	51	92	1.94	6993	86
1915	NY AL	19	16	.543	305	266	107	130	2.89	4060	68
1916	NY AL	5	12	.294	166	142	65	76	2.99	-4301	-2
1917	NY AL	13	16	.448	236	199	76	102	2.86	-580	32
1918	NY AL	9	8	.529	177	173	62	59	3.06	816	39
1919	Bos AL	7	4	.636	86	92	31	23	3.96	1848	*
	Cle AL	5	1	.833	57	33	19	24	1.71	1434	63

Year	Club	W	L	Pct.	IP	H	BB	SO	ERA	WR	PTS
1920	Cle AL	20	10	.667	238	286	63	80	3.86	1140	59
1921	Cle AL	6	6	.500	147	159	49	76	4.90	-1440	19
12 years		134	120	.528	2242	2089	738	1006	3.22	13448	486

*Records of two clubs are totaled to obtain Faber System points for 1919.

World's Series record:

		W	L	Pct.	IP	H	BB	SO	ERA
1920	Cleveland AL	0	1	.000	1/3	2	1	0	27.00

After his release by the Indians, Caldwell spent three years with the Kansas City Blues of the Class AA American Association. In 1922 he won 22 games, the most wins he ever garnered in one season during his 24 years in professional baseball. He posted a 16–10 mark for the championship Kansas City team of 1923, but managed only nine victories the next year. With the exception of two partial seasons in Milwaukee and Akron, he pitched in the Class A Southern Association for the next seven years, compiling a record of 88 wins and 82 losses, with a majority of the losses coming from 1925 to 1927, when he toiled for the last-place Little Rock Travelers, His record those three years was 11–12, 13–22, and 11–20. He had 10 wins and seven losses for Memphis in 1928. After his return from the Central League in 1929 he had four wins and two losses for the Birmingham Barons, and improved to 20–12 and 19–7 in 1930 and 1931 respectively. Then his work slacked off, and he retired after the 1933 season.

Probably the highlight of his minor league career came in the opening game of the 1931 Dixie Series. At the age of 43, Caldwell faced the sensational 20-year-old phenom of the Houston Buffaloes, Dizzy Dean. The oldster won 1 to 0 in a game that many consider the greatest game ever played in Birmingham's Rockwood Field. Four days later it was Dean's turn to throw a shutout, as the Buffaloes prevailed 2–0. In the seventh game, with the series tied at three games each, Birmingham took a 6–2 lead into the bottom of the ninth inning. Houston mounted a comeback threat. The Buffs had already scored one run, when with one out, Caldwell was summoned from the bullpen. He struck out future Hall of Famer Joe Medwick and induced Homer Peel, a Texas League legend, to hit an infield grounder to give Caldwell a save and his team the Dixie Series championship. In 1943 Caldwell was named to the Birmingham Barons Hall of Fame.

On April 13, 1933, the 45-year old Caldwell announced he was through with organized baseball. His request for voluntary retirement was granted by manager Clyde Milan of the Birmingham Barons. The old right arm was as good as ever, Ray maintained, but a leg injury suffered the previous season had slowed him down. The Associated Press report said: "The passing of Caldwell, one of the few grandfathers of the game, has taken from baseball one of its most colorful and widely known figures."[32]

After all those years in the game, Caldwell found it hard to leave baseball. During the spring of 1933 he managed a semipro team in Kansas City. On June 20, he signed with the Charlotte Hornets of the Piedmont League. He pitched two games for the Hornets, winning one and losing one, and going the distance in each game. He finished the season with Keokuk Indians of the Mississippi Valley League. The Keokuk club disbanded at the end of the season and the league folded as the Great Depression wreaked havoc on minor league baseball.

Ray spent one season as a minor league manager, guiding the Fremont Green Sox to a last-place finish in the six-team Class D Ohio State League in 1940. At the age of 51, Caldwell said that he might pitch an occasional game for the Sox but the record does not show any appearances for him as a Green Sox pitcher.

His minor league pitching record:

Year	Club	W	L	Pct.	IP	H	BB	SO	ERA
1910	McKeesport	18	14	.563	181	210	75	167	
1922	Kansas City	22	12	.647	263	269	62	85	3.59
1923	Kansas City	16	10	.615	238	273	73	95	4.39
1924	Kansas City	9	14	.391	198	210	44	86	3.95
1925	Little Rock	11	12	.478	190	204	43	63	4.12
1926	Little Rock	13	22.	.371	**298**	325	55	100	3.41
1927	Little Rock	11	20	.365	225	285	53	48	5.28
	Milwaukee	0	3	.000	26	30	8	7	4.15
1928	Memphis	10	7	.588	146	180	34	45	4.93
1929	Akron	2	4	.333	49	63	7	20	6.24
	Birmingham	4	2	.667	65	63	12	10	1.80
1930	Birmingham	20	12	.625	250	272	58	46	4.43
1931	Birmingham	19	7	.731	248	260	36	57	3.45
1932	Birmingham	2	0	1.000	21	17	4	2	1.29
1933	Birmingham/ Atlanta	0	4	.000	22	33	3	7	10.64
	Charlotte	1	1	.500	17	16	3	9	4.24
	Keokuk	1	3	.250	31	34	7	21	4.06
Total — 13 years		159	147	.520	2468	2746	577	868	3.85

Bold italics indicates he led the league.

League affiliations: McKeesport, Ohio-Pennsylvania; Kansas City and Milwaukee, American Association; Little Rock, Memphis, Birmingham and Atlanta, Southern Association; Akron, Central League; Charlotte, Piedmont League; Keokuk, Mississippi Valley League.

After he finally retired for good from professional baseball, Caldwell returned to his home in Salamanca on the banks of the Allegheny River in western New York, where for many years he had enjoyed his favorite wintertime activity of hunting for small game amid the beautiful, rolling hills of Cattaraugus County.

In the late 1950s, Caldwell's eyesight began to fail. His doctor recommended eye surgery. As he had played in a time of low salaries, before the days of free agency, and prior to the introduction of the pension plan for major league ballplayers, Ray had never accumulated much money. He had certainly not saved enough to pay for an expensive eye operation. The Lions Club of Randolph, New York, organized a benefit to raise funds. On May 7, 1961, the Lions hosted a chicken barbecue, one of the biggest events of its kind ever held in western New York state. Within a month an operation to remove cataracts from Ray's right eye was performed at a hospital in Jamestown, New York. Proceeds from the barbecue helped defray the expense of the operation.[33]

Ray Caldwell died on August 17, 1967, in the Salamanca District Hospital at the age of 79. He was survived by his widow, Estelle; his son, James; and four stepdaughters. Ray was buried in the Randolph Cemetery in nearby Randolph, New York.

Clarence Mitchell

He was a major league pitcher for 18 years, but the best-remembered pitch of his life is not one he threw from the mound, but one he hit while standing in the batter's box. It was Sunday, October 10, 1920, the fifth game of the World's Series between Cleveland and Brooklyn. The series was tied at two games each, but in this game the Indians had knocked out Burleigh Grimes early and were leading 7–0 at the end of four innings. Pete Kilduff led off the top of the fifth for the Dodgers with a single to left field. Otto Miller followed with a single to center. So there were two men on base and nobody out. Up to the plate stepped pitcher Clarence Mitchell, who had entered the game in relief of Grimes. He hit a line shot up the middle, just to the second baseman's right, a rising liner that looked like a sure base hit. But second baseman Bill Wambsganss was off with the crack of the bat, running toward second, and made a tremendously high leap to spear the ball. One out. Wamby's motion carried him toward second and he tagged the bag to double up Kilduff, who was still running toward third. Two out. Then Wamby noticed Miller, who had come down from first base, was just standing there a few feet away, so he tagged him for the third out. Shortstop Joe Sewell later said that he thought that Wambsganss was going to throw to first to double off Miller, but that he yelled "Tag him!" Either way would have been a triple play, but by tagging Miller Wamby had made the first and so far the only *unassisted* triple play in World's Series history.

Both men agreed that it took the fans a while to realize what had happened. For a few moments there was silence. Then as it dawned on them what they had seen the fans began cheering louder and louder and throwing straw hats down onto the field. They threw so many hats that time had to be called so the grounds crew could pick them all up. So what did Clarence Mitchell do on this at bat? He made a hero out of Bill Wambsganss and made himself the answer to a trivia question. The next time up, Mitchell hit into a double play, making himself responsible for five outs in two consecutive trips to the plate.

Clarence Elmer Mitchell was born February 22, 1891, in a sod house in Franklin County, Nebraska, on the Republican River just a few miles from the Kansas border. Raised on his father's farm, he played sandlot baseball throughout his childhood, whenever he could take time from his farm work. By 1908 he was the star pitcher for Franklin High School. During the summer he pitched for the town teams of both Franklin and

Cowles, in adjoining Webster County.[1] His desire to become a professional baseball player may have been the reason he dropped out of high school to take a clerking job in Cowles in April 1909. This gave him time to play for any club needing his services, usually as a pitcher, but also as an outfielder or first baseman. He won five games and lost two for the Franklin club in the independent Nebraska State League that summer, but pitched mainly for a semipro team in Alliance in the far western part of the state. Andrea Paul wrote that he won 40 games and lost only four that summer.[2]

Clarence broke into professional baseball with Red Cloud of the Class D Nebraska State League in 1910. When the decennial census was taken that summer he was listed as a baseball player living in Marion Township, Franklin County, in the household of his mother, Kittie, and his stepfather, Samuel H. Braden, a farmer. At the end of the season he was signed by the Detroit Tigers and ordered to report to the Bengals' spring training camp in Louisiana in 1911.

He divided the 1911 season between Saginaw of the Southern Michigan League and the big league club, where he was used mainly as a batting practice pitcher. Making his major league debut with the Detroit Tigers on June 2, 1911, he appeared in five games, winning one and losing none that year. His win came on June 18 at Bennett Park in Detroit as the Tigers overcame a 12-run deficit to defeat the Chicago White Sox. (The Bengals had been behind 13–1 in the fifth inning.) The 20-year-old rookie entered the game in the eighth inning with his team trailing 15–8. He shut the Sox down in the top half of the inning. In the home half he collected his first major league hit as he singled off the third base bag, and eventually scored as did four of his teammates, making the score 15–13. Clarence retired the side in order in the top of the ninth. In the bottom of the ninth, the Tigers tallied three times to win the game 16–15. Clarence was credited with the win, and Hall of Fame pitcher Ed Walsh was charged with the loss. It was the first time in the 20th century that a team had overcome a 12-run deficit to win a major league game.[3] Mitchell was cut from the Detroit team before the 1912 season began.

Regarding Clarence's dismissal from the Tigers, Andrea Paul repeated a widely told story that she said may have been apocryphal. "According to observers at the scene," she wrote, "Mitchell was warming up while being watched by Detroit manager Hughie Jennings. After observing a few pitches that behaved oddly, Jennings asked. 'Say, what the hell are you throwing?'

'A spitball,' says Clarence.

'And with a left hand?' roared Jennings. 'There ain't no such animal. Get out of here!'"[4]

Jennings was very nearly right. A lefthanded spitballer is among the rarest of all animals. Clarence Mitchell was the only legal lefthanded spitball pitcher to appear in a major league game since 1920, and there were few, if any, before that. Mitchell doctored the baseball with slippery elm sliced from a special tree on the farm of a neighbor, Jess Williams, in Franklin County.[5] For a while he collected his own supply. Later, when Clarence was a teammate of Burleigh Grimes on the Brooklyn Dodgers, Wallace Mitchell cut out pieces of wood from that same tree for his father and Grimes to use.

In 1912 and 1913 he played outfield and did some pitching for the Providence Grays of the International League. He hit .288 in 1912 and .333 in 1913. His won-lost record was 7–6 and 4–5 in the two years. He earned a reputation as one of the best fielding outfielders in the International League. Mitchell would have preferred to pitch, but his hitting and fielding were so good that his manager wanted him to be an every day player.

In 1914 Mitchell played for the Denver Bears of the Western League, hoping to be used only as a pitcher. He won eight games and lost six. However, his hitting and fielding prompted manager Jack Coffey to insert him as the regular left fielder. Paul quoted a Denver newspaper as reporting, "If Mitchell was Christy Mathewson himself Denver couldn't afford to take him out of left field now, because he is hitting at a .400 clip and covering worlds of ground in the garden."[6]

The following year, Denver's weak pitching staff needed bolstering, and Mitchell was used almost exclusively as a pitcher. He responded by winning 22 games, his only 20-win season in nearly 30 years in organized baseball. After the end of the season, Clarence joined Frank Bancroft's National League All-Stars on a West Coast tour. He won three out of the four games in which he pitched. He also pitched one game for the American League team and won that one, too. Bancroft was the business manager of the Cincinnati Reds, and Mitchell's performance led to his signing a major league contract with the Reds in 1916.

Mitchell's minor league record:

Year	Club	W	L	Pct.	IP	H	BB	SO	ERA
1910	Red Cloud	14	13	.519	46	195			
1911	Saginaw	statistics unavailable							
1912	Providence	7	6	.538	109	117	43	59	
1913	Providence	4	5	.444	100	116	31	31	
1914	Denver	8	6	.571	142	150	42	70	4.25
1915	Denver	22	11	.667	250	202	69	107	2.77
1934	Mission	19	12	.613	253	282	70	63	3.67
1935	Mission	6	11	.353	152	197	31	32	5.09
1936	Omaha	7	4	.636	101	101	36	27	3.39
1937	Mayfield	4	2	.667	50	33	3	14	1.98
1940	Meridian	0	0	—	2	statistics not available			
Incomplete totals—11 years		91	70	.565	1159	1198	371	598	

League affiliations: Red Cloud, Nebraska State League; Saginaw, Southern Michigan League; Providence, International League; Denver, Western League; Mission, Pacific Coast League; Omaha, Western League; Mayfield, Kitty League; Meridian, Southeastern League.

The Reds tied for last place in the National League in 1916, so Mitchell's 11–10 record was quite good under the circumstances. Paul wrote that the lack of run support cost Clarence eight losses—games the Reds lost by one run.[7] If that is accurate, and had the Reds scored two more runs in each of those games, Mitchell's record would have been a sensational 19–2. Unfortunately for the spitballer, it did not happen.

Despite a respectable 3.22 earned run average, lack of run support contributed to a 9–15 record in 1917. Mitchell was waived by the Reds and picked up by the Brooklyn Dodgers. For the Robins, Clarence had absolutely no luck at all in 1918. He started one game and retired only one batter, giving up four runs for an astronomical earned run average of 108.00. He also played a few games at first base and in the outfield with some success. In 10 games he hit .250 and had a respectable slugging average of .375. However, he joined the army and missed most of the season. While stationed at Camp Mills with the 342nd Field Artillery, he received a furlough and played in a game on June 13 against the Reds at Ebbets Field for the benefit of the Bat and Ball Fund Day. The two clubs agreed to give a percentage of the receipts to the fund, which was established by Clark Griffith to provide balls, bats, uniforms, and other baseball paraphernalia to armed services training camps. In addition, schoolchildren from Brooklyn were admitted to the grandstand back of third base for a nominal charge of 10 cents. Nine cents of this went to the Ball and Bat Fund and the remaining one cent to the government as a war tax.[8] Unlike some ballplayers who stayed stateside during the entire war, Mitchell went to France with his unit, where he starred on the American Expeditionary Force baseball team. He played first base; fellow Nebraskan Grover Cleveland "Pete" Alexander was the team's outstanding pitcher.

During the winter of 1918–19, the Dodgers considered converting Mitchell into a first baseman and playing him regularly at that position as a replacement for long-time star Jake Daubert, who had been released. Before Clarence got back from France, however, the Robins purchased Ed Konetchy from the Pirates, so Mitchell continued as a pitcher and pinch hitter. In 34 games he hit .367 and compiled a slugging average of .449. On the mound he went 7–5.

As a pitcher in 1920 Clarence won five and lost two. He played a few games at first base and in the outfield. As a pinch hitter he collect six safeties in 18 attempts. For the first time in his career, he made it to the World's Series, where he made his place in history by hitting into that famous triple play, followed by a double play. However, he did make a hit in his other time at bat. On the hill in relief of Burleigh Grimes, he performed admirably, pitching four and two-thirds innings without giving up a run.

In 1921, as the only lefthanded spitball pitcher in the majors, Mitchell had an apparent advantage. Batters faced no one like him and only a few right-handed spitballers who had been grandfathered, so they had little opportunity to practice hitting the spitball. In addition, Mitchell had a three-way spitter. The usual spitball dropped when it reached the plate. Mitchell could make his break down, up or away, as he desired, so the batter could not anticipate its location even if he could discern that a spitter was on its way. He had his best major league season yet, with 11 wins, nine losses, and an ERA of 2.89, which was excellent in that first year of the post-deadball era, and he tied for the league lead in shutouts.

Clarence was looking forward to a good year in 1922. Those hopes fell by the wayside. As a pitcher, the spitball artist got into only five games, losing all of his three decisions. Konetchy had retired, and manager Wilbert Robinson inserted Mitchell at first base. He performed well, fielding almost flawlessly and hitting .290. However, he hurt his right knee in a game in Boston in June. Although the injury was not believed to be serious and he stayed in the game, the leg grew steadily worse and finally Robbie had to sit him down.

On February 15, 1923, Brooklyn traded Mitchell to the Phillies for Columbia

Clarence Mitchell was a major league pitcher for 18 years but is perhaps best remembered as the only batter to hit into an unassisted triple play in a World Series game. (PHOTOGRAPH COURTESY OF NATIONAL HALL OF FAME LIBRARY, COOPERSTOWN.)

George Smith, a right-handed pitcher. In commenting on the trade, the *New York Times* stated Mitchell is as good a first baseman as a pitcher, can hit and field and is fairly fast afoot.[9] The fact that Clarence was a holdout influenced the Brooklyn club to trade him, President Charles Ebbets admitted. "We reduced Mitchell's figure because it was felt he would be useful in only a utility capacity."[10] As usually happened when a grandfathered spitballer was traded, the team giving up the grandfather got the worst of the deal. In the remainder of his major league career, Smith won three games and lost six. The 1923 Phillies were a last-place team, as they usually were in the 1920s. Hugh Fullerton sized them up correctly during spring training when he wrote: "It is a sad duty to chronicle the fact that I came to find a baseball team and failed to find anything but ... a lot of second raters, has-beens, and never wases ... Clarence Mitchell, who was used all round at Brooklyn, may prove a real help to the Phils. Brooklyn used Mitchell as first baseman, pinch hitter, pitcher and what not, and Fletcher (the Philadelphia manager) intends to keep him steadily on the pitching job.... It is a bad ball club which will have to have a world of luck to win fifty games and beat any one out."[11] Fullerton hit it right on the nose. The Phillies won exactly 50 games and finished in last place. Mitchell won nine and lost 10 for the cellar dwellers.

Then came several more losing seasons as Mitchell continued toiling for mediocre teams in Philadelphia. His record from 1923 through 1927 was 40 wins and 57 losses as the Phillies finished in eighth place three of his five years with them. By this time Clarence was a bit beyond prime time for pitchers and had slowed down somewhat in his delivery. As he did not have a good fastball, he had to get by on his spitter and his smarts. If he threw 120 pitches in a game, as many as 75 or 80 of them would be spitballs. His former Brooklyn teammates nicknamed him "Old Bullet Ball" in good-natured recognition of the fact that his pitch did not resemble a speeding bullet. However, his hometown supporters believed he could still pitch. Paul quoted the *Franklin County Sentinel* of June 17, 1926: "Maybe there isn't much on the ball except the cover and maybe the fellows do poke it here and there for many hits, but trying to get a run off this cunning old timer is like trying to take a bone from a cross dog."[12]

The Phillies gave Mitchell his unconditional release on May 28, 1928. Losing one's job may not seem like a lucky break, but for Clarence it was. He left the perennial tailenders who were on their way to a 109-loss season. One week later he was signed by the St. Louis Cardinals, who were on their way to the World's Series. On June 6 his new team faced the New York Giants and fell behind 5–0 in the second inning as the Giants pounded Grover Alexander. From the third frame on, the McGrawmen scored only one more run, as the Cards turned around to win the game. "The main reason for this," wrote Richards Vidmer, "was an old, worn out, cast-off, left-handed spitball pitcher by the name of Clarence Mitchell.[13]

Clarence allowed the Giants only three hits in the remaining seven innings of that game and was the winning pitcher as the Cards moved ahead of the Giants into second place in the National League. He helped the Redbirds take over first place in the pennant chase and in one notable game on August 5 pitched into the fifteenth inning as they defeated the clan of McGraw and young Carl Hubbell and pulled six and one-half games ahead of the second-place Giants. After the Cardinals clinched the pennant, the *Los Angeles Times* ran a feature on five outstanding Redbird players who played a big part in the winning of the pennant for St. Louis. Among the quintet was Mitchell, of whom the feature writer stated, "his signing by the Cardinals was a master stroke for Breadon. Mitchell has taken part in some twenty-nine games and they do say that he has deserved to lose only one of these games. The veteran has pitched marvelous ball against all the four other contenders.... Mitchell should have as much credit as any man on the team. He is the only left-handed spitballer in captivity.... He is smart, cool, and game."[14]

Cardinal manager Bill McKechnie agreed with that assessment: "I'd say he has done as much as any other ball player on the club to win the championship for us."[15]

Despite the fact that the New York Yankees had swept the Pittsburgh Pirates in the 1927 World's Series, they were decided underdogs in the 1928 fall classic. The majority opinion held that superior pitching would bring the crown to St. Louis. How wrong this opinion was! The Cardinals never had a chance as the Yankees swept their second consecutive World's Series. In game 2, Mitchell relieved his fellow Nebraskan, Grover Cleveland Alexander, with one out in the third inning, the bases loaded, and the Cards already trailing 6–3. The veteran spitballer hit a batter and allowed one base hit, permitting two runs to score, both of which were charged to Old Alex. Mitchell allowed only one more hit and one run in the remainder of the game. But the contest was already lost. The Yankees won 9–3. A *Washington Post* writer opined that had Clarence started the game instead of Old Pete, the series might then be tied at one game apiece. He wrote that Mitchell deserved to start one of the games in the Mound City.[16] However, the Cardinals manager had other ideas, and St. Louis lost both games.

Mitchell won eight games for St. Louis in 1929 and started the 1930 season with them. After winning the only game he appeared in for the Cardinals, he was traded to the New York Giants on May 15 for a right-handed pitcher named Ralph Judd. True to the tradition that spitball grandfathers outperform those for whom they are traded, Clarence had one of his best major league seasons ever, winning 11 games while losing only three for a league-leading .786 percentage in 1930. On the other hand, Judd never won a single game for the Cardinals or any other major league team in 1930. By the end of the season he was gone from the majors, never to return.

Mitchell's 1930 performance was cause for celebration in Nebraska. When the veteran returned to Franklin, he was met at the train station by an enthusiastic reception, complete with a band concert and a ceremonial presentation of a new hunting outfit. Hunting was always Clarence's main off-season avocation. He owned hunting dogs and enjoyed chasing after rabbits and coyotes. He became the official coyote catcher of Franklin County. During the 1936–37 off-season, he received $7 per pelt and averaged six kills per week.[17] Often he hosted other baseball stars, such as Alexander, Burleigh Grimes, "Sunny" Jim Bottomley, and Red Ruffing on hunting trips in the nearby Nebraska and Kansas countryside. Frequently he pitched for local semipro teams and sometimes enticed fellow major leaguers to appear in the games with him.[18]

Throughout his life Mitchell considered Nebraska his home. Even when he was away playing baseball he was listed in the Franklin County censuses of 1910, 1920, and 1930, for that is where his family lived year round and where he always joined them during the off-season. The 1930 census listed his wife, Marion; his son, Clarence, Jr.; and a stepson, Wallace. Clarence Jr., also became a professional baseball player. Among teams the younger Mitchell played with were the Oklahoma City Indians of the Texas League.

In 1931 Mitchell won 13 games for the Giants. Surprisingly that was the most victories he ever posted in any of his 18 major league seasons. In a game at Philadelphia's Baker Bowl on July 11, Clarence benefited from some extraordinary hitting by his teammates. The Giants amassed 28 hits and tied the modern major league record of 58 at-bats in a nine-inning game.[19] Mitchell coasted to a 23–5 win, allowing four runs before turning the game over to the 20-year-old rookie, Hal Schumacher, in the ninth inning.

A New York sports columnist was quoted as writing: "Clarence is no Dazzy Vance for speed and curves and he hangs up few strikeouts, but he has a slow ball that has a tantalizing break when properly moistened and he gets results that keep him in the big show."[20]

Before the 1932 season started Mitchell celebrated his forty-first birthday. He had been pitching since he was a child, and it was thought that his arm was starting to wear out. He was used sparingly that spring. On April 20 he won a major league game for the last time, pitching a complete game and defeating the Philadelphia Phillies 14–5. The task was made easy for the ancient hurler by the heavy clouting of his teammates, especially Bill Terry, who for the second day in a row hit two home runs in a game. Clarence's last start came against the St. Louis Cardinals on June 21. Mitchell pitched well in a losing effort, giving up only six hits in six innings, but three of the hits were bunched with the only free pass the pitcher allowed and an error to plate three runs for the Cardinals in the second inning. Meanwhile, the Cards' young and eccentric right-hander, Dizzy Dean, shut the Giants down until the last frame of the 5–1 game. In late June, manager Bill Terry removed Mitchell from the active roster, but retained him as a coach. On November 30, Clarence was given his unconditional release.

Mitchell's major league record:

Year	Club	W	L	Pct.	IP	H	BB	SO	ERA	WR	PTS
1911	Det AL	1	0	1.000	14	26	7	4	8.16	425	6
1916	Cin NL	11	10	.524	195	211	45	52	3.14	3213	53
1917	Cin NL	9	15	.375	159	166	34	37	3.22	-3744	9
1918	Brk NL	0	1	.000	1/3	4	0	0	108.00	-398	-2
1919	Brk NL	7	5	.583	109	123	23	43	3.05	1176	36
1920	Brk NL	5	2	.714	79	85	23	18	3.09	1380	29
1921	Brk NL	11	9	.550	190	206	46	39	2.89	1000	44
1922	Brk NL	0	3	.000	13	28	7	1	13.85	-1515	-8
1923	Phi NL	9	10	.474	139	170	46	42	4.73	3230	49
1924	Phi NL	6	13	.316	165	223	58	36	5.62	-1045	17
1925	Phi NL	10	17	.370	199	245	51	46	5.29	-2430	17
1926	Phi NL	9	14	.391	179	232	55	52	4.58	184	30
1927	Phi NL	6	3	.667	95	99	28	17	4.07	2313	42
1928	Phi NL	0	0	—	6	13	2	0	3.30	0	*
	StL NL	8	9	.471	150	149	38	31	3.53	-2788	18
1929	StL NL	8	11	.421	173	221	60	39	4.27	-1995	19
1930	StL NL	1	0	1.000	3	5	2	1	6.00	405	*
	NY NL	10	3	.769	129	151	36	40	3.98	3029	65

Year	Club	W	L	Pct.	IP	H	BB	SO	ERA	WR	PTS
1931	NY N	13	11	.542	190	221	52	39	4.07	-864	36
1932	NY NL	1	3	.250	30	41	11	7	4.15	-892	0
Total — 18 years		125	139	.473	2217	1613	624	543	4.12	684	454

World's Series record:

		W	L	Pct.	IP	H	BB	SO	ERA
1920	Brooklyn NL	0	0	—	5	3	3	1	0.00
1928	St. Louis NL	0	0	—	6	2	2	2	1.59
Total		0	0	—	11	5	5	3	0.87

But the veteran spitballer's arm was not yet gone. Near the end of January 1934, the Mission Reds of the Pacific Coast League let it be known that if the league would let down the spitball bar down for Mitchell, they would sign him. By a six to two vote the coast magnates approved his admission. Clarence joined Jack Quinn as one of the two spitball grandfathers to toss the moist delivery on the shores of the Pacific in 1934. Mitchell had far greater success than Quinn did on the coast. Clarence won 19 games for the Reds in 1935 and six more the following season. In 1936 he won seven and lost four as a player-manager for Omaha in the Western League. Later, when he was manager of minor league clubs in Mayfield, Kentucky, and Meridian, Mississippi, he made an occasional appearance on the mound. He pitched two innings for Meridian in 1940 at the age of 49. He pitched and managed semiprofessional teams in Broken Bow, Nebraska, and Marysville, Kansas, for a year or so. He helped establish the Cornhusker League, a semipro circuit that operated in Nebraska until 1953 and played with and managed the Aurora team in that league for several years.[21]

During the early years of World War II, Mitchell worked at the Cornhusker Ordnance Plant in Grand Island. In 1943 he and his wife moved to Aurora, where they operated a tavern. To commemorate his Fall Classic fiasco, Mitchell had a key chain made in the shape of a baseball bat. On one side was inscribed an advertisement for his tavern. On the reverse these words appeared: "Beat this Record, Two times at Bat, Result Five Outs in Brooklyn-Cleveland World Series, 1920."[22]

In 1953 Mitchell was named to the Nebraska Sports Hall of Fame. When baseball historian Jerry Clark chose his All-Nebraska All-Star team, he selected four starting pitchers — Grover Cleveland Alexander, Bob Gibson, Mel Harder, and Clarence Mitchell.[23] What a fearsome foursome that was!

Mitchell suffered a circulatory ailment in the late 1950s. His right foot was amputated at Lutheran Hospital in Grand Island on December 29, 1958. Eventually both legs were amputated and he was confined to a wheelchair for the last five years of his life.

On November 6, 1963, Clarence Mitchell died of a heart ailment about one hour after entering the Veterans Hospital in Grand Island, Nebraska. Funeral services were held November 9 in Aurora. He was survived by his widow and two sons, Wallace and Clarence Jr.

9

Dutch Leonard

He pitched two no-hit, no-run games and is credited with the all-time record for the lowest earned run average posted in the American League, an astounding 0.96. In pitching two World's Series games, he hurled a complete game each time and gave up a total of two earned runs, eight hits, and four bases on balls in 18 innings. The losing pitchers in his two fall classic starts were Hall of Famers Grover Cleveland Alexander and Rube Marquard. Yet among many fans, Dutch Leonard is better remembered for his charges against baseball immortals Ty Cobb and Tris Speaker than he is for his exploits on the mound. Sometimes he is confused with another Dutch Leonard, Emil John, an accomplished knuckleball pitcher who came along some two decades after the original.

Hubert Benjamin Leonard was born April 16, 1892, in Birmingham, Ohio, a son of Ella and David C. Leonard, a carpenter. When the lad was nine years old, the family moved to Fresno, California, because of his David's health. During his public school days in Fresno, Hub received the nickname Dutch because someone said he looked so much like a Dutchman. The Leonards were a musical family. Hub's older brother Cuyler was a professional musician. His mother was an accomplished pianist; one brother, Culver, played a cornet; another brother, Ralph, played a slide trombone; and Dutch was a drummer. According to the Associated Press, until success as a pitcher altered his plans, the star slabster was considering taking up professional orchestra work.[1]

For two years, Hub attended St. Mary's College, which was located at the time in Oakland, where he established a considerable local reputation as a pitcher and attracted the attention of a scout for the Philadelphia Athletics and John I. Taylor, former president of the Boston Red Sox. During spring training 1911, he had a brief tryout with the A's, but nothing came of it. Hub pitched for the Visalia clubs of the independent San Joaquin Valley League in 1911.

On June 22, 1911, Chief Bender, one of the A's star pitchers, was ejected from the game by an umpire for throwing a ball over the grandstand in the sixth inning. The Associated Press reported that he was replaced by Leonard, formerly of St. Mary's College, California. According to the record books this was not Hub, but Elmer Leonard. It was a coincidence that two St. Mary's alumni, both named Leonard, were with the Philadelphia club for at least part of the year in 1911.

The following spring, Dutch reported to the Red Sox at their spring training camp in Hot Springs, Arkansas. In his first appearances he was hit hard. Club president James McAleer asked him if he had nothing more than he was showing. Leonard replied that he did not want to use his best stuff against his veteran teammates, for fear of making them angry at him. McAleer advised him to go all out the next day, as it was up to him to earn a place for himself on the team. In the next day's batting practice the veterans had trouble even getting a loud foul off Hub's pitches. He made the team but when the season opened he was sent down to Worcester in the Class B New England League. In his first start he was hit hard, and the Busters returned him to Boston. McAleer asked him what had happened, Dutch replied, "Oh, that field out there is too small to play on, and besides, they gave me an old uniform." The exasperated president shouted, "Gave you an old uniform did they? Well, they ought to have charged you rent for it, and you will be lucky to get even an old one again."[2]

Leonard was about ready to return to Fresno, when Jack Hendricks, manager of the Denver club of the Western League, put in a bid for the southpaw and got him, but with strings attached. McAleer reserved the right to repurchase his contract. The young lefty had a great season, winning 22 games and losing only nine for a percentage of .710 and having almost as many strikeouts as innings pitched. He led the Grizzlies to the pennant and won the final game of the post-season series between Denver and the Minneapolis Millers, the American Association champions. (One publication reported that Leonard won 29 games that year for the Denver club of the Rocky Mountain League.[3] Not only did the book have him in the wrong league, but it also overstated the number of victories by seven.)

His minor league record, excluding the one game he pitched for Worcester in 1912, and the games he pitched in the independent San Joaquin Valley League, consisted of only one season.

Year	Club	League	W	L	Pct.	IP	H	BB	SO
1912	Denver	Western	22	9	.710	241	231	62	226

During the off-season, the Red Sox got Leonard back, at a cost far greater than what Denver had paid for him a few months earlier. Dutch made his major league debut against the New York Yankees at the Polo Grounds on April 26, 1913. He pitched six and two-thirds innings and allowed only two hits. However, he was wild and walked seven batters. After giving up but one run in the first six innings, wildness caused his downfall in the seventh when the Yankees took a 4–3 lead, and Leonard was replaced on the mound by Hugh Bedient. However, the Red Sox rallied to win the game 8–5 and Leonard was credited with no decision in his first major league start. In addition to his excellent pitching, Dutch collected two hits in three trips to the plate. He finished his rookie season with a 14–17 record.

In 1914 Dutch had an outstanding year. He won 19 games while losing only five for a winning percentage of .792. But his most spectacular achievement of the season was compiling an incredible earned run average of 0.96. Among hurlers with enough innings pitched to be eligible for the ERA crown, he is the only pitcher in the history of the American League to allow an average of less than one ERA per game and the only one in any major league to accomplish that feat since 1880, when the pitching distance was only 45 feet. He also had the lowest opponents' batting average and the fewest bases on balls of AL pitchers in 1914. He tied for second in winning percentage, ranked third in strikeouts, and tied for fourth in wins. He ranked fourth in Weighted Rating and was number one in Faber System ratings. Thorn and Holway designated him as their choice for the best pitcher in the American League by naming him their Jim Creighton Award winner. Quite a sophomore season!

On July 11, 1914, a young pitcher up from Baltimore made his major league debut for the Red Sox. Called Babe Ruth, he pitched well for seven innings, holding Cleveland to a 3–3 tie. In the bottom of the seventh, manager Rough Carrigan lifted the Babe for a pinch hitter, Duffy Lewis, who delivered a single. Shortly thereafter, Everett Scott scored the go-ahead run on a single by Tris Speaker. With the Sox on top 4–3, Hub came in to finish the game, striking out four of the six batters he faced. Babe Ruth had won his first major league start thanks to the fine relief pitching of Dutch Leonard.

When Leonard started his major league career he had control problems, but he worked hours on end every day to improve his control. Good control does not mean simply the ability to put the ball over the plate. It means putting it in the exact location desired. A good control pitcher will use only five inches of the strike zone — two and one-half inches on the inside, two and one-half on the outside. Babe Ruth wrote that Ernie Shore could just about drive a nail at 60 feet and Dutch Leonard was just as good. When they pitched they did not guess where the ball was going. They knew.[4]

While Leonard did not again match his 1914 record, he continued pitching well for several more seasons. In 1915 he won 15 games while losing seven. He held opponents to a .208 batting average, the lowest in the league.

The Red Sox were favored in the 1915 World's Series against the Philadelphia Phillies, who were making their first appearance in the fall classic. Although the Phillies had Grover Cleveland Alexander, arguably the best pitcher in baseball that year, the Sox had much greater depth on their pitching staff. Rube Foster, Ernie Shore, Babe Ruth, Dutch Leonard, and Smoky Joe Wood had each won 15 or more games that season. Veteran star Ray Collins and rookie Carl Mays were available if needed. The Phils took the first game as Alexander outpitched Shore 3–1. The Sox evened the series in the next game as Foster defeated Erskine Mayer in another pitchers' battle 2–1.

In the third game it was Leonard's turn to face Alexander the Great. Dutch proved to be the greater one in this game, hurling a masterful three-hitter and allowing no bases on balls, and the Sox prevailed 2–1 on Duffy Lewis's game-winning single in the bottom of the ninth. The Associated Press reported that: "Old Dutch Leonard of Fresno, Cal., a portside twirler, brave of heart, steady of nerve and determined of spirit ... had nothing but speed, a fine change of pace, a curve that seemed to jump first one way then another and had the same effect upon the Philly batsmen, and a control that gave no man an easy speaking acquaintance with the initial bag.... Leonard was a man of mystery to the Phillies. His wide sweeping curves and cross-fire delivery repeatedly fooled the best batters among the National League champions, there being called strikes without the slightest attempt on the part of the batters to connect."[5] In this account there was no mention of the use of a spitball. Why the story referred to the 23-year-old youngster as "Old Dutch Leonard" is not clear.

That was the crucial game of the series, as Shore and Foster wrapped it up with route-going performances in games four and five. During the series the Sox had found it necessary to employ only three hurlers from their deep pitching staff.

Although he started 34 games in 1916, Leonard also was used 14 times in relief and picked up six saves, enough to tie for second in the junior circuit. Ty Cobb never said what year it happened, but it may have been during 1916 that he deliberately tried to spike Hub. (Cobb insisted that he intentionally tried to spike an opposing player on only two occasions in his entire career.) According to the Georgia Peach, Leonard threw a lot of bean balls. So Ty dragged a bunt down the first base line, and when Dutch beat him to the bag, Cobb slid right through the coach's box at him, but missed.[6]

The defending champion Red Sox were fighting for the pennant in 1916 in a six-way race involving every team except Philadelphia and Washington. On August 28 the *Washington Post* stated it was the most contested race in a decade. On August 29 the Crimson Hose had a five-game lead when Dutch Leonard faced the St. Louis Browns in the first game of a doubleheader. During his entire career, Hub had lost only once to the Brownies, and he expected another victory. However, he did not last through the first inning. Two hits, a walk, and a hit batsman gave the Browns two quick runs, and Leonard departed with only one out in the opening stanza. The Sox came back to take the lead but Babe Ruth and Carl Mays could not hold it, and the Browns won 5–3. Leonard asked to start the second game, but manager Rough Carrigan opted to go with Ernie Shore, who was hit hard and frequently. The Browns took this game 8–2. Meanwhile, the Detroit Tigers swept a doubleheader from the Yankees and cut the Sox lead to three games.

Leonard got his chance for revenge the very next day, and did he ever take advantage of it! For seven innings he was perfect — no hits, no runs, no base runners. In the eighth inning he walked the opposing catcher, Hank Severeid. In the ninth he walked pinch hitter Grover Hartley. Neither man reached second base. Dutch Leonard had pitched a no-hit, no-run game and the Red Sox salvaged one game from the series, 4–0. Joe Lannin, who had succeeded McAleer as president of the Sox, presented Hub with $100 as a reward for his no-hitter. One month later, Leonard had the distinction of pitching the game that clinched for the Boston club at least a tie for the league championship by shutting out the New York Yankees 1–0 in 10 innings of brilliant pitching, in which he allowed only six hits and one walk.

The Red Sox were again favored to win the 1916 World's Series. They were facing the Brooklyn Robins, a club that like the Phillies of the previous year had never been in a World's Series before. The Bostonians won the first two games of the series, but the Dodgers came back to win the third. In the fourth game, Leonard faced Rube Marquard, and Dutch got off to a rocky start. Jimmy Johnston hit Hub's first pitch for a triple and scored on a single by Hi Myers. Fred Merkle drew a base on balls, but was retired on a fielder's choice grounder by Zach Wheat, who soon advanced to second base on a wild pitch. George Cutshaw reached on an error, with Myers scoring and Wheat advancing to third. A reporter for the *New York Times* wrote that, "It certainly

Pitcher Hubert "Dutch" Leonard (left) and manager Bill "Rough" Carrigan (right) led the Boston Red Sox to the 1916 World's Series championship. In 1914, Leonard posted the lowest earned run average ever recorded in the major leagues since the 60 feet 6 inches pitching distance was established. (PHOTOGRAPH COURTESY OF LIBRARY OF CONGRESS, LC-USZ62-23245.)

looked like a shower bath, a suit of pajamas, and a nap for Mr. Leonard."[7] However, Wheat was picked off third base and Mike Mowrey struck out to end the inning. Leonard had given up two runs, only one of which was earned, and got out of the first inning with a two-run deficit. He allowed the Robins no more runs and only three hits during the remainder of the contest. Boston came back to win the game 6–2 and wrapped up the series the next day.

The *Times* scribe wrote of Leonard's turnaround: "Leonard began like a man possessed of wide human sympathies and kindness of heart. For just one inning all Brooklyn was fond of him. Then the man's entire nature seemed to become woefully transformed. Whether it was he had exhausted his day's supply of Dr. Jekyll spirit and perforce became Mr. Hyde, or that Brooklyn, on closer acquaintance, palled on him and irritated him, may never be known. At any rate, after giving the hopes of local fandom the pleasant thrills of a rapid ascent to the mountain peak, he cast them from the summit and they were dashed to bits on the cruel rocks below."[8]

During spring training 1917, Leonard held out, demanding a salary of $6,000, which would be a $1,000 raise over his 1916 salary. Eventually he signed for an undisclosed sum. He won 16 games against 17 losses that season, but posted an excellent earned run average of 2.17. On June 28, 1917, Leonard married Sibyl Maud Hitt of Los Angeles. Sportswriters were interested to learn that Miss Hitt was better known as Muriel Worth, who was described as a "dainty and fascinating vaudevillian and danseuse, who has charmed audiences on the Orpheum circuit for the last two seasons."[9] The young couple resided in Boston until the end of the baseball season, when they moved to Leonard's farm in Fresno, the products of which earned Leonard the name "the raisin prince of Fresno." Hub put all of his savings since the first semipro game he ever pitched into his vineyard. By 1917 his vineyard comprised 90 acres, 50 acres of which produced grapes that were marketed regularly, while 40 acres were allocated to the production of raisins. After their marriage, Sibyl gave up her vaudeville career. The 1920 census for Fresno listed Hube Leonard, 27, farmer, and wife Sibyl, 23, no occupation.

After the end of the 1917 season, Hub enlisted in the Navy and was assigned as a yeoman to the Charlestown Navy Yard. He missed part of the 1918 season due to his naval service, but was back with the Red Sox in time to compile a record of eight wins and six losses. On June 3 he pitched a no-hit, no-run game, defeating the Detroit Tigers 5–0. It was his second no-hitter in two years. He was the third American League hurler to toss multiple no-hitters, being preceded by only Cy Young and Addie Joss. It would be another 29 years before Bob Feller became the fourth AL pitcher to achieve that feat.

On December 18, 1918, the Red Sox exchanged Duffy Lewis, Ernie Shore, and Dutch Leonard to the New York Yankees for outfielder Frank Gilhooley, catcher Roxy Walters, pitchers Ray Caldwell and Slim Love, and $15,000 cash. When Leonard read of the transaction in the newspapers, the husky southpaw decided that he was entitled to part of the cash involved in the deal and announced that he would not play for the Yankees unless he received part of the purchase money. Of course, that position was unacceptable to the Yankee owners. Leonard went back to Fresno and pitched for a semipro team called the Sunmaids, probably named after a brand of raisins. The Chicago Cubs stopped in Fresno on their way back from spring training and played an exhibition game against the Sunmaids. With Dutch pitching for Fresno against Shufflin' Phil Douglas, the semipros won 6–1. Leonard shut the major league team out on three hits during the six innings he worked.

The New York club sold Leonard on May 18, 1919, to the Detroit Tigers for $7,500. He probably did not get any of that money either, but the Tigers did make him an offer he could accept and he signed quickly. At the time of his signing, his wife was dancing at the Orpheum theatre in Los Angeles, using her stage name, Muriel Worth. The *Los Angeles Times* quoted Leonard as saying that he would let his wife join him on a trip over the American League circuit later in the season. In their two years of marriage she had seen him pitch only once. "I'd sort of feel her presence and become overanxious to make a good showing and probably ruin my game," the spitballer said. "On the one occasion that she saw me play, late in the sixth inning, a swift liner knocked my thumbs out, and I was forced to retire from the game. Muriel thought that I was killed and couldn't get over it for the longest time. That only strengthened my belief that it is better for her to stay away from the games for a while anyway."[10] He won 14 games for the Bengals in 1919.

Leonard posted double-figure wins for Detroit in each of the next two seasons. He also lost more games than he won for the second-division Tigers, both in 1920 and 1921. His winning percentage both years was slightly less than that of the team as a whole. Hub's value to the team was somewhat less than he thought it to be. Along with

Clarence Mitchell, he was one of the only two lefthanders to be certified as spitball grandfathers. His spitball became his best pitch, although he also had a good fastball and a good curve.

Following the 1921 season Leonard demanded a salary of $15,000 for the next year. The Tigers offered $9,000. The two sides were too far apart to reach a compromise satisfactory to either. Leonard went back to California and signed with Fresno of the independent San Joaquin Valley League. Pitching mainly on Sundays, he compiled a 12–4 record in 1922 and went 10–7 in 1923. He pitched his last game for Fresno on August 6, 1923. The following January, he applied for reinstatement in organized baseball. He was reinstated effective one year after the last date he had pitched in the outlaw league. While waiting for the year to pass, he kept in shape by pitching for the semipro Elks Club in Fresno. On August 6, 1924, the very day his suspension expired, he rejoined the Detroit Tigers. He won three games while losing two in the remainder of that season. Despite having a sore arm, he compiled an 11–4 record in 1925, making most of his starts in the first half of the season. Either because of the sore arm or a dispute with Detroit's player-manager Ty Cobb, Leonard was used sparingly in the latter part of the season. On September 13, Leonard was sent along with six other players and cash to the Vernon club of the Pacific Coast League for third baseman J. R. "Jack" Warner, who never quite achieved the big league stardom that was predicted for him. Dutch Leonard's career in professional baseball was over.

Leonard's major league record:

Year	Club	W	L	Pct.	IP	H	BB	SO	ERA	WR	PTS
1913	Bos AL	14	17	.452	259	245	94	144	2.39	2914	22
1914	Bos AL	19	5	.792	225	139	60	176	**0.96**	5592	87
1915	Bos AL	15	7	.682	183	130	67	116	2.36	330	54
1916	Bos AL	18	12	.600	274	244	66	144	2.36	300	50
1917	Bos AL	16	17	.485	294	257	72	144	2.17	-4521	17
1918	Bos AL	8	6	.571	126	119	53	47	2.72	-378	33
1919	Det AL	14	13	.519	217	212	65	102	2.77	-1755	31
1920	Det AL	10	17	.370	191	192	63	76	4.33	-864	25
1921	Det AL	11	13	.458	245	273	63	120	3.75	-168	33
1924	Det AL	3	2	.600	51	68	18	26	4.56	215	15
1925	Det AL	11	4	.733	126	143	43	65	4.51	3435	64
Total — 11 years		139	113	.552	2192	2022	664	1160	2.76	-728	431

Bold italics indicates he led the league. This is also the lowest ERA ever achieved in American League history.

World's Series record:

		W	L	Pct.	IP	H	BB	SO	ERA
1915	Boston AL	1	0	1.000	9	3	0	6	1.00
1916	Boston AL	1	0	1.000	9	6	4	3	1.00
Total		2	0	1.000	18	9	4	9	1.00

Leonard never played for Vernon. Instead he returned to Fresno to tend his grapes and raisins and to engage in his favorite pastimes of hunting and fishing. However, in 1926 he dropped a bombshell, which shook baseball to its very foundations. It cast a black mark on the reputations of two of the greatest players who ever lived, Ty Cobb and Tris Speaker, and led to the resignation of American League president Ban Johnson. According to Leonard, he and Cobb, both of the Tigers, met with Speaker and Wood of the Indians under the stands at Navin Field on September 24, 1919. Cleveland had already clinched second place, and Detroit needed one more win to finish third. The four men agreed that Detroit would win the game between the two clubs the next day.

Leonard asserted that the four agreed to pool some money and place a bet on Detroit to win. Cobb agreed to put up $2000, Leonard $1500, and Speaker and Wood $1000 each. The bet was to be placed by Detroit's clubhouse attendant Fred West. Despite two triples and a single by Speaker, Detroit won the game 9–5. Cobb went one for five, while Leonard and the washed-up Wood did not play. The season over, the players scattered before there was an opportunity to discuss the bet or divide up the winnings. Some time went by before Leonard received the following letters from Cobb and Wood.

Augusta, Georgia, October 23rd, 1919
Dear Dutch,

Well, old boy, guess you are out in old California by this time and enjoying life.

I arrived home and found Mrs. Cobb only fair, but the baby girl was fine and at this time Mrs. Cobb is very well, but I have been very busy getting acquainted with my family and have not tried to do any correspondence, hence my delay.

Wood and myself were considerably disappointed in our business proposition, as we had $2000 each to put into it and the other side quoted us $1,400 and when we finally secured that much money it was about 2 o'clock and they refused to deal with me, as they had men in Chicago to take up the matter with and they had no more time, so we completely fell down and of course we felt badly over it.

Everything was open to Wood and he can tell you about it when we get together. It was quite a responsibility and I don't care for it again, I can assure you.

Well, I hope you found everything in fine shape at home and all your troubles will be little ones. I made a this year's share of world series in cotton since I came home and expect to make more.

I thought the White Sox should have won, but I am satisfied they were too overconfident. Well, old scout, drop me a line when you can. We have had some dandy fishing since I arrived home.

With kindest regards to Mrs. Leonard, I remain,
Sincerely, Ty

Cleveland, Ohio, Friday
Dear Friend Dutch,

Enclosed please find certified check for sixteen hundred and thirty dollars.

The only bet West could get down was $600 against $420. Cobb did not get up a cent. He told us that and I believed him. Could have made some at 5 to 2 on Detroit, but did not, as that would make us put up $1,000 to win $400.

We won the $420. I gave West $30, leaving $390 or $130 for each of us. Would not have cashed your check at all, but West thought he could get it up at 10 to 7, and I was going to put it all up at those odds. We would have won $1,750 for the $2,500 if we could have placed it.

If we ever have another chance like this we will know enough to try to get down early.

Let me hear from you, Dutch. With all good wishes to Mrs. Leonard and yourself, I am.
Joe Wood

According to one source, Leonard tried to sell the letters to the press in 1926, but found no buyers. He then took them to Ban Johnson and Detroit owner Frank Navin, who paid Leonard $20,000 for the letters.[11] Johnson met with Cobb and Speaker and told them he would keep the scandal quiet if they resigned as managers. (Wood was out of organized baseball at the time, coaching at Yale.) Cobb resigned on November 3, and Speaker retired on November 29. Both immortals were also released by their clubs as players.

What happened next is a matter of dispute. Dan Gutman wrote that Johnson mentioned the matter in a meeting of club presidents and the group voted to turn the evidence over to Commissioner Landis.[12] On December 21, Landis shocked the baseball world by releasing to the press Leonard's charges against the superstars. Landis held a hearing in Chicago to ascertain the facts. Leonard refused to leave his California home to make his accusations face to face. Cobb admitted writing the letter, but claimed he was only discussing a business proposition. Both he and Speaker denied that a meeting had taken place beneath the grandstand. Speaker insisted he knew nothing about the whole affair. Wood backed up the testimony of the two managers. Fred West said he had placed the bet on a horse race, not on a baseball game. For two months Landis deliberated. On January 27, 1927, he exonerated everyone involved, except Leonard. Cobb and Speaker were signed by other major league teams. Dutch was unofficially barred from participating in any future organized baseball activities, such as old-timers games. Humiliated by the commissioner's overruling him, Johnson suffered a breakdown, was granted an indefinite leave of absence, and resigned permanently in October 1927.

Another version of the affair held that Leonard told Tigers outfielder Harry Heilmann about the letters. Heilmann then told Navin, who reported the matter to Landis. One source reported that the commissioner paid Leonard $15,000 to $25,000 for the letters, which Dutch invested in California farmland.[13]

What really happened will probably never be known. No evidence was ever presented against Speaker. However, it seems very likely that Wood and Leonard did bet on the game and that Cobb tried to do so.

Leonard lived out the remainder of his life in the Fresno area. He expanded his vineyards and became a prominent vintner, producing and selling wine. He died on July 11, 1952, at the age of 60. He was buried in Mountain View Cemetery in Fresno.

10

Ray Fisher

It was late in a game between the New York Highlanders and the Chicago White Sox late in the 1910 season. The score was tied and Sox infielder Rollie Zeider was on third base. Fred Mitchell was catching for New York. On the mound was a tall, skinny rookie who had just been called up from the minors. The kid was pitching a great game. As one writer described it, his fastball had a baffling hop and his curve darted like a butterfly and left the hitters swinging at the air. The rookie glanced at the catcher, and nodded in agreement as Mitchell called for a curve. As he started his windup, Zeider suddenly broke from third. He was trying to steal home! Panic stricken, the kid forgot about the curve he was supposed to throw and heaved a fast one toward the plate. The bewildered catcher, expecting a curve, was completely fooled. The ball got past him, and the winning run crossed the plate. More than 30 years later, the pitcher, Ray Fisher, recalled this as the most embarrassing moment in his long and illustrious baseball career.[1]

Ray Lyle Fisher was born October 4, 1887, in Middlebury, Vermont, the fourth and youngest child of Emerette New and Albert Fisher. Albert was a hardworking farmer and a lumberman who traced his ancestry back to Anthony Fisher, who had come to Massachusetts from England in the 1640s. As a child, Ray loved sports. He was glad that his athletic ability gave him an opportunity to escape the prospect of a life as a farmer with its daily grind. In high school and college he played baseball, basketball, football, and track and field. He was a pole vaulter and at one time held the Middlebury College record for the shot put. In football he was a left tackle, and in baseball he was a catcher in high school but changed to pitching as a freshman at Middlebury, where he also played third base. He also played for amateur town teams in the area. His first semipro game was for a team in Valleyfield, Quebec, following the end of his freshman year at Middlebury. He was paid $1.35 a day for working as an assistant to a machinist in a factory and received $10 a game plus room and board for his pitching, more than enough to hire a hand to do his work back on the farm for $1 a day.

In 1908 Fisher started his professional career with Hartford in the Connecticut State League. In 1908 he won 12 games with only one loss. His .923 winning percentage was the best in the league, but he was not in enough decisions to be the official leader. In 1909 he won 24 games against five losses for a percentage of .828. He also had 243 strikeouts that year, one of the greatest performances in a single season in the history of the league. While Ray was pitching for Hartford, Arthur Irwin, a scout for the New York Highlanders, approached Ray with an offer of a contract. The lad jumped at the chance, thinking, "Here's my opportunity for a career in baseball and a ticket off the farm."[2] He signed with the provision that he could finish college first. A few days later he learned that both the New York Giants and the Boston Red Sox, two teams far superior to the Highlanders, were interested in his services, but it was too late. On August 10, 1909, his contract was purchased by the Highlanders from Hartford for $500.

His minor league record to the extent data are available:

Year	Club	League	W	L	Pct.	BB	SO
1908	Hartford	Connecticut	12	1	**.923**		
1909	Hartford	Connecticut	**24**	5	.828	85	**243**
Two years			36	6	.857		

Bold italics indicates he led or tied for the league lead.

Fisher graduated from Middlebury in the spring of 1910. When he reported to the Highlanders, he had never seen a big league game before. Ray showed up with his own homemade bat from off the farm.[3] On July 2 he made his big league debut in an 8–3 loss to the Philadelphia Athletics. He pitched three innings in relief, giving up only one unearned run on one hit and struck out two Mackmen. The next day, he started the first game of a doubleheader and pitched seven innings, leaving with the score tied 3–3. His teammates scored four runs in the top of the eighth and went on to win 7–3. Used mainly in relief, Fisher won five games while losing three during his rookie season and had a respectable 2.95 earned run average.

Ray was vague about how he learned to throw the spitball. Although he never used it at Hartford, he said he already knew how to throw it when he came up to the big leagues. He told an interviewer, "Well, I'll tell you when I came up I never used it. But when I came up to the big league, I was a little country boy and I read about big leaguers and never expected to be amongst them. I'd wake up and realize I was 2–0 or 3–1 and had to come in. But I knew I could throw a spitter, so I threw a spitter. And it helped me ... I always used slippery elm; that's all I used."[4]

Contrary to popular opinion that the spitball was hard to control, Fisher claimed he could get the spitter over the plate better than his other pitches. By the time the spitball was banned, Fisher was using the moist delivery less frequently. He said that when he got acclimated and knew more about how to handle himself, he would just sneak it over for a strike now and then. However, he kept slippery elm in his mouth anyway, just in case.[5]

On September 26, 1912, Fisher married Alice Helen Seeley, a former schoolmate, at the Congregational Church in Middlebury. Their only child, Janet Seeley Fisher (Mrs. John Leidy, Sr.), was born April 28, 1919.

Ray spent eight seasons in New York, enjoying moderate success with a team that finished in the first division only twice during his tenure in the Big Apple. His best season was 1915, when he won 18 games against 11 losses for a fifth-place club. His earned run average that season was a sparkling 2.11, fifth best in the league. His weighted rating was second best in the circuit, as was his Faber System rating. In 1916 he developed pleurisy, which made pitching very difficult. He had fever, sweating, and wheezy breathing. He wore plasters on his chest for a year. Nevertheless, he had a winning season in 1916, with 11 wins and eight losses. New York newspapers dubbed Fisher the "Vermont Schoolmaster" for his off-season vocation of teaching school. His friends from Middlebury, however, called him "Pick."

During the 1917 off-season, the Yankees worked out a deal to obtain second baseman Del Pratt from the St. Louis Browns. The New York club was to receive Pratt, Eddie Plank, and cash from St. Louis in return for Les Nunamaker, Fritz Maisel, Nick Cullop, Joe Gedeon, and Fisher. However, before the deal was consummated, Ray was drafted into the army. Urban Shocker was then substituted for Fisher and the trade went through. What a break for the Browns! Fisher was a good pitcher, but he was no Urban Shocker.

Ray had registered for the draft in Middlebury, Vermont, and it was the Middlebury draft board that called him up, much to his annoyance. He was 29 years old, married, had a career going in New York, and thought that Middlebury had plenty of single, young men they could draft instead of him. John Leidy, Jr., wrote that at first Ray was bitter toward those in Middlebury responsible for his being drafted. However, his feelings changed after he got out of the army and saw that his arm and stamina seemed to have benefited by the time spent in service.[6]

Although Fisher was unhappy about being drafted, the army was very good to him. He spent his entire army career (December 13, 1917-December 2, 1918) at Fort Slocum, near New Rochelle, New York, where he was appointed assistant to the camp's athletic director. He coached and played for the basketball and baseball teams. By the time he was discharged he had been promoted to sergeant.

For a Deadball Era pitcher, Fisher was well paid by the Highlanders (or the Yankees, as they were later called). In 1914 he received $4,000; then he signed a three-year contract at $6,500 per season. When the upstart Federal League showed an interest in him, the Yankees renegotiated his contract, giving him a small raise. He came out of the army a veteran member of the Yankees, looking forward to leading the club, bolstered by recent trades with the Red Sox, to new heights. However, on March 15, he was traded to the Cincinnati Reds for Pete Schneider, a right-handed pitcher who had once won 20 games for the Reds but posted not a single victory for the Yankees and was out of the majors long before the 1919 season was over.

When his contract from Cincinnati arrived, Fisher was astounded to learn that his salary was to be only $3,500 a year. However, he did not protest the cut in pay as he had a soreness in his arm and did not know how he would fare after missing the 1918 season because of army service. In his first National League game, the Schoolmaster defeated the St. Louis Cardinals, helped by a base-running blunder when Cliff Heathcote stopped before reaching second base and was forced out on what should have been a hit by Rogers Hornsby. Ray won his first five starts for the Reds, then ran into tough times. However, he finished the season with a flourish. On August 13 the New York Giants came to the Queen City with a lead of only one-half game over the charging Reds, whom they were to play in three consecutive doubleheaders. The Reds took three

Ray Fisher was traded away from the Yankees before they became pennant contenders. Because of a misunderstanding with his new club, the Cincinnati Reds, he was blacklisted by organized baseball, but went on to become one of the most successful college baseball coaches of all time. (PHOTOGRAPH COURTESY OF NATIONAL BASEBALL HALL OF FAME LIBRARY, COOPERSTOWN.)

of the first five games to take a half-game lead. In the nightcap of the August 15 game, Ray Fisher shut out the Giants 4–0, and the Reds went on to win their first National League pennant of the 20th century. Fisher led the way with eight consecutive victories, finishing the season with 14 wins and five losses. Among National League hurlers he ranked fourth in fewest base runners allowed per nine innings and also held opponents to the fourth lowest batting average in the circuit. He compiled a glittering 2.17 earned run average, one of the best in the league.

In the World's Series which followed, the Reds won a tainted crown when the Chicago Black Sox allegedly "threw" the series. Fisher started the third game and pitched well, losing 3–0, as Dickie Kerr, one of the "clean" Sox threw a three-hit shutout. Ray contributed to his own defeat by mishandling a bunt in the second inning. "Shoeless Joe" Jackson had singled. When Happy Felsch bunted, Fisher tried to force the Shoeless one at second, but threw the ball over Morrie Rath's head, putting runners on second and third. The wild throw may have been caused by his grabbing the ball on the spot that had slippery elm on it. Both runners scored on a single by Chick Gandil. All three Hose players responsible for this rally — Jackson, Felsch, and Gandil — were later barred from baseball for life for their part in the gambling conspiracy. Fisher made a brief appearance in Game 7 of the series, relieving Slim Sallee in the fifth inning of an eventual 4–1 loss. With two runners on base, only one out, and two runs already across the plate, Ray came in and made quick work of the Sox. He fielded Chick Gandil's grounder and threw him out at first base, then struck out Swede Risberg to end the inning. In the next inning, manager Pat Moran removed Fisher for a pinch hitter, and the Vermont Schoolmaster's World's Series career was over.

Despite Fisher's contributions to the Reds' 1919 world championship, club president Garry Herrmann offered the spitballer a raise of only $150 for the 1920 season. When Ray threatened to quit the club, Herrmann eventually granted him a $1,500 increase. Fisher won 10 games against 11 losses in 1920 and again posted a fine earned run average at 2.73. Herrmann responded by offering Fisher a contract for $4,500 for the next season — a cut of $1,000. Ray protested this cut as unfair, but had little choice other than to sign for what the Reds were willing to pay.

On October 2, 1920, Ray made what turned out to be his final major league start, pitching a complete game 13–4 victory over the Pittsburgh Pirates and clinching third place in the National League for the Reds. This was the first game of a tripleheader, the only triple bill played in the majors during the 20th century.[7] The unusual event came about because the games scheduled for the two previous days had been rained out, and the Pirates still had a mathematical chance of catching the third-place Reds if the games were made up and resulted in a Pittsburgh sweep.

In February 1921 Billy Evans wrote that Fisher had once been a spitball pitcher almost exclusively, but of later years he had been getting by without using it except in a pinch. The umpire opined banning the damp delivery would not injure Ray's effectiveness.[8]

Unbeknownst to Evans, during 1921 spring training Fisher perfected what has been called the most deadly spitter ever seen.[9] Working with catcher Ivy Wingo, Fisher developed a a spitball which broke more sharply than that thrown by any other master of the moist delivery. He found a new way to use slippery elm. In addition to wetting the first two fingers of his right hand, he also placed a small wad of chewed-up bark on top of the ball. The slight weight of this wad caused the ball to break downward so sharply that teammates who hit against Fisher in practice found the ball almost impossible to hit solidly. Whether this was legal or not was never tested. As the ball sped toward the plate, the bark fell off and no evidence remained to show that Ray had used it.

The Reds were in Oklahoma City about to wind up spring training when Fisher saw in a newspaper that the University of Michigan was in the market for a baseball coach. On April 3, he telegraphed Michigan to inquire about the position and was invited to come for an interview. According to Fisher, he asked for and received permission from manager Pat Moran to go to Michigan for the interview. The *Cincinnati Enquirer* reported that Moran had granted permission, but the manager denied it. Moran's denial was not known about by Fisher until he saw the letter in the commissioner's files in 1951. The confusion may have been caused by different interpretations of the nature of the permission. Moran may have granted Fisher permission to go to Michigan for an interview, but had not meant to give him permission to take the job.[10] The manager had no authority to release the pitcher from his contract. The release would have to come from the owners.

The university offered Fisher the position at $5,000 per year. On April 8 the Reds offered Pick a $1,000 increase to stay, but Ray countered by asking for a three-year contract. When Herrmann refused to grant that demand, Fisher picked up the telephone on the club president's desk and called Michigan, accepting the job.[11]

As a result of the conversation in the president's office, Fisher thought he would be placed on the "voluntarily retired" list. On April 11 the Associated Press reported that Fisher had been given his "unconditional release." During Michigan's season, Ray began receiving inquiries about his availability to pitch during the summer months. Branch Rickey, in particular, wanted him to come to the Cardinals as a relief pitcher and pitching coach. On April 22, Pick wrote to Herrmann inquiring about his status, saying that he was receiving offers from other teams but realized the Reds had first call on his services. Herrmann replied that Ray was to be placed on the "ineligible list" for violation of contract. Fisher applied to Commissioner Landis for reinstatement. On June 14, 1921, Landis refused reinstatement and Fisher was banned from organized baseball for life.[12]

Fisher's major league record:

Year	Club	W	L	Pct.	IP	H	BB	SO	ERA	WR	PTS
1910	NY AL	5	3	.625	92	95	18	42	2.92	360	24
1911	NY AL	10	11	.476	172	178	55	99	3.25	-798	30
1912	NY AL	2	8	.200	90	107	32	47	5.88	-1370	2
1913	NY AL	12	16	.429	246	244	71	92	3.18	1764	41
1914	NY AL	10	12	.455	209	177	61	86	2.28	22	33
1915	NY AL	18	11	.621	248	219	62	97	2.11	6264	80
1916	NY AL	11	8	.579	179	191	51	56	3.17	1292	46
1917	NY AL	8	9	.471	144	126	43	64	2.19	119	33
1919	Cin NL	14	5	.737	174	141	38	41	2.11	1140	57
1920	Cin NL	10	11	.476	201	189	50	56	2.73	-1449	27
10 years		100	94	.515	1756	1667	481	680	2.82	7344	373

His World Series record:

		W	L	Pct.	IP	H	BB	SO	ERA
1919	Cincinnati NL	0	1	.000	8	7	2	2	2.35

At the University of Michigan, Fisher became one of the most successful coaches in the history of college baseball. In 38 years his teams won 636 games, lost 295, and tied eight for a percentage of .686. They won or tied for the Big Ten championship 15 times, going undefeated through three seasons. The College World Series did not start until near the end of Fisher's coaching career, but even so his team won one championship — in 1953. He was also named the college baseball coach of the year that season. During most of his tenure he also coached freshman football and served as an assistant coach in basketball. Among the freshman football players he coached were Heisman Trophy winner Tom Harmon and President Gerald Ford. Ray retired from the University of Michigan after the 1958 season.

Because of his blacklisting by organized baseball, Fisher was unable to obtain a position in the major leagues during his summers off from Michigan. Consequently, he managed or coached various semipro teams. At various times he managed the Burlington, Montpelier, and Twin City teams in the Northern League in Vermont; and the Fredericton and Blacks Harbour clubs in Canada. He also pitched one season for the outlaw Franklin, Pennsylvania, club during the summer of 1921.

In the early 1930s Fisher received in the mail a silver pass entitling him to free admission to any major league ballpark. It was inscribed: "To Ray Fisher in appreciation of long and meritorious service" and it was signed by the National and American League presidents, Ford Frick and Will Harridge, respectively. Ray assumed from the statement about meritorious service that all had been forgiven. He regarded it as a reinstatement in the good graces of organized baseball. When the Cellar Committee, a subcommittee of the U. S. House Judiciary Committee, held hearing on the monopoly of power in baseball in 1951, Fisher was called to testify. Feeling that he was being used by the attorneys who called him to testify, Fisher did not take a slap at the profession that had given him his career. If he felt any bitterness about the blacklisting, he did not reveal it to the committee.[13]

Apparently, others believed that the blacklist was no longer in effect. Fisher worked as a pitching instructor with the Milwaukee Braves for their minor leagues during spring training at Waycross, Georgia, in 1960 and 1961. From 1963 through 1965 he worked in a similar position for the Detroit Tigers at their Tigertown spring training base in Florida. (Perhaps the ban was only on him as a player, not extending to other positions in organized baseball.)

However, an investigation by University of Michigan-Dearborn professor Don Proctor revealed that Fisher was still officially on the ineligible list in 1980. Proctor wrote to the baseball commissioner's office, but received no reply. Another friend of Fisher, Henry Caswell, wrote a letter, which may have caused Kuhn to alter his stance somewhat on Fisher's status. Then John Leidy, Jr., wrote a letter to Gerald Ford, asking the former president to intervene on his grandfather's behalf.[14] It is not unusual for a baseball commissioner to receive letters pleading for the reinstatement of banned players. Many such letters have been written on behalf of Pete Rose, "Shoeless Joe" Jackson, Buck Weaver, and others. But the letter Bowie Kuhn received was different. It was signed by a former president of the United States, and in conjunction with the other letters, it produced results (of a sort).

The ex-president's letter read in part as follows:

You have previously been contacted about the case of Ray Fisher, who is an old and dear friend of mine. He was my football coach at the University of Michigan and our friendship has grown over these years. I can tell you from personal experience that Ray was one of the most respected coaches by his players, and all others of any sport at the University. His whole life has been one of the highest standards. Until I received the enclosed letter from Ray's grandson, John B. Leidy, Jr., I never knew that Ray Fisher had been blacklisted by professional baseball. I have carefully read the detailed article on the case by Professor Donald J. Proctor. From the facts he presents, and because I have such high regard for Ray Fisher, I am convinced that it would be proper for remedial action at this time. I do most fervently hope that you will take a careful look at the record and consider the current circumstances of a wonderful 93-year-old gentleman who has given so much of his life to baseball. Gerald Ford.

The commissioner replied that he considered Fisher to be "a retired player in good standing." Kuhn did not specifically repudiate the blacklisting, nor did he declare Fisher restored to the eligibility list. How can we declare a 93-year-old man eligible, asked his spokesperson.[15] The injustice done to Fisher by Landis is now recognized by serious students of baseball. Many researchers now agree with the entry in *The Ballplayers* that states that Fisher "was the victim of the petulance and pettiness of Cincinnati owner Garry Herrmann and Commissioner Landis, [who was] often a capricious tyrant."[16]

During his retirement years, Fisher spent many of his summers at a cottage on Lake Champlain, where he fished almost daily. He used minnow to fish for perch and walleye, the only kind he ever kept. As a young man growing up in Vermont, he had been an avid hunter, but in his later days he confined his hunting mainly to trips to Nebraska or South Dakota to hunt pheasants or ducks. When at home he spent much of his time following whatever sport was in season and keeping in touch with University of Michigan baseball via the two coaches who followed him. Of course, he followed baseball most closely, but he also watched football, basketball, and hockey — even occasionally boxing matches. When watching baseball on TV he often turned the sound off and listened to the radio commentary.

His wife and their only daughter preceded him in death. Ray died at the age of 95 in Ann Arbor, Michigan, on November 3, 1982. He was buried in Washtenong Memorial Park in Ann Arbor.

11

Dick Rudolph

During the 1890s the Boston Beaneaters and the Baltimore Orioles had battled for supremacy in the National League. But the Orioles had dropped out of the major leagues, and ill times befell the Bostonians in the early years of the 20th century. From 1901 through 1913, the team, now called the Braves, had finished in the first division only once, back in 1902. Going into the 1914 season, the Braves had 11 consecutive second division finishes, including last-place finishes four years in a row from 1909 through 1912.

On July 4, 1914, the Braves were in their accustomed place—the National League cellar 15 games behind the league-leading New York Giants. Then the Boston contingent mounted a charge that earned them the name Miracle Braves. Leading the charge were three pitchers—Bill James, Lefty Tyler, and Dick Rudolph. Down the stretch, Rudolph won nine in a row. The Braves went into first place briefly on September 2 and were tied with the Giants at the start of a Labor Day morning-afternoon doubleheader. Before 35,000 fans Rudolph outpitched Christy Mathewson to win the morning game 5 to 4 to retake first place. The Giants won the second game in front of nearly 40,000 fans to again tie the race. The attendance for the day was announced at 74,163, the largest paid attendance for any one day in Boston. On the day after Labor Day, the Braves won again and were on their way to the miracle finish.

In the year's official records, Rudolph was credited with 27 wins, tying for the league lead in that category with Grover Cleveland Alexander, but the editors of the *Baseball Encyclopedia* more than half a century later took one of the wins away from him because he had not pitched the requisite five innings as a starting pitcher in one of his victories.

Richard Rudolph was born in New York City on August 27, 1887. His parents, who were of German ancestry, resided at Stanton and Delancey streets in Manhattan. While Dick was still a child, the family moved to the Bronx. Like many small boys of the era, Dick was greatly attracted to the game of baseball. Also like most youngsters, he craved to become a great pitcher. As a schoolboy he made a careful study of the prerequisites for pitching success and remained an astute student of the art throughout his career. He began pitching as an elementary school pupil and became a star at Morris High School in the Bronx. He also hurled for several semipro teams in the area.

According to Ray Nemec, the 17-year-old lad made his professional debut with

Providence of the Eastern League on September 10, 1904, pitching three innings in which he gave up no hits or runs, walked one, and struck out one. Apparently, this brief outing escaped the notice of other baseball authorities. Rudolph's name does not appear on the roster of the 1904 Providence Grays, which was published in Marshall Wright's history of the International League. Nor is his association with the Providence club mentioned in biographical sketches in *Deadball Stars of the National League* and the *Baseball Magazine*. In 1905 Rudolph attended Fordham University and played on the university baseball team the following spring, so any adventure in Providence was unknown to or overlooked by college officials. Dick's first big outing as a collegian occurred in a major league ballpark as he pitched Fordham to a 3–2 victory over Yale at the Polo Grounds.

In the summer of 1906, Rudolph pitched for Rutland of the independent Northern League. When that team folded, he joined the New Haven Blues of the Connecticut League, pitching under an assumed name (King.) Before the season was over, he gave up the pseudonym and forfeited his college eligibility. He was ready for a full-time professional career.

In 1907 he signed with the Newark club of the Eastern League, but failed to impress manager Walter Burnham, who advised him to seek another line of work. Apparently Newark dropped him before he appeared in a single official game. However, he caught on with the Toronto Maple Leafs of the same league, where he compiled a remarkable record over the next several years, averaging 20 wins per season from 1907 through 1912. In 1910 he pitched no-hit ball against Montreal for 10 innings, but lost 1–0 in the 12th.

Despite his great success at Toronto, Dick had difficulty making the major leagues. His brother, a compositor at the *New York Press*, tried to help him by getting sports editor Jim Price to plant stories in the newspaper to the effect that it was a crime that someone of Rudolph's ability was not called up. More effective was the recommendation of the Toronto manager, Joe Kelley, who said: "He has terrific speed, good control, is a quick thinker, and mixes up his assortment as well as any twirler in the big leagues. I look for him in a few years to be as great as Mathewson."[1]

Rudolph was given a tryout by the Giants that fall. He made his major league debut on September 30 in Boston. The Giants had the game well in hand, leading 17–7, when Rudolph entered the game in the ninth inning. Dick retired the first two big league batters he faced, Fred Beck and Doc Miller. The next man up, Bill Sweeney, hit a single to right field, stole second and third, and scored on a single by Pete Burg. Then Rudolph struck out Bill Rariden to end the game. Wanting to give the young spitballer another look, McGraw brought Dick into the eighth inning of the next day's game, with the Giants leading 11–2. The Doves collected four hits and two runs off Rudolph in the two innings he worked. The record books credit Rudolph with saves in both of these games, but this is ridiculous, given that he came in late in the games with a huge lead both times. He also made one start that September. He pitched a complete game and lost, giving up 15 hits and 8 runs. Not a very auspicious beginning to a major league career in which he accomplished some outstanding feats a few years later.

In 1911 Larry Doyle famously said, "It's great to be young and a Giant." In the late winter and early spring of that year, the young man from the Bronx surely shared the sentiments of his more famous teammate. On January 30 the Giants signed Rudolph to a contract. On February 11 he was among the contingent of Giants that sailed from New York aboard the Southern Pacific steamship *Proteus* for New Orleans. After a delightful sea voyage, the group arrived in the Crescent City, from whence they took a train to the Giants' spring training site at Marlin, Texas, in Falls County, near the Brazos, south of Waco. The morning of February 11 found the squad out at the ball yard running, fielding, and batting. The *New York Times* reported that Rudolph "is a finished ball player and looks like he would be one of New York's best pitchers. Dick Rudolph can hit, too," the paper concluded.[2] The *Times* was a bit premature in its judgment. In 1911 Rudolph pitched only two innings for McGraw before being sent back to Toronto, where he had another banner year.

In 1912, Baldy led the International League in both wins and winning percentage, but received a 25-percent pay cut for 1913 when the league passed a rule limiting salaries. Rudolph signed his contract, but soon after the season started he requested a restoration of his former salary or a chance at the big leagues, threatening to quit baseball and go into business if his petition was denied. Thinking (correctly) that his success in Toronto boded well for a major league career and frustrated at not getting another opportunity in the show, he tried to buy his release from the Maple Leafs so he could try his luck as a free agent. He offered the owners $3,500 cash for his release, but they turned him down, believing they could get a better deal from a major league club.[3] Garry Herrmann of the Cincinnati Reds reportedly made an offer, but Toronto officials turned him down. On April 19, Rudolph pitched a three-hitter against Newark but lost 1–0. It was the last game he ever pitched in the International League, as the former Eastern League was now called. He left the club and said he was going to join his brother in business in New York City.

Realizing at last that Rudolph was serious, Toronto sold him on May 4 to the Boston Braves for $4,000 (some sources say $5,000) and pitcher Buster Brown, one of the highest prices ever paid up to that date for a minor league player.

Rudolph's minor league record:

Year	Club	W	L	Pct.	IP	H	BB	SO	ERA
1904	Providence	0	0	—	3	0	1	1	0.00
1906	New Haven	3	3	.500	54	36	8	32	
1907	Toronto	13	8	.619	223	190	47	82	
1908	Toronto	18	12	.600	262	243	48	117	
1909	Toronto	23	14	.622	326	261	50	116	
1910	Toronto	23	15	.605	304	242	69	125	
1911	Toronto	18	11	.621	276	266	64	136	
1912	Toronto	***25***	10	***.714***	299	295	63	137	
1913	Toronto	0	1	.000	8	3	0	1	1.13
Total—9 years		123	74	.625	1753	1536	350	747	

Bold italics means he led the league.

League affiliations: Providence, Eastern; New Haven, Connecticut; Toronto 1907–1911, Eastern; Toronto 1912–1913 International.

In his first start for Boston, Dick relieved with two men on and walked the first batter he faced to load the bases. With three balls on the next batter, he threw three straight curves over the plate to end the inning. Before long, manager George Stallings was calling Rudolph the smartest pitcher he had ever seen.[4] An unimpressive physical specimen at 5' 9½" and 160 pounds, with a receding hairline that earned him the nickname "Baldy," Rudolph made up for physical inadequacies with mental acumen. He copied Christy Mathewson's curve and Bill James's spitball, which together with his excellent control made him the most dependable pitcher on the Miracle Braves of 1914. Baldy turned in a 12-game winning streak during the Braves' run for the flag, and pitched six shutouts, all after the Fourth of July. The diminutive Rudolph and the 6' 3" James were called Mutt and Jeff after popular cartoon characters of the day. Of all the pitchers in the National League, Dick allowed the fewest base runners per nine innings, tied for first in lowest batting average by opponents, ranked second in complete games and in innings pitched, tied for second most wins, tied for third in winning percentage, and ranked fourth in fewest bases on balls allowed per game.

The Philadelphia Athletics were 2 to 1 favorites to win the World Series. The Braves had pulled off one miracle by coming from last place to cop the National League flag, but it was too much to expect them to defeat the A's with their $100,000 infield and the all-star pitching lineup of Chief Bender, Eddie Plank, "Bullet Joe" Bush, Bob Shawkey, and Herb Pennock. In the first game, Stallings chose Rudolph to face Bender, who had led the A's staff with a formidable 17 and 3 record. It was an easy 7–1 victory for the Braves as Baldy threw a five-hitter and the Chief was knocked out of a World's Series game for the first time in 10 starts. The only run scored off Rudolph was unearned. When asked if he was nervous during the game, Baldy replied, "Yes, I was thinking about my daughter Marion who was being born in New York."[5]

Bill James defeated Plank in game two 1–0, and was credited with the win in game three as he relieved Lefty Tyler in the 11th and was the pitcher of record when the Braves rallied to take the contest 5–4 in 12 innings.

Rudolph was back on the mound to start game four against Shawkey and pitched a masterpiece as the Braves won 3–1 to sweep the series in four straight games, the first time that feat had ever been accomplished. In the opinion of some baseball researchers, this was the greatest upset in the history of the game. Boston never witnessed a wilder celebration than that which followed the fourth game. Thousands of fans swarmed the Boston dugout, and paraded around the Fens, down Washington Avenue to Copley Square.

Connie Mack was so shaken by the experience that he immediately broke up his $100,000 infield and spent the next 10 years in the second division. The A's were the first American League club to win the pennant one year and finish in last place the next.

Opposite: **The pitching of Dick Rudolph was one of the reasons the Miracle Braves of 1914 were able to come from last place in July to win the National League pennant and defeat the heavily favored Philadelphia Athletics in the World's Series. (PHOTOGRAPH COURTESY OF NATIONAL BASEBALL HALL OF FAME LIBRARY, COOPERSTOWN.)**

All four victories in the sweep had been won by spitball pitchers, two each by James and Rudolph. Rudolph had pitched two complete games, allowing a total of only two runs, one of which was unearned, 12 hits, and four bases on balls. He struck out 15 White Elephants.

By pitching complete games in each of his two starts, Rudolph set a record of 18 innings pitched in a four-game World Series. This record has never been broken, and has been tied only three times in the last 90 years. Waite Hoyt in 1928, Red Ruffing in

1938, and Sandy Koufax in 1963 all matched Baldy's feat, but none has exceeded it. Rudolph's 15 strikeouts also set a standard for a four-game series which lasted until Koufax notched 24 K's in 1963.

After the 1914 World's Series, Connie Mack was reported to have said: "James is a great pitcher and Rudolph is a wise one." F. C. Lane applauded this distinction. He wrote:

> Rudolph is of slighter build. His height militates against him. He possesses little of James' whizzing speed. But he displays a world of cautious craft, a wealth of shrewd experience, the harvest of years of close application and strict observation. He pitches with his head. The distinction is obvious, clear cut, and well established in baseball.... His whole career has borne out the assertion of Connie Mack that he is a wise pitcher, one who makes use of the gifts at his disposal and supplements whatever he may lack of speed or curve with craft and ready knowledge of the opposing players and the manner in which their talents may be offset. He is first, last, and all the time a head pitcher, and his stepping stones to success are knowledge of the game, wisdom in handling himself in tight places, and control.[6]

Rudolph agreed with this assessment:

> What good would it do me if I had the greatest curve in the world or the most speed, if I couldn't use them to advantage. It isn't what I have on the ball, it's how I use what I have that counts.... My favorite delivery is a slow ball, bearing in mind that a slow ball is valuable only as a change of pace. That is the main thing, mixing them up, never giving the batter what he is looking for, but springing the unexpected, particularly at critical moments of the game. I used to pitch the spit ball a good deal. In fact they call me a spitball pitcher now. Well, I do use it a little. I use it as it ought to be used, once in a while. It takes a great pitcher to pitch a spit ball and depend on that delivery altogether.... A spit ball is a very useful ball to mix in with other types if you can control it. Personally I never had any great trouble in controlling a spit ball. Even now when I use one I would just as soon send a spit ball over the plate for a third strike as a fast one. I believe I can control my spit ball as well as I can my fast ball, and I use it occasionally in just that situation.[7]

In an article credited to Rudolph in the May 1918 issue of *Baseball Magazine*, the pitcher said: "I use a fast ball a great deal, in spite of what they say. I also use curves, spit balls, and slow balls. True, I used spit balls mostly as a blind. But the batter can never tell when I am bluffing and when I am actually going to cut loose with a spit ball, so it has the same effect as though I used it more frequently."[8]

Writing in the same magazine a year later, F. C. Lane added a similar assessment: "Dick Rudolph is a wise pitcher who uses everything that is lawful for the pitcher. He is too wise to depend overmuch on the spit ball, but he does throw a spitter occasionally, just often enough to remind the batter that he can expect a freak break once in a while. What Rudolph does, however, is to bluff throwing the spitter, and this is just as bad as actually using the twister, as far as the batter is concerned."[9]

In 1915 Lane interviewed a number of pitchers on whether they try to outguess the hitter by throwing a pitch that the batter is not expecting. Some, including Christy Mathewson and Walter Johnson, denied ever doing so. Others, such as Grover Alexander and Red Faber, said they tried to cross up the batter most of the time. Of all the pitchers interviewed, Rudolph was the most outspoken and pronounced. In fact, he said:

I spend practically all my time trying to fool the batter.... It is the whole science of pitching to my mind. Most batters try to foresee what the pitcher will give them a good share of the time and upon their ability to do this depends their success as batters. Conversely the good pitcher is the one who is the most successful at fooling the batters, by giving them something in the line of a delivery that they are not prepared for. I would easily rank this as first in a pitcher's assortment.[10]

Rudolph's threat to quit baseball if he were not given an opportunity to pitch in the majors certainly paid off for him. Although the $2,900 he received from the Braves in 1913 was only a few hundred more than he would have received in Toronto, financial advancement came quickly. He signed for $3,500 in 1914, received a $1,500 gift for outstanding performance, and was awarded a contract of $7,500 for the next season. Perhaps more important than the salary was the satisfaction of becoming a major league star, one of the elite pitchers in the world.

In 1915 Baldy again won more than 20 games, but the miracle was over. Boston did not win another pennant until 1948. Rudolph did his part for the Braves, ranking second in wins, complete games, and innings pitched, and fifth in bases on balls per game.

Dick had another good year in 1916, falling one game short of the 20 victory total. He held opponents to the lowest batting average in the league, gave up the fewest bases on balls per game, tied for second fewest base runners allowed per nine innings, and ranked third in complete games and innings pitched. That was his last winning season, as he fell below the .500 mark in each of his remaining years. As a married man, he was not drafted into the armed services and pitched throughout World War I. In 1919, pitching for a second division club, he ranked fourth in both innings pitched and complete games. From 1921 through 1927 he served as a coach for the Braves, and occasionally pitched a game. After the 1927 season, he was released.

Of all the grandfathered spitball pitchers, Rudolph had the fewest bases on balls per nine innings pitched and the best strikeouts to walks ratio. He also held opponents to the lowest on base average. His reputation as a great control pitcher is certainly validated by the statistical records.

Major League record:

Year	Club	W	L	Pct.	IP	H	BB	SO	ERA	WR	PIS
1910	NY NL	0	0	—	12	21	2	9	7.50	-595	-3
1911	NY NL	0	0	—	2	2	0	0	9.00	0	0
1913	Bos NL	14	13	.519	249	258	59	109	2.92	1998	50
1914	Bos NL	26	10	.720	336	288	61	138	2.35	5513	91
1915	Bos NL	22	19	.537	341	304	64	147	2.37	-574	46
1916	Bos NL	19	12	.613	312	266	38	133	2.16	1054	55
1917	Bos NL	13	14	.481	243	252	54	96	3.41	351	39
1918	Bos NL	9	10	.474	154	144	30	48	2.57	1064	38
1919	Bos NL	13	18	.419	274	283	54	76	2.17	341	36
1920	Bos NL	4	8	.333	89	104	24	24	4.04	-984	14
1922	Bos NL	0	2	.000	16	22	5	3	5.06	-704	-4

Year	Club	W	L	Pct.	IP	H	BB	SO	ERA	WR	PIS
1923	Bos NL	1	2	.333	19	27	10	3	3.72	-51	4
1927	Bos NL	0	0	.000	1	1	1	0	0.00	0	0
Total — 13 years		121	109	.526	2049	1941	402	786	2.66	7411	366

World's Series record:

		W	L	Pct.	IP	H	BB	SO	ERA
1914	Boston NL	2	0	1.000	18	12	4	15	0.50

In 1928 Rudolph and a friend bought the Waterbury club in the Eastern League. The club disbanded after one losing season. In 1929 he became New England sales representative for the truck division of General Motors. One report said Dick joined his brother for a few years in the undertaking business in Nyack, New York. From 1932 to 1945 he was affiliated with the Walter B. Cooke Funeral Home in the Bronx as a licensed undertaker and arrangement man at their main office in the Bronx. A recurrence of diabetes forced him to retire from that position, but he soon returned to baseball as a supervisor for Stevens Brothers Concessionaires at the Polo Grounds and Yankee Stadium. In 1947 or 1948 he became a volunteer baseball coach for the freshman team at Fordham University.

On October 20, 1949, he died of a heart attack at the home in the Bronx that he shared with his daughter, Marion Rudolph Prediger. He was also survived by his wife, the former Alice Craig, whom he had married on October 8, 1912; another daughter, Ethel Rudolph Trull; and four grandchildren. He was just two months past his 62nd birthday when he passed away. He was buried in Woodlawn Cemetery in New York City.

12

Allen Sothoron

Although he was recognized by his peers as one of the smartest pitchers in all of baseball, the name of the veteran spitballer was not a household word to the fans of America. For his entire career he had pitched in relative obscurity, toiling for the lowly St. Louis Browns on the west side of the Mississippi River, far from the population centers of the East where ballplayers gained national renown. In 1921 he got off to a poor start with the Browns. After losing two of three decisions, he was waived to the Boston Red Sox. With the Crimson Hose he lost both of his starts. Then he found new life with the Cleveland Indians. What a break it was to be picked up by the defending world champions! The spitballer took full advantage of the opportunity. With the Tribe he won 12 games and lost only four, keeping the Indians in first place much of the season. It appeared he would finally get to a World's Series and receive the recognition that was his due. Alas, it was not to be. The surging New York Yankees caught and then passed Cleveland to take the American League pennant. The spitballer never again enjoyed a season such as 1921. He is destined to be remembered mainly for a one-liner penned by Bugs Baer: "Allen S. Sothoron pitched his initials off yesterday."

Allen Sutton Sothoron was born in Bradford, a small city in western Ohio, on April 27, 1893, a son of Ida and Bernard Sothoron, a tinner. When he was 18 or 19 years old, Allen played baseball for Juniata College in Pennsylvania.[1]

He started his professional career as an outfielder, playing for both Troy and Binghamton in the Class B New York State League in 1912. The following season, he played for York in the Tri-State League and Columbus in the South Atlantic before taking the mound for Fall River in the New England League. He split the 1914 and 1915 seasons between the St. Louis Browns and two minor league clubs.

In 1916, with the Portland Beavers of the Pacific Coast League, he had his first winning season, and it was a dandy. A sportswriter for the *Los Angeles Times* was impressed by Al's pitching. After one game in June he wrote: "Sothoron, running true to a peculiar habit which he has, allowed only three hits and was strongly opposed to anybody getting further than second base. He believes that base-runners should be confined to the southwest side of the diamond." But the scribe was more impressed by Al's batting stance: "Al got mighty fresh with his feet. He attracted a lot of unfavorable attention to them by not keeping them in the box, and when at bat in the sixth he spraddled all over the plate, in this way leaving Oscar [Horstman, the opposing pitcher] nothing to throw at. Sothoron's feet are the most unconventional feet seen here since Bill Piercey was in town last. They chafe at confinement, and don't seem to care who points the finger of scorn at them. They simply wander around regardless of what anybody thinks of them. It was even rumored that Al sleeps with them sticking out the window on clear, calm nights."[2]

By August of that year he had a 15–15 record; then he reeled off win after win. On October 21 he shut out Los Angeles 6–0 for his 15th consecutive victory and his 30th win of the season. He was just one game short of the league record for consecutive wins, but he lost his last two games and did not break the record. However, he led the league in wins and in shutouts, and was second in strikeouts, just one behind the league leader.[3]

This fine performance earned him a promotion to the majors, where he pitched for the next 10 years, with the exception of a stint with Louisville of the American Association in 1923.

His minor league pitching record:

Year	Club	W	L	Pct.	IP	H	BB	SO	ERA
1913	Fall River	5	6	.455	not available				
1914	Haverhill	15	18	.455	259	235	90	152	
1915	Wichita	16	17	.485	262	262	106	156	3.15
1916	Portland	***30***	17	.638	397	341	158	202	2.65
1923	Louisville	6	9	.400	108	112	57	43	4.67
Total — 5 years		72	67	.518	1026+	950+	411+	553+	

Bold italics indicates led the league in that category.

League affiliations: Troy, Binghamton, New York State; York, Tri-State; Columbus, South Atlantic; Fall River, Haverhill, New England; Wichita, Western; Portland, Pacific Coast; Louisville, American Association.

Sothoron made his major league debut for the St. Louis Browns on September 17, 1914. He entered the game in the top of the fourth inning with the Washington Nationals leading the Browns 8 to 2. The *Washington Post* reported: "Rickey introduced young Southern [sic] just up from the bushes. He just arrived yesterday. Southern went along well enough for five of the six innings that he slabbed. But in the seventh the Nationals took a sudden and fond liking for his offerings and hammered out four more runs."[4] In all Sothoron gave up six hits and four runs. He walked four and struck out three in his only appearance of the season as the Browns went down to a 12–2 defeat. (The *New York Times* also spelled Allen's name Southern in its report of the game.) In 1915 Allen appeared in three major league games, losing his only decision.

In 1917, his first full major league season. Al pitched reasonably well, as attested by his 2.83 earned run average, but received little support from his teammates. He and fellow Brown pitcher Bob Groom tied for the league lead with 19 losses each as the St. Louis club finished seventh in the American League. In 1918 Sothoron improved his ERA to 1.94, third best in the league, and broke even in the won-lost column. Dixie, as he was called because his frequently mispronounced name led people to think he was from the South, held opponents to a .205 batting average, lowest in the league. Among American League pitchers he held opponents to the second lowest on-base percentage and allowed the third fewest base runners per nine innings.

In 1919 Al had his most successful season in the major leagues, winning 20 games and posting a fine 2.20 earned run average. He tied for fifth in the number of wins and had the fifth best ERA in the league. He had the third best Weighted Rating and tied for fifth in the Faber System rankings. In 1920 he was unable to repeat that success, falling to an eight and 15 mark. In his four full seasons with the Browns, the club never had a winning record, making it difficult for Sothoron to compile the record that his ability seemed to warrant. Another reason Al did not enjoy greater success in the majors may have been his inability to field bunts. More about that later.

His 1921 season has been reviewed above. One of his best efforts was a three-hit shutout over the New York Yankees, which temporarily stopped the Yanks from taking over first place in their drive to their first American League pennant. Dixie's .750 winning percentage for the Indians was not bested by any pitcher in the junior circuit that year, but his earlier losses with St. Louis and Boston brought his overall percentage down to a more modest .619. Perhaps his most outstanding accomplishment that season was pitching 178 innings without giving up a home run. No other pitcher in the post–Deadball Era has pitched that many innings while allowing no homers.[5]

After getting off to a poor start in 1922, Sothoron was released by the Indians. He pitched for Louisville of the American Association in 1923 and returned to the majors with the St. Louis Cardinals in 1924. Upon his purchase by the Cardinals, a sportwriter for the *Washington Post* reviewed his career, putting special emphasis on his difficulty fielding bunts:

> The psychology students in the ranks of fandom will have something to mull over.... Around the half-way mark of the 1920 campaign in the closing innings of a tight game at Cleveland ... the pitcher, fielding a bunt, chucked the ball into the stands, for the Indians' margin of victory. From then on it became a habit, and Sothoron's appearance in the box was the signal for a concerted bunting attack by the enemy that always wound up in the same way — wild heave and early exit.[6]

According to the *Post* article, Sothoron's difficulty fielding bunts led to a temporary end to his major league career and even plagued him at Louisville. The writer thought that Branch Rickey's mastery of psychology might enable him to get the spitballer back on the track even after three other managers had failed. Perhaps Rickey's magic worked for a while. Al made no errors in 1924. However, his fielding average plummeted to .864 in 1925 and a mind-boggling .778 in 1926. His career fielding average of .871 was by far the worst of any of the spitball grandfathers.

Among the tricks of this master trickster was one worked by raising a corrugation on the side of the ball without the aid of any foreign substance. By the use of a strong forefinger and thumb Sothoron would work up the seam of the ball until it stood out. Then the pitch would act much like the outlawed emery ball that Russell Ford had used.[7]

Sothoron won 10 games for the Redbirds in both the 1924 and 1925 seasons. In 1926 he won only three games for the Cardinals, but one of his victories was crucial to

Allen Sothoron spent most of his major league career in St. Louis, starting with the Browns and finishing with the Cardinals. Later he was a successful minor league manager. (PHOTOGRAPH COURTESY OF NATIONAL BASEBALL HALL OF FAME LIBRARY, COOPERSTOWN.)

the Redbirds' winning their first National League pennant. In late August the Cards were locked in a tight race with Pittsburgh and St. Louis. On the morning of August 31, the world champion Pittsburgh Pirates were in first place, Cincinnati was second, and St. Louis third, only a few percentage points behind the leaders. In the day's action, the Reds lost to the Cubs, and St. Louis moved into first place by sweeping the Pittsburgh Pirates in a doubleheader. Sothoron won the nightcap 2–1 with a masterful performance, holding the champs to only three hits. The Corsairs scored their only run in the fourth inning when Hal Rhyne singled, Kiki Cuyler beat out a bunt, Clyde Barnhart singled, and George Grantham sacrificed Rhyne home. Two bunts were involved in getting the Pirates their run, but Al did not throw either of them away. He held the Pirates to one hit during the rest of the game, and the Cardinals won it by scoring two runs in the seventh inning. Sothoron went the route for his only complete game of the season. For the first time in their history, the Cardinals entered September in first place. They held on, of course, to cop their first National League flag.

However, Sothoron did not get a chance to pitch in the Cards' World's Series triumph over the Yankees that October. Al wound up his major league pitching career at the end of the 1926 season, but he was not through with baseball yet.

His major league record:

Year	Club	W	L	Pct.	IP	H	BB	SO	ERA	WR	PTS
1914	StL AL	0	0	—	6	6	4	3	6.00	0	0
1915	StL AL	0	1	.000	4	8	5	2	7.36	-412	-2
1917	StL AL	14	19	.424	277	259	96	85	2.83	2277	46
1918	StL AL	12	12	.500	209	152	67	71	1.94	800	41
1919	StL AL	20	12	.625	270	256	87	106	2.20	5920	81
1920	StL AL	8	15	.348	218	263	89	81	4.70	-4025	5
1921	StL AL	1	2	.333	28	33	8	9	5.20	-579	*
	Bos AL	0	2	.000	6	15	5	2	13.50	-986	*
	Cle AL	12	4	.750	143	146	58	61	3.24	2624	49
1922	Cle AL	1	3	.250	25	26	14	8	6.39	-1052	-2
1924	StL NL	10	16	.385	197	209	84	62	3.57	-1170	23
1925	StL NL	10	10	.500	156	173	63	67	4.05	-60	35
1926	StL NL	3	3	.500	43	37	16	19	4.22	-492	11
Total — 11 years		91	99	.479	1582	1583	596	576	3.31	2845	291

Following the end of his playing career, Al stayed with the Cardinals as a coach for two years. In 1928 he signed as a coach with the Boston Braves under manager Rogers Hornsby. In 1929 Sothoron became the manager of a second division Louisville club in the American Association. The very next season he led them to the league crown.

Sothoron had been regarded as one of the cleverest pitchers in the majors. He proved to be a very intelligent manager as well. In 1930 outfielder Johnny Marcum was leading Louisville in hitting with a .395 average, but toward the end of the season the Colonels needed pitching help. Knowing that Marcum had once been a pitcher, Sothoron asked Johnny to try pitching again.[8] The young Kentuckian responded with four straight wins to help the Colonels win the pennant. Marcum went on to play in the majors for seven years — as a pitcher. At Louisville Sothoron earned a reputation as a great teacher of young players. Although Louisville did not repeat as league champion, Al had shown enough managerial acumen to earn another chance in the major leagues. In 1932 he became a coach for the St. Louis Browns.

On July 19, 1933, with the Browns in last place and in financial difficulty brought on by the Great Depression and aggravated by their own lack of competitiveness, Bill

Killefer resigned as St. Louis manager. His good friend and coach Al Sothoron was appointed acting manager in his stead. Al knew the limitations of the team: "I'll simply try to get the most out of the material at hand and see if I can't get the Browns in the winning habit."[9]

Sothoron did not have much of a chance to instill a winning habit in the Browns. Under his tutelage the cellar-dwellers won only one of four games before Al was replaced as manager by Rogers Hornsby. The Browns had never intended for Sothoron to be a long-term manager. They employed him only as a stopgap until they could complete arrangements for Hornsby to take over. The Rajah was unable to get the Browns out of last place. The club never finished higher than sixth place during his five years at the helm.

In 1934 Sothoron became manager of the Milwaukee Brewers of the American Association. He enjoyed considerable success with the Brew Crew, finishing in the first division in four of his five years as skipper. One of the problems with being a minor league manager is that your best players are likely to be promoted to a higher league. The champion 1936 Brewers were led by two powerful sluggers, Chet Laabs and Rudy York, who hit .324 and .334, respectively, and between them had 79 home runs and 299 runs batted in. Both were in the major leagues in 1937. Two of Al's 19-game-winning pitchers, Luke Hamlin and Joe Heving, were also called up, as was Clyde Hatten, who went 16–6 and led the association with 190 strikeouts. Also promoted to the majors from the 1936 team was a third baseman whom Sothoron had discovered as a teenager playing on the sandlots of Milwaukee the previous season. Ken Keltner went on to have a distinguished major league career, mostly with the Cleveland Indians. After his Brewers finished third in the 1938 season, Sothoron was released as manager, and his career in professional baseball was over.

In 1928 Sothoron married a young woman from Kansas named Harriett. The couple was living in Louisville at the time of the 1930 census. By 1937 the marriage had ended, and Al wed a St. Louis socialite, Dorothy Clemens, at St. Bartholomew's Church in the Mound City in October of that year. The daughter of a prominent physician, Dorothy was a member of the Colony Club and the Junior League.

On June 17, 1939, the former spitballer died at St. John's Hospital in St. Louis from a complication of diseases after a three-week illness. According to Bill Lee, Allen died from heart trouble, acute hepatitis, and alcoholism. He was buried in New York.[10] Sothoron was only 46 years old. He was survived by his wife, Dorothy.

13

Phil Douglas

The veteran spitball pitcher should have been on top of the world in the summer of 1922. He had won two games for the New York Giants in the 1921 World Series and was regarded as one of the heroes, perhaps the number one hero, of the fall classic. He got off to a great start for the defending world champions that spring, winning 10 of his first 11 decisions. In July his pitching faltered somewhat, but going into the last days of the month he had 11 wins and only three losses and was leading the league in winning percentage, earned run average, and other statistical categories.

He had a drinking problem, but he kept his drinking under control that summer. However, John McGraw, his manager, did not trust him and assigned a Giant scout, Jesse Burkett, known as The Crab, to guard him. The Giants were in the thick of a pennant race with the St. Louis Cardinals and two or three other clubs. As always, McGraw hated to lose and in the stress of the pennant race became more and more caustic. He saved his sharpest words for his ace spitballer, Phil Douglas. On July 30 Phil started against the Pittsburgh Pirates in a game at the Polo Grounds and was hit hard, losing for only the fourth time that season. After the game the veteran pitcher was already feeling low. Then his manager launched an abusive verbal attack on him that made Phil's ears burn. The pitcher protested: "I do not care to be humiliated this way. What you are doing is getting to be more than a man can stand."

The events of the next few days led to Phil's expulsion from organized baseball. According to his biographer, in order to understand why Douglas reacted the way he did, we must understand Phil's background and the culture in which he grew up.[1]

Phillip Brooks Douglas was born June 17, 1890, in Cedartown, a northwest Georgia hill country town noted for its ironworks. He was a son of John A. Douglas and his second wife, the former Lucy Jane Hawkins of Cowan, Tennessee, a Cumberland Mountain town that was the site of an iron foundry. Phil grew up in a large, unpainted frame house in downtown Cowan. The Douglases were a large family. John's first wife had given birth to three sons and two daughters before she died in the 1880s. Lucy Jane gave him another son and a daughter.

According to Phil's biographer, Phil's father and his older half-brothers were all foundry workers with a similar lifestyle. Big and agile, they drank corn whiskey, told good stories, and were honest, good-natured men who worked hard when they wanted to, and were left to do whatever they pleased when they did not feel like working.[2]

Sometimes headstrong, the Douglas men thrived on praise and chafed under criticism and pressure.

Although the family was not wealthy, Phil attended the Brandon Training School in Wartrace, Tennessee, a private academy. In the summers he did occasional day labor in local mills and mines, but his weekends were for playing ball. At the precocious age of nine, he was sometimes allowed to play with a team of local railroad men. Two years later he was playing regularly with the Cowan town team. At the age of 13 he was playing every weekend for Cowan and other semipro teams within a radius of 100 miles. In his early teens he was already taller and sturdier than most adults. Because of his size, he started out as a catcher, but he threw so hard that he was made into a pitcher.[3]

Between his weekend games, the teenaged lad loafed, fished, drank, and traveled. In 1910 he signed with the Rome club of the Southeastern League and had already won 12 games when the club folded in midseason. A few weeks after his 20th birthday, he became a married man. On August 15, 1910, he wed Louise Wepf, in Stevenson, Alabama. In the fall his daughter Mary Louise was born in Tracy City, Tennessee. In 1912 a second daughter, Eunice, was born in Georgia. Life changed for Phil Douglas. The carefree life that he had enjoyed in semipro ball was not possible in organized baseball. Baseball had rules, schedules, and no room for optional weekday vacations. The sacrifice of his fishing and drinking days and of his independence was almost more than he could endure.

He was called "Shufflin' Phil" because of the way he walked. Douglas started his professional baseball career with Rome of the Class D Southeastern League in 1910. The following year, he pitched for the Macon Peaches in the South Atlantic League. He led the Sally League in wins with 28, and captured the attention of Charles Comiskey, owner of the Chicago White Sox, who purchased his release from Macon. In March 1912 Douglas went to spring training with the White Sox, who sent him to Des Moines of the Class A Western League for the 1912 season. On August 28 the Sox called him up for a major league trial. He got into only two games for the Pale Hose, but spent two weeks with Sox ace Ed Walsh, who taught him how to use his spitball more effectively. Phil later said that Walsh was the only player who ever was considerate enough to try to teach him how to pitch.[4] In preparation of his spitter, Phil used tender new twigs of slippery elm, which were procured for him by a friend who climbed to the top of the tallest slippery elm tree in Pikeville, Tennessee, to obtain them.[5]

In 1913 the Sox optioned Douglas to San Francisco in the Double A Pacific Coast League. In June the Seals released him to the Spokane Indians of the Class B Northwestern League. After the season, Spokane sold him to the Cincinnati Reds.

He spent 1914 and 1915 in the majors and had his final minor league experience with St. Paul of the Class AA American Association in 1916. His minor league career was notable for permitting few base runners per game and maintaining an excellent ratio of strikeouts to walks.

His minor league record:

Year	Club	W	L	Pct.	IP	H	BB	SO	ERA
1910	Rome	12	6	.667	156	110	37	116	
	Macon	0	1	.000					
1911	Macon	**28**	11	.718	356	249	94	228	
1912	Des Moines	15	16	.484	249	217	71	211	
1913	San Francisco	6	8	.429	147	180	54	87	
	Spokane	10	10	.500	173	136	61	167	
1916	St. Paul	12	11	.522	226	185	72	134	2.11
Total — 5 years		83	63	.568	1307	1077	389	943	

Bold italics indicates he led the league.

League affiliations: Rome, Southeastern; Macon, South Atlantic; Des Moines, Western; San Francisco, Pacific Coast; Spokane, Northwestern; St. Paul, American Association.

Douglas made his major league debut on August 30, 1912, for the Chicago White Sox, starting against the Cleveland Indians. He had a rough outing, giving up nine hits and five bases on balls in seven innings and being charged with the loss as the Hose fell 7–2. Another rookie made his major league debut in this game. Ray Chapman played shortstop for the Indians. It is ironic that both of the men who initiated their major league careers in this contest had their baseball lives cut short by tragedy. (Chapman, of course, was killed by a pitch delivered by Carl Mays in a 1920 game, while Douglas was banished from organized baseball in 1922.)

Although Phil lost his first start, sportswriter I. E. Sanborn was impressed with his potential, even though he reported the name as Bill Douglass, rather than Phil Douglas. The scribe wrote:

> It was the young man's first day in fast company and he went in without knowing half the first names of the men who were supporting him. Stated frankly, he didn't look too pretty in spots, but did look pretty in others, and the good spots were frequent enough that Manager Jim [Nixey Callahan] would have sent him the full route but for a chance to start something in the eighth, which brought in Easterly as pinch hitter. Douglass was nervous and wild at the start, and gave the Naps three passes, out of which they manufactured two runs. Then he set the enemy down three in a row for a couple of rounds, whereupon Cleveland started bunting on him and found him a bit slow in going after the little rollers, which mean so much or so little, depending on how they are handled. ... Douglass is a whale of a fellow, a lot over 6 feet tall, and favored with the shoulders and back of the stroke of a varsity crew. He is far from a stripling, but will weigh more when he gets a little older. He showed a lot of stuff, including speed that smoked and a curve that hooked.... What he does possess is so much more than what he does not possess that he will get a lot more opportunities to show what he has and to learn what he lacks.[6]

When Douglas returned to the major leagues in 1914, it was as a member of the Cincinnati Reds, who had acquired him from Spokane. The Reds were a last-place team that year, so Phil's record of 11 wins and 18 losses was not as bad as it seems. He had a fine earned run average of 2.56 and held his opponents to a batting average of .223, fifth best in the league. However, he had numerous clashes with manager Buck Herzog and was fined $100 for breaking training rules.

During the first week of May 1915, Douglas was suspended briefly for excessive drinking. Herzog decided to get rid of his problem. On June 13, Douglas was sold to the Brooklyn Robins in a straight cash transaction with no other player involved. The highlight of Phil's season came on July 7 when he shut out the Boston Braves for 16 innings as Brooklyn and Boston battled to a scoreless tie. However, the Shuffler's drinking problems caused the Robins to lose patience with him. When club president Charles Ebbets asked for waivers on Phil because of repeated violations of the club's training rules, both the Chicago Cubs and the Boston Braves claimed him. By lot, National League president John Tener awarded the spitballer to the Cubs on September 8. For the three clubs combined Shufflin' Phil won only seven games during the 1915 season. The Cubs shipped him to St. Paul but brought him back in 1917. He won 14 games for Chicago in that season. He appeared in 51 games (the most of any National League pitcher), ranked third in strikeouts, and tied for fourth in fewest bases on balls allowed per nine innings.

In the war-shortened 1918 season, Douglas won 10 games as the Cubs took the National League pennant. In the fourth game of the fall classic, with the Red Sox leading two games to one, the Bruin's Lefty Tyler faced Babe Ruth. The Red Sox pitcher, whom his teammates called Tarzan, put his team ahead in the fourth inning with a two-run triple. The Cubs came back in the eighth inning to tie the game 2–2, ending Ruth's record streak of 29⅔ consecutive scoreless innings of World's Series pitching. In the bottom of the inning, Phil Douglas shuffled in to relieve Tyler.

What happened to Douglas was reported by the *New York Times* in vivid prose:

> The dogged, uphill fight of the Chicago Cubs today to wrest victory from the Boston Red Sox at Fenway Park in the fourth game of the world's series was depressingly thwarted this afternoon by one of their own players. Shuffling Phil Douglas, the big, awkward pitcher, sent the Boston men riding to victory on the wings of an impetuous, violent throw past first base which allowed Wally Schang to race home from second base with the run that lacerated the 2 to 2 tie and brought the Athens of America home in front by a score of 3 to 2.
>
> It was the tricky, moist ball which brought disaster tumbling down on Douglas's head. He thoroughly moistened the ball in serving a deceptive jumping tangent to Harry Hooper in the eighth inning. Hooper laid down a bunt on the infield lawn and when Douglas picked the ball up the wet, slippery sphere skidded in his hand and went hopping to the right field stand.
>
> With the Boston crowd in a hysterical agitation of excitement, Schang, perched on second base cut loose and speeded over the plate. The trickery pitching of Douglas had turned on him like a boomerang and he succumbed to his own faulty artfulness.[7]

Douglas allowed no hits or bases on balls in his stint on the mound, but the unearned run scored off his error was enough as Carl Mays saved the game for Babe Ruth. The loss put the Cubs in the hole three games to one, a disadvantage from which they were unable to recover. For the Cubs, one of baseball's dominant teams of the Deadball Era, it meant they had now gone 10 years since winning their last World's Series. By 2004 that string had extended to 96 years. Equally surprising, the Red Sox, who won their fifth world championship that year, failed to capture another during the next 86 years before finally breaking the "Curse of the Bambino" in 2004.

In 1919 Douglas got off to a good start for the Cubs, winning 10 games before July 25, when he was traded to the New York Giants for Dave Robertson, an outfielder who had quit baseball rather than continue playing for manager John McGraw. The Little

Napoleon had blamed the loss of the 1917 World's Series on Robertson's error. Dave felt this was unfair, inasmuch as he had led his team with 11 hits, three runs scored, two stolen bases, and a .500 batting average. His error was only one of 11 miscues committed by the Giants in the series. Robertson quickly agreed to return to baseball in order to play for Chicago.

Billy Evans thought the spitball ban would cause Douglas to be much less effective, but the grandfather clause bailed the Shuffler out. During the next two seasons, Phil enjoyed a fair amount of success for the Giants, winning 14 in 1920 and 15 in 1921 against 10 losses each year. In the latter season, his pitching was instrumental in the McGrawmen winning the National League championship. He lost the first game of the 1921 World's Series to Carl Mays, now pitching for the Yankees in Gotham's first subway series. But Douglas atoned for this loss and the 1918 debacle by defeating Mays 4–2 in game four and outpitching him 2–1 in the seventh game as the Giants defeated their fellow Polo Grounds tenants to take the fall classic five games to three.

After his World's Series triumphs of 1921, Douglas got off to his best big league start ever in 1922. But his drinking problem became his undoing. Ever since he came up to the majors at the age of 21, he had been plagued by alcohol abuse. He sometimes went on what he called vacations—binges during which he would get drunk and disappear for a week or so. His unreliability was one reason why he had been dropped by or traded away from four teams between 1912 and 1919. John McGraw thought he could reform the big spitballer or at least prevent him from going on benders. Mac hired Jesse Burkett, a former big league star, to keep an eye on the pitcher.

Douglas pitched his last big league game on July 30, 1922. Although his season ended early, Phil had already pitched enough innings to qualify for listing among the league leaders. He led the National League in more categories than any other pitcher that year, ranking first in winning percentage, earned run average, lowest batting average by opponents, and opponents' on base percentage. He ranked second in fewest base runners allowed per nine innings. It was by far the best season he had experienced during his nine years in the major leagues. Things appeared to be looking up for the Shuffler. The hero of the 1921 World's Series was well on his way to leading his team to a second straight National League pennant when disaster struck.

His major league record:

Year	Club	W	L	Pct.	IP	H	BB	SO	ERA	WR	PTS
1912	Chi AL	0	1	.000	12	21	6	7	7.30	-510	-3
1914	Cin NL	11	18	.379	239	186	92	121	2.56	-348	28
1915	Cin NL	1	5	.167	47	53	23	29	5.40	-1836	*
	Brk NL	5	5	.500	117	104	17	63	2.62	-280	*
	Chi NL	1	1	.500	25	17	7	18	2.16	46	15
1917	Chi NL	14	20	.412	293	269	50	151	2.55	-2288	24
1918	Chi NL	10	9	.526	157	145	31	51	2.12	-2793	21
1919	Chi NL	10	6	.625	162	152	34	63	2.00	1616	*
	NY NL	2	4	.333	51	53	6	21	2.10	-1818	38
1920	NY NL	14	10	.583	226	225	55	71	2.71	696	46

Year	Club	W	L	Pct.	IP	H	BB	SO	ERA	WR	PTS
1921	NY NL	15	10	.600	222	266	55	119	4.22	-400	43
1922	NY NL	11	4	**.733**	158	154	35	33	**2.63**	2145	59
Total — 9 years		94	93	.503	1708	1626	411	683	2.80	-6264	271

*Faber System points are computed on total record for all clubs in 1915 and 1919.
Bold italics indicates he led the league in these categories.

His World Series record:

		W	L	Pct.	IP	H	BB	SO	ERA
1918	Chicago NL	0	1	.000	1	1	0	0	0.00
1921	New York NL	2	1	.667	26	24	5	17	2.08
Total		2	2	.500	27	25	5	17	2.00

After the loss to Pittsburgh on July 30, 1922, Phil's world came crashing down. Accounts differ as to how Douglas eluded his bodyguard. John Lardner wrote an unlikely tale about Phil walking in the front door of a Prohibition era speakeasy with Burkett tailing him. Jesse thought the Shuffler went to the men's room and was guarding the door to that room when Phil slipped out a back exit and disappeared.[8] Probably more accurate is the version provided by Tom Clark: "Phil walked out of the Polo Grounds an unhappy man that midsummer evening, with Jesse Burkett at his side. Phil told Burkett he wanted to go downtown for a meal because he felt too bad to go home. They dined together at a chop house on Broadway.... When they had finished dining Phil told Burkett he wanted to walk over to Times Square to buy some cigars and a newspaper, before going home. Burkett, of course, accompanied him. But the streets were crowded, and somewhere along the way Phil slipped the clutches of The Crab and lost himself in the passing stream of humanity that filled Broadway."[9]

A few nights later, some of New York's finest, responding to a call from neighbors, found Douglas passed out at a party in an apartment near his home in Manhattan. The police dragged him out of bed and took him to the 135th Street police station, where they telephoned a Giants official for advice on what to do with the star pitcher. At the behest of the Giants, Shufflin' Phil was taken to the West End Sanitarium, a hospital on Central Park West. His clothes were taken away, he was given sedatives, and was not allowed to call his wife.[10] Such hospitals were sometimes called snake pits because of the conditions residents had to endure. According to Stant and Johnson: "In those days treatment for alcoholism could be as debilitating as the disease itself, often consisting of forcible stomach-pumping, hot baths, massive sedation by narcotics, and injection of substances such as double chloride of gold. Such cures often lasted weeks and left patients weakened and dazed."[11]

Douglas did not wait to be cured. He escaped or was released from the sanitarium, got drunk again, and went to the Polo Grounds, but the day's game had been rained out. Going through his mail, he found a bill from the Giants for $224.30 to cover the sanitarium charges. Adding insult to injury, McGraw called Phil into his office, bawled him out, fined him $100, and docked him five days' pay. Suffering from a hangover and speaking with difficulty he mumbled a few words of protest and walked out of the manager's office. The Little Napoleon followed him out and in front of other players gave him a vicious tongue-lashing. This was too much for the Shuffler to take.

He sat down and wrote a letter on New York Giants stationery to his friend Les Mann, an outfielder on the St. Louis Cardinals.

Dear Leslie:
  I want to leave here but I want some inducement. I don't want this guy to win the pennant and I feel if I stay here I will win it for him. You know I can pitch and win. So you see the fellows, and if you want to send a man over here with the goods, and I will leave for home on the next train, send him to my house so nobody will know, and send him at night. I am living at 145 Wadsworth Ave., Apartment 1R. Nobody will ever know. I will go down to fishing camp and stay there. I am asking you this way so there can't be any trouble to any one. Call me up if you all are sending a man. Wadsworth 3210. Do this right away. Let me know. Regards to all.
  Phil Douglas

When he sobered up, Phil realized writing the letter was a mistake. He later claimed he called Mann and told him to tear up the letter when it arrived. Mann said he never received the call.

Meanwhile newspapers such as the *New York Times* and the *Chicago Tribune* covered up the story about Phil's disappearance. On August 5 the *Washington Post* ran a short piece: "The atmosphere of mystery in which Shufflin' Phil Douglas moved last year surrounded the Giant dugout at the Polo Grounds today. Douglas, it was rumored, had disappeared and no one could account for his absence. Last year he was constantly chaperoned by Coach Jesse Burkett, but it was not believed a chaperon would be

Shufflin' Phil Douglas was an extraordinarily gifted spitball pitcher whose problems with alcoholism and bad judgment brought a premature end to his major league career. In the midst of one of his best seasons he was banned from organized baseball for life. (PHOTOGRAPH COURTESY OF NATIONAL BASEBALL HALL OF FAME LIBRARY, COOPERSTOWN.)

needed this season. Douglas had promised to stay close to the straight and narrow path, and has done so."[12]

Four days later the *Post* reported: "Shufflin' Phil Douglas, of the Giants, reported to have disappeared last week, shuffled into the press box here after the game, and threatened a writer, telling him never to print anything more about him, good or bad. The press representatives, the writer in question [later identified as Fred Lieb] included, made a few remarks to Douglas on their own account. Incidentally, Douglas admitted that he had been fined for breaking training rules, and is now in the custody of Jess Burkett, scout for the club, to see he doesn't get into any mischief or break the last amendment to the Constitution."[13]

When Mann received Phil's letter, he was in a quandary. Should he ignore the letter or report it to authorities? After thinking about it for 24 hours he took the letter to Branch Rickey, manager of the Cardinals. What happened next is a matter of dispute. Most of the recent articles on the subject indicate that Rickey or Mann took the letter to Baseball Commissioner Kenesaw Mountain Landis, and the commissioner banished Douglas from baseball for life.[14]

However, contemporary newspaper accounts gave a slightly different version of the events. According to the *New York Times,* the *Chicago Tribune,* and the *Los Angeles Times,* among others, Rickey took the letter to John McGraw and it was the Giants manager, not Commissioner Landis, who placed Douglas on the permanent ineligibility list, and notified other clubs. This action occurred after Douglas confessed to McGraw in Pittsburgh on August 16. Douglas was barred not only from playing with any other club in organized baseball, but also barred from all parks. Some accounts said that Landis came to Pittsburgh at McGraw's request and endorsed the manager's action after the fact.[15] Other accounts said that Landis and National League president John K. Heydler were present when McGraw banned Douglas and concurred in the action but took no part in it.[16] The *Trib* reported Landis as saying, "In cases where a player is placed on the ineligibility list by a club the player has a right to appeal to me, if he feels he has a just grievance, but in this case I do not expect an appeal, for Douglas has admitted the truth of the charges made by Mr. McGraw."[17]

On August 21, Landis announced that he would not consider a hearing asked by lawyers representing Douglas: "The guilty party has been found and punished, and so far as our office is concerned the matter is a closed incident."[18] So it did not really matter whether the ban had been issued by the Giants or the commissioner. Douglas was out of organized baseball. Ironically, the Giants won the 1922 pennant without the benefit of the Shuffler's help during the last two months of the season.

Broken in spirit and abed, the victim of a nervous breakdown, a sobbing Phil Douglas told his side of the story in an effort to clear his name and win reinstatement. According to his version, he pitched his last game for the Giants on July 30, losing to the Pittsburgh Pirates 7–0. It was his fourth defeat of the year against 11 wins. That night he drowned his troubles in drink. While he was sleeping off the effects in the apartment of a friend, he alleged, two detectives broke into the place and attempted to drag him out. When he resisted they threatened to blackjack him and dragged him, half-dressed, into a waiting taxicab in which were three other strong-arm men. He was taken to a police station and then to a sanitarium, where his clothes were taken from him and he was kept prisoner for five days. When he returned to the Polo Grounds he was fined $100, docked five days' pay, and presented with a bill for his sanatorium treatment and taxicab fare.[19]

The Shuffler asserted that he was not in possession of his senses when he wrote the letter to Mann, that he had tried to retrieve it, and that he had no intention of harming the Giants. He hired a lawyer and, alleging kidnapping and unlawful imprisonment, threatened a $300,000 lawsuit if he were not reinstated.[20]

About this time Douglas suffered a severe nervous attack. He was advised by his physician to take a complete rest and not to assume any active part for the present in an attempt to have his case brought before Landis.[21] Apparently that ended any further effort to bring legal action to clear his name.

The baseball establishment was almost unanimously against Douglas. The *Sporting News*, with its promanagement bias, was particularly hard on the Shuffler. One columnist wrote: "Douglas always had been regarded as a good-natured, simple-minded, over-grown boy, not a vindictive, deep-dyed villain ready to throw down the men who had befriended and protected him. Probably no one was more bitterly disappointed in the well-known Shuffler than McGraw, who had forgiven his frequent outbursts and tried so hard to make a man of him."[22]

Another columnist in the same paper tried to show some sympathy for Shufflin' Phil: "Some degree of pity must be felt for this physical giant with the undeveloped mind of a young boy, with his lack of education and training, with his apparently incurable weakness for drink, and with his lack of self-control and general irresponsibility; and a greater degree for his unfortunate wife and children."[23]

When he recovered sufficiently to pitch again, the spitballer latched onto a semipro team in Lakeland, Florida. At the end of the season, Phil and his family returned to Birmingham, Alabama, his former home. On October 11 police officers were called to the Douglas home by Louise Douglas, who said the pitcher had beaten her. Arresting officers found Louise with both eyes blackened. She claimed that her husband had abused her in front of her two children. Phil was taken to the city jail.[24] He was released the next day when his wife refused to press charges, but was fined $10 for drunkenness and disorderly conduct.[25]

During the next season, Douglas pitched briefly for a number of semipro teams in the southeast. In August he signed with the Forest City, North Carolina, team in the semipro Blue Ridge League to a great deal of fanfare. The locals thought that a former big league star would draw a lot of fans to their small town, and they were right—at first. Then Commissioner Landis issued an edict that any player under contract to clubs in organized baseball would be declared ineligible if he played with or against Douglas.[26] That pronouncement plus some ineffective pitching by Douglas convinced the Forest City management that Douglas was not worth the $75 a week they were paying him. In 1936 Douglas again applied for reinstatement in baseball, but was turned down.

For the next several years, Douglas pitched for various semipro clubs in the South, many of them sponsored by cotton mills and providing a high level of competition. In 1926 Phil was in Bluefield, West Virginia, earning $275 a month as a coal miner and manager of the company baseball team. The next year he was back in Tennessee, but out of a job. On November 28, 1927, Louise Douglas died of cancer. In late August 1928, Phil married a widow from Cowan, Tennessee, Jacqueline Hodges. He rented a farm in the Sequatchie Valley and continued playing semipro baseball. During the Depression he was unable to secure employment and fell upon hard times. The farm was sold out from under him. He worked at whatever odd jobs as a laborer he could get. The New Deal eased the situation somewhat, and Phil worked for a time on the WPA. Then a childhood friend got him a job with the Tennessee State Highway Department as a road maintenance man. He held the job for eight years, keeping sober, and getting back on his feet.

In 1949 Phil was mowing grass along the side of state highway when he got his foot caught in the blade of a power lawnmower. The injury led to a blood clot, which in turn caused a stroke, costing him his job. In 1951 he suffered a second stroke, which left him barely able to speak or move. A third stroke late in July 1952 nearly deprived him of his power of speech.[27]

In 1990 some supporters petitioned Commissioner Fay Vincent to reinstate Douglas posthumously, asserting that the cause of his letter to Mann was the brutal rehabilitation program forced upon him, not any intention to hurt the team. The commissioner's office replied: "It is our opinion that a resurrection of the Phil Douglas case today would not be appropriate. The events surrounding the matter cannot be recreated in sufficient detail to provide an adequate basis to reverse Commissioner Landis's decision. Commissioner Vincent cannot substitute his judgment nearly 70 years after the fact for the judgment of a commissioner with a reputation for the highest degree of integrity."[28]

Douglas never recovered from his strokes and died in his sleep in the night of July 31–August 1, 1952, at the age of 62. He was buried in the city cemetery in Tracy City, Tennessee, not far from his home. In 1971 the mayor of Tracy City organized an Old Timers Benefit game for Phil Douglas. The proceeds, along with a contribution from the city council, were used to buy a headstone for the old spitballer's grave. The marker is a large rounded white stone with the seams of a baseball carved into its face. The inscription reads Phil Douglas, 1890–1952. Across the base are the words Outstanding Baseball Figure. At the top is a star.[29]

14

Allan Russell

One of the tenets of the Puritan work ethic was that a man finished what he started; a man did not quit when the going got tough. Not all baseball people at the turn of the century were Puritans, by any means, but most of them held the conviction that a pitcher who started a game should finish it. Words such as long relief, middle relief, short relief, set-up man, and closer were not in their vocabularies. The idea that there would be a specialist whose job was to pitch only to left-handed batters in the eighth inning would have been incomprehensible to them. During the first two decades of the twentieth century the number of complete games declined drastically—from nearly 90 percent to less than 60 percent, but the era of the relief specialist was not yet here. When the starting pitcher ran into trouble and had to be removed, the usual response was to send in another starter to put out the fire.

Clark Griffith, manager of the Washington Nationals, was one of the first to try a new strategy—developing a full-time fireman. The Old Fox had been a pitcher in his playing days and a good one. He had pitched 337 complete games during his career—finishing what he started more than 90 percent of the time. But he recognized that the times called for a new approach. He converted his spitballer, Allan Russell, into a relief specialist. The experiment that started with Russell came to fruition with Fred Marberry. Baseball was changed forever.

It was always Griffith's idea to have men in the bullpen who did not start regularly. When other clubs took up the practice of having a reliever who was not also a starter, they usually picked a hurler who had been around for years and could no longer go the distance. When he was unable to last nine innings anymore, he was sent to the bull pen. For a pitcher to be assigned to the bull pen was rather like a position player being relegated to the bench, a demotion. This was the practice that Griffith changed with Russell and Marberry.

Allan E. Russell was born in Baltimore, Maryland, on July 31, 1893, of Scottish and English ancestry. In contemporary news accounts his first name was spelled indiscriminately as Allan or Allen. His signature on a questionnaire in the National Baseball Hall of Fame in Cooperstown is spelled Allen. His Social Security death record gives his name as Allan. Most present-day references use the Allan spelling, so we shall go along with that option. He was a younger brother of Clarence "Lefty" Russell, who had a brief major league career with the Philadelphia Athletics. Allan attended Waverly

Elementary School #51 in Baltimore and completed one year at Baltimore Polytechnic High School.

At the age of 18, Allan got his start in professional baseball. He was given a trial with Baltimore and then sent down to Reading of the Class B Tri-State League for experience. Baltimore took him back in 1913, and sent him down to the Tri-State League again, where he won 22 games for Wilmington. In the fall Baltimore recalled him to their club in the Double A International League. In 1915 he won 21 games for Richmond and led the International League in strikeouts, earning a late-season promotion to the New York Yankees. After an 11-year career in the show, he returned to the International League to pitch for Reading, Buffalo, and Newark in 1927–1928. On his second stint in this league he had difficulty winning because he was not allowed to use the spitball, previously his most effective pitch.

His minor league record:

Year	Club	W	L	Pct.	IP	H	BB	SO	ERA
1912	Reading	10	16	.385	not available				
1913	Wilmington	22	8	.733	not available				
	Baltimore	4	3	.571	60	53	32	35	
1914	Baltimore	11	16	.407	286	248	143	164	
1915	Richmond	21	15	.583	317	276	164	***239***	
1927	Reading/Buffalo	3	12	.200	123	155	42	27	4.24
1928	Newark	0	2	.000	not available				
Total—6 years		71	72	.497	not available				

Bold italics indicates he led the league in this category.

League affiliations: Reading and Wilmington, Tri-State; Baltimore, Richmond, Reading, Buffalo, and Newark, International League.

Babe Ruth, Allan's one-time Yankee teammate, was an admirer of Russell's moist delivery. In discussing various types of pitches, the Bambino wrote:

> The chief difference between the so-called screwball and the spitter, as I see it is that the screw ball can be thrown only overhand, while the spitter can be thrown overhand or sidearm. Neither pitch can be used by an underhand pitcher. The side-arm spitter is by far the more difficult to handle. Allan Russell, the old time Yankee pitcher who was later with the Washington Senators, was the most successful side-arm spitball pitcher I ever knew. Allan could break the spitter where he wanted it and since he threw it with the same sweeping side-arm motion with which he delivered his fast ball, it was doubly hard to gauge.[1]

In September 1915 the New York Yankees acquired several young players from the minor leagues. The highest priced and most touted among them was Big Dan Tipple from Indianapolis, who started three games for the Highlanders that fall, won one, lost one, and was never heard of again. More lasting was the 22-year old lad from Richmond, Allan Russell.

Russell made his first major league start for the Yankees on September 17, 1915. He earned his only big league victory that fall by defeating the Chicago White Sox 3–2. The *New York Times* scribe was impressed:

A likely young busher named Allan Russell, from Richmond, snuffed all the brilliancy out of the Chicago stars. He held the Sox to six hits and struck out eight. In the ninth inning when the Sox had two on, nobody out, and visions of launching a rally, he struck out Happy Felsch, Shano Collins, and Eddie Collins in succession. Young Russell isn't very big, but he was cool as a fresh gallon of ice cream. Manager Clarence Rowland tried several times to encourage Russell to uncork some wild pitches, but the busher turned down the invitation, with a smile. Rowland couldn't get the youngster's goat, because he doesn't have any goat to get. Jack Dunn, who has been Russell's supervisor at Richmond all season, was on hand to give his pupil encouragement. Take it from Jack, the lad is going to make a big rep for himself next season.[2]

Fred Lieb of the *New York Press* wrote: "The blanket was taken from another of Donovan's cold pitchers yesterday, a youth named Allan Russell.... He pitched a smart game for a kid. He held the Rowland maulers to six hits. His control was a little shaky, as he walked eight, but he breezed as many. Twice he struck out Eddie Collins who is one of the hardest men to fan in baseball. In the ninth Allan struck out the side. With men on second and third he fanned the two Collinses. Eddie did a wooden Injun and stood stock still as Russ curved over three."[3]

Despite the promising start, the story of Allan's stay with the New York team is a tale of misfortune after misfortune. We are unable to document a story that he collapsed on the mound with a cerebral hemorrhage in July 1916, but recovered to continue his major league career. In 1917 he had a sore arm and missed the second half of the season. On July 16, 1918, to the annoyance of Miller Huggins and Jake Ruppert he left the team without informing the manager or the owner in order to join the Sparrows Point shipyard team in Baltimore.[4]

During World War I, many players joined steel mill or shipyard teams to work in the defense industry, play ball, and avoid the draft. In Russell's case, however, the motive may have been different. As a married man, he was not likely to be drafted, although some benedicts were called up. At any rate, he never served in the armed forces.

In parts of five seasons in the Polo Grounds, the sidearming spitballer failed to post a winning record. On July 29, 1919, Yankees sent Russell, pitcher Bob McGraw and $40,000 in cash to the Boston Red Sox for pitcher Carl Mays. The change of scenery was good for Russell. During the last half of the season he won 10 games while losing only four for the Sox. For the year he won 15 games, the most victories he ever posted in a major league season. As a relief pitcher, Al saved four games for the Crimson Hose that season, which added to the one he had saved for the Yankees before the trade gave him a league-leading total of five saves for the year.

In 1920 Russell suffered a blood clot in the brain, the result of an earlier beaning, which left his right side paralyzed for five weeks.[5] His health problems were responsible for holding him to only five wins that year. Furthermore, the spitball ban threatened his career. Billy Evans wrote that the case of Allan Russell was similar to that of Stanley Coveleskie. "To use the words of many American League players," the umpire wrote, "those two start with a spitball and finish with one. There is little or no hope of getting a cripple to pick on."[6]

However, Russell was granted a lifetime exemption from the spitball ban, and he recovered his health. He resumed pitching for the Red Sox, but not primarily as a starter. In both 1921 and 1922 he appeared in more games as a reliever than as a starter.

On February 10, 1923, the Sox traded Russell and catcher Muddy Ruel to the Washington Nationals for catcher Val Picinich, outfielder-third baseman Howard Shanks, and outfield prospect Ed Goebel. Opinions among baseball men were that the Red Sox got the better of the deal because of Goebel's potential. As it turned out, the phenom never played a game for Boston, while Ruel and Russell were to help the Nats win two pennants. Although Russell had been used in relief throughout his career, the Nats made him an almost full-time relief specialist. Al became one of the earliest pitchers in major league history to hold that distinction. His ability to go to the mound day after day earned him the nickname "Rubberarm." During the 1923 season, Russell appeared in 52 games, all but five of them in relief. He led the league in saves with nine and had the circuit's third best earned run average. Furthermore, he won nine games and lost seven in relief, both marks being tops in the American League.

While with the Washington Nationals, Allan Russell became one of baseball's earliest relief specialists. (PHOTOGRAPH COURTESY OF NATIONAL BASEBALL HALL OF FAME LIBRARY, COOPERSTOWN.)

Although some feel that Russell represented a landmark in the development of relief pitching, Bill James was more inclined to dismiss him as a footnote.[7] If Russell was a footnote, we hold that he was a very important footnote. He paved the way for Fred "Firpo" Marberry, who everybody agrees was definitely a landmark.

In 1924 Russell ranked second in the American League in saves with eight. In addition he won five games and lost one, all in relief. He became the first pitcher in major league history to relieve in 200 games. However, by now his teammate Marberry had emerged as the leading relief pitcher of the decade and Russell's appearances declined in frequency. The two relievers won or saved 39 of the Nats' 92 wins that season as Washington won its first American League pennant.

In the 1924 World's Series youthful playing-manager Bucky Harris pulled a surprise by starting Marberry, his ace reliever, in the third game. At this point the series was tied at one game apiece. The New York Giants had won the first game 4–3, defeating Walter Johnson in his first World's Series start after 18 years in the majors. The Nationals evened the series, taking the second game by an identical 4–3 score, with Marberry picking up the save by getting the final out of the game.

The very next day Marberry came back to make the start, but he was victimized by the Boy Manager. Playing second base, Harris made an error in the second inning on an attempted double play, setting up two runs for the Giants. With one out and Bill Terry on first base, Travis Jackson hit a grounder to third base. Ossie Bluege flipped the ball to Harris, but Bucky missed the low throw and both men were safe. Hank Gowdy knocked in Terry with a single, and Jackson scored on Marberry's wild pitch, giving the Giants a 2–0 lead. The Giants got another run in the third.

In the top of the fourth the Senators scored two runs, knocking out starter Hughie McQuillen, who was replaced by Rosy Ryan. In the home half of the fourth inning, Allan Russell entered the game in relief of Marberry, with the Senators trailing 3–2. The spitballer got Hank Gowdy to fly out. Up to the plate stepped Rosy Ryan. With the count two balls and one strike, Ryan hit a home run into the upper tier of the rightfield stands, the first homer hit in a World's Series game by a National League hurler. Russell pitched three innings, giving up four hits and two runs, one of which was unearned. The Giants won the game 6–4, but the Senators came back to take the series 4 games to 3, with Walter Johnson finally getting his first World's Series win — in relief, in the seventh game.

In 1925 the Nats again won the American League pennant, but Russell did not pitch in the World's Series that year. His final major league game occurred on September 19 of that year. He did not go out in a blaze of glory. Relieving Tom Zachary in the fourth inning and trailing the White Sox 7–0, Allan pitched one scoreless inning and then got blasted in the next, giving up a total of eight hits in one and two-thirds innings. Win Ballou, who relieved Russell, fared little better, being roughed up for nine hits in the remainder of the game. All told the three Washington pitchers gave up 26 hits and 17 runs, while their mates collected only one hit off Ted Lyons in a 17–0 loss. The hit, a solid single by Bobby Veach, came with two out in the last of the ninth inning. After the game, Veach went to the visitor's clubhouse and apologized to Lyons for depriving him of what would have been the American League's first no-hitter in more than two years.

Russell's major league record:

Year	Club	W	L	Pct.	IP	H	BB	SO	ERA	WR	PTS
1915	NY AL	1	2	.333	27	21	21	21	2.67	-369	2
1916	NY AL	6	10	.375	171	138	75	104	3.20	-2576	11
1917	NY AL	7	8	.467	104	89	39	55	2.24	45	30
1918	NY AL	7	11	.389	141	139	73	54	3.26	-2088	16
1919	NY AL	5	5	.500	91	89	32	50	3.47	-810	*
	Bos AL	10	4	.714	121	105	39	63	2.52	3626	60

Year	Club	W	L	Pct.	IP	H	BB	SO	ERA	WR	PTS
1920	Bos AL	5	6	.455	108	100	38	53	3.01	-187	21
1921	Bos AL	6	11	.389	173	204	77	60	4.11	-1998	16
1922	Bos AL	6	7	.462	126	152	57	34	5.01	884	30
1923	Was AL	10	7	.588	181	177	77	67	3.03	1870	48
1924	Was AL	5	1	.833	82	83	45	17	4.37	1470	29
1925	Was AL	2	4	.333	69	85	37	25	5.77	-1890	0
Total — 11 years		70	76	.479	1394	1382	610	603	3.52	-940	263

*Records with two clubs are combined for Faber System points in 1919.

World's Series record:

		W	L	Pct.	IP	H	BB	SO	ERA
1924	Washington AL	0	0	—	3	4	0	0	3.00

On July 8, 1915, Russell married Myrtle Rebecca Covington. Their daughter, also named Myrtle, was born in 1925. After he retired from baseball, Russell returned to his hometown, Baltimore. The 1930 census showed the Russell household as consisting of Allan, the two Myrtles, and his mother-in-law, Ella Covington. Allan's occupation was listed as professional ballplayer, although there is no record of him having played in organized baseball after 1928. In a questionnaire in the National Baseball Hall of Fame, Russell stated that his last year of professional baseball was 1930. We surmise that he must have played a couple of years in an independent league after leaving organized baseball. Later he worked for the States Marin-Isthmian Lines, Inc., as a clerk in charge of deliveries.

Allan Russell died suddenly in Baltimore on October 20, 1972, at the age of 79. He was buried in Loudon Park Memorial Cemetery in the Maryland metropolis.

15

Doc Ayers

If the young man who took the mound that September afternoon in 1913 at the American League Park in the nation's capital was nervous, he had a right to be. Called up after a sensational season with the Richmond Colts in the Virginia League, he was making his first major league appearance at the age of 23 with only two years of experience in the lower minors. Although he had mowed down the opposition with ease for the Colts, he knew there was a great difference in the caliber of hitters he had faced in the lowly Class C circuit and those who toiled in the major leagues. However, any nervousness manifested in the game was exhibited by his supporting cast, not by the young spitballer.

Doc, as he was called, pitched well, allowing only five hits in seven innings, three of which were flukes. Not a run should have been scored off him. In the seventh inning the home team's defense fell apart. Misplays came thick and fast. The opposing St. Louis Browns scored five unearned runs in that inning alone, seven in the game as the Washington fielders committed a total of seven errors. The *Washington Post* reported: "The Nationals staged their worst exhibition of the season at the Georgia avenue grounds yesterday afternoon." The young pitcher was tagged with an undeserved defeat. Undaunted, he came back a few days later to shut out the Philadelphia Athletics on four hits to gain his first major league victory. Admittedly, the Mackmen had already clinched the American League pennant and were resting some of their regulars, but the win served notice that Doc Ayers was on his way.

Yancey Wyatt Ayers was born in southwestern Virginia, near Fancy Gap in Carroll County on May 20, 1890, the son of Jefferson Davis Ayers. When he was a high school student at nearby Woodlawn, he tried out for the baseball team. As he was big for his age, with powerful shoulders and arms, he was sent behind the plate for a trial as a catcher. He did not make the grade as a backstop, but developed a love for the game and determined to find a spot where he could play. In 1911 he enrolled in the Medical College of Virginia in Richmond. While there he bought a book on how to become a pitcher, and when the call came for baseball tryouts he reported as a pitcher. He immediately made the team and pitched for the college during the spring of 1912. At the end of the spring term, a scout for the Richmond club of the Virginia League signed him. He left college to become a professional baseball player. However, because of his one year in medical school the nickname "Doc" stuck with him.[1]

We have been unable to find out when Doc first started throwing the spitball, but he was on the list of hurlers exempted when the pitch was banned. Several newspaper accounts from his playing days refer to him as pitching underhand, which was almost unheard of among spitball pitchers. One article in the *Washington Post* stated that "Ayers is one of the most peculiar pitchers in the business. His greatest asset is an underhand ball which he shoves up from his shoe tops, about the same style as Carl Mays of the Boston Red Sox. He hasn't a great curve ball, but has a fast one that is mighty hard to get hold of."[2]

The strong young man started off with a bang, winning 25 games for the Richmond Colts in the Class C Virginia League in his very first year in organized baseball. The next spring, Washington manager Clark Griffith ordered Ayers to report to the Nationals' training camp in Charlottesville. Doc refused to report on the designated date, apparently wanting to complete the school year first. Did Griffith show the young man any compassion? No. That was not the custom of baseball officials in those days, and sportswriters backed up the powers-that-be. The *Washington Post* reported:

> Manager Griffith announced tonight that he had recommended to President Ban Johnson of the American League that Doc Ayers, the Richmond hurler, who has refused to report here despite orders, be placed on the ineligible list. There is no question but that the American League president has already complied with the request. This means that Ayers will be forced to pay a $100 fine before he is allowed to join the Nationals or any other professional team. The Old Dominion city boy is touted as one of the likeliest looking pitchers that has ever worked in the Virginia State League, and there is no question that he made a serious mistake in not agreeing to forsake his studies in order to take a chance in the big league, where he might have made his fortune.[3]

How much of a fortune did the *Post* think Ayers would have foregone had he stayed in medical school rather than becoming a baseball professional? Ban Johnson, president of the American League, wrote that salaries to major league players came to approximately $800,000 per year.[4] With 16 teams of 25 players each there would be 400 players to divide the money among. That comes to an average of $2,000 per player. Of course, a few stars made considerably more than the average. Perhaps half a dozen were getting in excess of $10,000 with Tris Speaker probably topping the list. The Grand Old Man of Baseball, Nicholas E. "Uncle Nick" Young, former president of the National League, said baseball had about reached its limit in regard to salaries. "Take, for instance, the sum of $16,000 the Boston Red Sox are said to be paying Tris Speaker. He may be worth this much money if his ability is strictly compared to some of the other players who are wearing big league regalia, but it certainly is pushing the stipend to mighty near the topmost rung.... The time is drawing near when a maximum salary will be agreed on, and it would not at all surprise me if the players themselves would be the first to ask for such a ruling."[5]

On May 1, 1913, Ayers was optioned back to Richmond after agreeing to pay his fine for failing to report on time. On May 3 he made his first appearance of the season, winning a two-hit shutout over Norfolk 2–0. Evidently, missing spring training did not diminish his effectiveness. Doc was the best pitcher in the league that year, with a league-leading 29 wins, and he also led the circuit in winning percentage at .784 and in strikeouts with 390, averaging well over a strikeout per inning pitched. His strikeouts to walks ratio was better than 13 to one. On July 27 and 28, 1913, he won three games in two playing days. In a Saturday doubleheader he pitched five scoreless innings in the first game and nine in the second game, winning both, putting Portsmouth down without a run in 14 innings. As no games were played on Sunday, the next playing day was Monday. Ayers came into a game against Norfolk in the ninth inning with the score tied 2–2. He held the opposition scoreless for three innings until Richmond won the game in the 11th. That extended his total to 17 shutout innings in two days.

Years later Shirley Povich wrote a column in the *Washington Post* in which he asserted that in 1913 Clark Griffith advertised in newspapers for pitchers, inviting any lads who could throw hard enough to try out with the team. Povich wrote that in those days the country was not blanketed with big league farm teams, and unattached talent abounded. He stated that Griffith got a veritable windfall. Among those who reported was Doc Ayers.[6] The main problem with this story is that Ayers was already the property of the Nationals and had been sent to Richmond under an option agreement.

Ayers spent parts of nine years in the majors before returning to the minors in 1921. Doc pitched with moderate success in the Double A American Association for nearly three seasons before retiring in 1923, winning 10 or more games each year.

His minor league record:

Year	Club	W	L	Pct.	IP	H	BB	SO	ERA
1912	Richmond	25	12	.676	346	271	35	197	
1913	Richmond	**29**	8	**.784**	342	233	29	**390**	
1921	Toledo	15	11	.577	219	235	63	82	4.40
1922	Toledo	12	13	.480	229	229	51	92	3.38
1923	Minneapolis	10	12	.455	199	247	98	94	5.20
Total — 5 years		91	56	.619	1335	1215	276	855	

Bold italics indicates he led the league in that category.

League affiliations: Richmond, Virginia League; Toledo and Minneapolis, American Association.

Ayers made his major league debut with the Washington Nationals on September 9, 1913. He appeared in four games that fall, winning one and losing one. Washington finished second that season to the Philadelphia Athletics, the eventual World's Series winners.

In 1914 one of the bitterest rivalries in baseball was between Washington and the world champion Athletics. In a game in the Quaker City on April 29, Doc Ayers entered the contest at a critical time. Nats pitcher Joe Engel had been pitching well up until the sixth inning, breezing along with a 3–1 lead. In the bottom of that frame, Eddie Collins led off by working Engel for a base on balls, then came three successive hits by Frank "Home Run" Baker, Stuffy McInnis, and Amos Strunk. Collins and Baker both scored to tie the game at 3–3 and knock Engel out of the game. In came the rookie, Doc Ayers, with runners on second and third, nobody out, and the dangerous Jack Barry at the plate. The A's were famous for executing the double squeeze and Barry was one of the best bunters in the game. Few teams attempt the double squeeze, but the A's were experts at it. As the pitcher winds up, both runners take a flying start, so when the ball leaves the pitcher's hand the runner on third is almost home and the runner who was originally on second has already passed third base. If the batter puts down a perfect bunt, both runners will score. On the first pitch by Ayers, the Mackmen attempted the double squeeze, but Barry fouled off the pitch. Washington's catcher John Henry did not expect the A's to try the double squeeze again, but just to be safe he called for a waste pitch, one so far outside it would be impossible to hit. Again the A's were off and running. The pitch came in high and outside, but not quite far enough outside. Barry reached out and hit a low liner toward first base. Chick Gandil raced in, caught the ball in the air, and threw it to third baseman Eddie Foster, who relayed the ball to George McBride at second base. Both base runners were caught off base for a triple play. Young Doc Ayers had thrown two pitches and had gotten three outs. According to *Harper's Weekly,* this was "An Unusual Peformance."[7] What an understatement!

Doc won the game 6–4, but the rest of the season was a bit of a disappointment as he finished the season by winning only 11 games while losing 15. According to J.C. Kofoed, Ayers set down the Tigers with only four hits in one 1914 game, but two of the hits were doubles, and two were triples. The writer used that as an example of bad luck. We think doubles and triples may represent something other than luck. Kofoed did not say who won the game.[8]

In 1915 Ayers came into his own, living up to the promise that had been seen in him. During a spring exhibition game against the Brooklyn Robins, he created a sensation by striking out eight consecutive batters. 1915 was to be his best year in the majors. He won 14 games against nine losses, had a fine earned run average of 2.21, and ranked fourth in the American League in fewest base runners allowed per nine innings and compiled the fifth lowest batting average by opponents.

Late in the spring of 1916, Ayers suffered a badly sprained thumb, which kept him out of action for much of the season. During the layoff he allowed himself to get out of shape, bulking up to 200 pounds, 15 pounds above his normal playing weight. When he did return to the mound, he did not pitch with his usual effectiveness. At this time Doc was living on a farm near Hillsville, Virginia. During the off-season he worked on the farm, got himself back into shape, and lost the excess baggage. The contract offered to him for 1917 called for a decrease in salary, based on his poor 1916 performance. Doc held out briefly but in late February he and manager Clark Griffith reached a compromise. A bonus clause was inserted in Doc's contract, providing that if the pitcher won a certain number of games in 1917 he would receive additional money. No figures were released.

Ayers won 11 games in 1917 and 10 games in the war-shortened 1918 season. As Doc had a wife and a child he was in a deferred draft classification. It was expected that

Opposite: Doc Ayers received his nickname because he had attended medical school. Sportswriters of the day delighted in working references to the practice of medicine into their accounts of his pitching. (PHOTOGRAPH COURTESY OF NATIONAL BASEBALL HALL OF FAME LIBRARY, COOPERSTOWN.)

he would join some of his teammates at the Alexandria Shipbuilding Company. Instead, he returned to Carroll County to work on his farm during the off-season.

In 1919 Doc got off to a terrible start with the Nationals, losing all six of his decisions. On June 25 the Washington club traded Ayers to the Detroit Tigers for Eric Erickson, a young Swedish-born pitcher who was believed to have lots of potential. Erickson did not quite deliver what was expected of him in the nation's capital, winning only 30 games in his four years in Washington. However, that was 18 victories more than Doc was able to garner for Detroit. His major league career ended in May 1921.

His major league record:

Year	Club	W	L	Pct.	IP	H	BB	SO	ERA	WR	PTS
1913	Was AL	1	1	.500	18	12	4	17	1.53	-172	3
1914	Was AL	11	15	.423	265	221	54	148	2.54	-3250	16
1915	Was AL	14	9	.609	211	178	38	96	2.21	1449	51
1916	Was AL	5	8	.385	157	173	52	69	3.78	-1573	14
1917	Was AL	11	10	.524	208	192	59	78	2.17	966	42
1918	Was AL	10	12	.455	220	215	63	67	2.83	-2860	19
1919	Was AL	0	6	.000	44	52	17	12	2.89	-2508	*
	Det AL	5	3	.625	94	88	31	32	2.69	456	12
1920	Det AL	7	14	.333	209	217	62	102	2.75	-1533	16
1921	Det AL	0	0	—	4	9	2	0	9.00	0	0
Total—9 years		64	78	.451	1429	1357	382	622	2.84		

The *Sporting News* printed a rather odd article about Doc's departure from the major leagues:

> The Detroit club last week asked waivers on Doc Ayres, and no one claimed him, the waiver price being $4000 these days and thereby more than one good man slipping by. Ayers in his sojourn with the Tigers more than earned his pay, but with a new pitching staff Cobb will not need him as a stop-gap. In Dr. Ayers' retirement from baseball ... the game loses one of its finest gentlemen, with manners and character that set him apart from the run of fellows. Having dentistry as a profession to fall back on the Doc, after 10 years of big league service, probably will return to his Virginia home and forget about baseball for the business of fixing teeth.[9]

Of course, Ayers did not retire from baseball at that point, but pitched three more years in the minors. However, what is unusual is the reference to dentistry. We have seen no other linkages of Doc to that profession and it is almost certain that he was never a dentist. Some sportswriters were fascinated by the fact that Doc had attended medical school and references to him as a physician are routine in the writings of the times. Some writers had already conferred the M. D. degree upon him.

For example, a 1917 report in the *Washington Post* read as follows: "Dr. Yancey Wyatt Ayers, the Nationals' underhand flinger, is in Washington, coming here from his mountain home in Hillsville, Va., for the express purpose of unraveling the tangle now existing between him and Manager Griffith over a contract for 1917. Just what the final settlement will be is strictly a matter of conjecture. The Hillsville M. D. and his boss will be closeted today, when it is expected that an amicable agreement will be reached."[10]

Perhaps one more example will suffice. Writing in the *Washington Post* about a game in Boston also in 1917, J. V. Fitzgerald penned these lines:

> Doc Ayers is a real honest-to-goodness doctor in the making. After today he can play physician as often as he likes to the world's champion Red Sox. The prescription he handed them in the seventh inning of the game with the Nationals at Fenway Park this afternoon pulled them out of the sick bed of defeat and put them on the road to rapid recovery. It read "Two runs to be filled at once," and that was enough to yield the Red Sox a 5 to 4 victory over the Griffmen. In the first six innings Physician Ayers didn't hold out much hope for the Red Sox. In that time he was acting as chief surgeon for the Nationals and making a good job of it with the aid of the Griffmen themselves. Had he kept at his task instead of helping the ailing Red Sox, all would have been well. But a doctor is bound to answer the call of distress and Ayers, as becomes his profession, answered the sick summons. He prescribed the most curing of all ills pills for a baseball club and the Red Sox took them as good children are supposed to take sugar-coated pellets and cry for more. His prescription was in the form of five bases on balls and these coupled with a sacrifice hit that the sickly, at the time, Red Sox injected to help themselves in their recovery, made for two runs, and the game.[11]

One leading baseball researcher, Tom Hufford, knew Doc Ayers personally. He wrote that to his knowledge Ayers never practiced either medicine or dentistry.[12] Doc was a part-time farmer who managed or coached a semipro team in Pulaski, Virginia, in the mid–1920s, and worked as an automobile salesman for various Pulaski car dealerships for the next 35–40 years or so.

Doc married Elizabeth Brown Dunlap in 1914 at the home of a Methodist minister in Pulaski. According to Hufford, Doc purchased a farm in Draper in Pulaski County, where the couple lived the rest of their lives in a big white frame house.[13] Their son Yancey Wyatt Ayers, Jr., was born in Washington, D. C., in 1917, and a daughter, Mildred, was born in 1923. The 1920 U. S. Census for Pulaski County listed Doc as a farmer; the 1930 census showed his occupation as automobile salesman.

Yancey Ayers died in a hospital in Pulaski, Virginia, on May 26, 1968. He, his wife, and their son are buried in a family cemetery on his farm, which lies along a frontage road alongside I-81, just west of the State Route 99 exit to Pulaski. Although there is no name sign on the cemetery, it is sometimes called the Grantham Cemetery, after Elizabeth's kinfolk, who are also buried there.[14]

16

Dana Fillingim

At the age of 27, the spitballer on the mound in Wrigley Field one unseasonably warm day in 1918 must have wondered if he would ever win a major league game. He had had a brief trial with the Philadelphia Athletics in 1915, but had lost all five of his decisions. He had been exiled to the minor leagues for three years. At last he was being given another chance in the show. On this date of May 18, 1918, his wet one was working wonderfully. He was an overhand pitcher and his spitter broke straight down. Occasionally he threw sidearm and the ball broke sideways. Ed Walsh, the great Chicago White Sox spitballer, had taught him how to throw the moist delivery years ago, but this was his most effective use of the wet one to date. Throughout the game, he kept the Cubs batters mystified. The Braves scored one run in the first inning and that would be enough, although they added four insurance runs later. Dana Fillingim shut out the Bruins 5–0, allowing but six hits and walking only one batsman. He had won the first of what would be 47 major league victories.

Dana Fillingim was born November 6, 1893, in Columbus, Georgia, a son of Terah Fort and Henry Vann Fillingim. He claimed to be of Scotch-Irish and English ancestry. Dan Daniel wrote in the *New York World-Telegram* that Dana was Greek, the first son of Athens to play professional baseball.[1] We suspect Daniel may have been mistaken. Fillingim may have known more about his own forebears than the scribe did. A son of the sunny southland, Dana spent most of his life in Georgia and Alabama. After elementary school, the lad attended Gordon Institute in Barnesville, Georgia, for four years.

Dana mastered the spitball while pitching for the Gordon Institute. As far as we can determine, he was the only one of the 17 spitball grandfathers to use the moist delivery while in secondary school. He became a star in prep school and on the Georgia sandlots at a tender age.

While only 16 years old, Dana pitched in two games for Albany of the South Atlantic League in 1912, but statistics are not available. In 1913 he hurled for Cordele of the Empire State League and posted a commendable 15–10 record. The league disbanded after that season, and the Cordele club became a member of the Georgia State League in 1914. Dana was sold to the Atlanta Crackers of the Southern Association on August 20 and appeared in four games for the Crackers that year. At the end of the season he was sent to Charleston and spent most of the next two seasons with the Sea Gulls of the South Atlantic League, with time out for a trial with the A's in 1915 and another with the Columbus Senators of the American Association in 1916. Fillingim had excellent success with Charleston, going 14–5 in 1915 and 20–7 the following year.

His stay in Charleston was interrupted by several transactions. On August 28, 1916, he was sold to the Philadephia Athletics for a reported sale price of $650. After the tryout period resulted in all losses, as noted above, he was returned to the South Carolina city. On June 15 he was sold to the Cleveland American League club for $800, but got into no games for the Indians before being loaned to Columbus for most of the month of July. On July 25, he was returned to Charleston again. In 1917 he had an outstanding season with the Indianapolis Indians of the American Association with a record of 20–9.

At the end of the 1917 season, Fillingim was drafted and chose the navy as his branch of service, but did not go on active duty until well into 1918. While he was in the service, Indianapolis sold his contract to the Boston Braves in return for two marginal players, first baseman Sam Covington and pitcher Cal Crum, plus an undisclosed amount of cash.

His minor league record:

Year	Club	W	L	Pct.	IP	H	BB	SO	ERA
1912	Albany	no statistics available							
1913	Cordele	15	10	.600					
1914	Cordele	5	4	.556					
	Atlanta	2	2	.500	29	35	10	11	
1915	Charleston	14	5	.737	174	128	46	129	
1916	Charleston	20	7	.741	243	155	80	205	
	Columbus	2	5	.286	59	60	27	21	4.42
1917	Indianapolis	20	9	.690	261	222	41	96	2.34
1925	Beaumont	7	15	.288	157	203	60	37	5.73
1926	Beaumont	15	8	.652	211	249	75	54	3.54
1927	San Antonio	12	10	.545	181	197	83	42	3.38
1928	San Antonio	7	10	.412	122	157	37	30	3.84
Partial totals—10 years		116	83	.583	1408	1371	449	634	

League affiliations: Albany, South Atlantic; Cordele 1913, Empire State; 1914, Georgia State; Atlanta, Southern Association; Charleston, South Atlantic; Columbus and Indianapolis, American Association; Beaumont and San Antonio, Texas League.

Although he showed flashes of brilliance, Fillingim did not have as much success in the major leagues as he could have hoped for. After going winless in 1915, he won his first major league game in 1918 as noted above. During the 1918 season, he won seven games and lost six before going into the navy. He had an absolutely sensational record pitching for the Newport Naval Reserves. He was credited with 20 wins and no defeats. Admittedly, the level of competition was not of major league caliber, but a record of 20 straight wins is a remarkable achievement under any circumstances.

He was discharged from the navy in January 1919. Based on his navy accomplishments, great things were expected of Dana in 1919. However, he did not live up to expectations, winning only six games that year.

Cliff Wheatley of the *Atlanta Consitution,* upon learning of Brad Hogg's retirement because of the spitball ban, expressed his concerns for Fillingim's future:

> The writer is reminded that another of Georgia's favorite sons in baseball's solar system must certainly be affected by the new legislation. We refer to Dana Fillingim, one of the well-known exponents of the water flinging pellet style. Fillingim has had a rather checkered career in the majors, but his pitching has been good enough to secure for him a splendid position among the spitball artists. What's Dana to do? If his major league delivery is the same he used in his bush league days, this Georgia twirler is going to be walloped by the freak delivery ban. He won his way through the sand lot ordeal by his mastery of the spitball. His major league try-out came after a record of minor league victories, obtained mostly through the bewildering slants of the outlawed style.[2]

As Fillingim relied heavily on the spitball, Billy Evans also predicted he would not be effective if he was not allowed to use the pitch in the future.[3] Of course, Dana was grandfathered in and did not have to try to live without his favorite pitch. Hurling for a really weak Boston team in 1920, Dana won 12 games, but lost 21.

On May 3, 1920, he pitched one of the most memorable games in baseball history. Facing Sherrod Smith of the Brooklyn Dodgers, Fillingim hurled a complete, 19-inning game. His mound opponent also went the route. No other National League pitcher has thrown a complete game in a winning effort of that length in the subsequent 80-plus years. (Bob Smith of the Boston Braves pitched a 22-inning complete game against the Chicago Cubs on May 17, 1927, but lost a heartbreaker when the Cubs pushed across the winning run in the top of the 22nd.)

In Fillingim's win, the two teams were scoreless until the fifth inning, when Brooklyn scored its lone run on three singles and an error. With one out, Smith and Ivy Olson each singled to left field. Bernie Neis then hit a little dribbler in front of the plate. Trying to force Smith at third base, catcher Mickey O'Neil threw low, loading the bases with one out. Jimmy Johnston then singled to right field, with Smith scoring, but the right fielder, John Sullivan, threw out Olson at the plate. Fillingim then induced Zack Wheat, the Brooklyn clean-up batter, to hit an easy fly to Sullivan. Dana got out of the jam with only one run scoring. In the next inning, Boston tied the score. Smith issued consecutive walks to Ray Powell and Charlie Pick. Leslie Mann beat out an infield single to load the bases with nobody out. Sullivan's infield grounder forced Powell at the plate, Walter Holke hit a sacrifice fly to score Pick and tie the game, and then Tony Boeckel popped up to end the rally.

The longer the game continued, the better the two hurlers pitched. With the score tied 1–1 in the 17th inning, manager Wilbert Robinson asked umpire Bill Hart to call the game on account of darkness, but Hart refused. Robbie then appealed to the other arbiter, Bill McCormick. Unluckily for Uncle Robbie, McCormick sided with his colleague. In the 19th inning, Fillingim gave up two of the four walks he allowed in the game, but the other batsmen were helpless against his spitters. In the Boston half of the frame, Boston collected three safeties to win the game and send Sherrod Smith down to an ill-deserved defeat. Sherry had nearly matched Dana pitch for pitch for 19 innings, but all the glory went to Fillingim when his team emerged victorious. The hard-luck Robins had played 58 innings in three successive games and had no victories to show for their efforts.

Despite the misgivings of Wheatley and Evans, in 1921 Dana had his best year in the majors, compiling a 15–10 record for a Boston club that finished only five games above the .500 mark. But that was to be his last winning season for the Braves. It was not the loss of his favorite pitch, but an injury that threw a crimp into his big league career. On July 10, 1922, while trying to field a short roller by Hack Miller of the Cubs, Dana slipped and wrenched his right knee. He had injured the same knee in high school, and never regained effectiveness after this misfortune. Dana won only five games in 1922, and only two more in what remained of his major league career. Both the amount and the quality of his pitching declined dramatically. He logged 100 innings on the mound in 1923, but only eight frames after that.

Dana Fillingim was the winner in one of the most memorable pitching performances in National League history. Pitching for the Boston Braves against the Brooklyn Robins on May 3, 1920, Fillingim was matched against Sherrod Smith. Both hurlers went the route as the Braves won 2–1 in 19 innings. (PHOTOGRAPH COURTESY OF NATIONAL BASEBALL HALL OF FAME LIBRARY, COOPERSTOWN.)

Dana pitched enough in 1923 to become involved in one controversial play. The Braves were leading the Pittsburgh Pirates with runners on first and third. Rabbit Maranville hit a foul ball. When the ball was returned to Dana, it did not suit him, so he tossed it into the dugout. The Pirate runner who was on third crossed the plate and the man on first moved up to third. An argument ensued. The umpires decided that since Fillingim had not stepped on the rubber before tossing the ball away, the ball was not in play. The runners were sent back to their respective bases with no damage done. Dana won only one game in 1923, then underwent a knee operation causing him to miss the entire 1924 season.

On December 10, 1924, the Braves sent Dana and pitcher Skinny O'Neal to the Philadelphia Phillies in return for cash and three players to be named later. During spring training, a sportswriter for a Philadelphia newspaper welcomed him back by writing that Fillingim was a typical southerner and fit in well with the number of citizens from below the Mason-Dixon line in the Phils' camp. O'Neal never won a game for the Phils and Fillingim did little better. He won one game in 1925—his last major league victory—and then it was back to the minors for the spitball pitcher. In May 1925 the Phillies released him to the Beaumont Exporters of the Texas League.

After the end of the 1925 season, a powerful politician became involved in an attempt to help Dana return to the major leagues. James M. Cox was a prominent newspaper publisher with a chain of papers in Ohio, a three-time governor of the Buckeye State, and the Democratic candidate for president of the United States in 1920, with Franklin D. Roosevelt as his running mate. How Cox became interested in Fillingim can be seen from this letter, dated December 16, 1925, and addressed to Garry Herrmann, president of the Cincinnati Reds:

> *My dear Garry:*
> *Every year I go to Alabama for a bird hunting trip. My headquarters are at Tuskegee. This is the home of Dana Fillingim. He's highly esteemed here, and seems to be a straight forward fellow.*
> *He was a top notcher at one time, but had trouble with his knee, and could stand little or no pressure upon the impaired leg. During the last year he had a cartilage removed, and he tells me the member is just as good as it ever was.*
> *He was sent to Beaumont in the Texas league by the Philadelphia Nationals. He's trying to purchase his release, and tells me he would like to play with Cincinnati. He likes Hendricks [Jack Hendricks was the Cincinnati manager], having worked for him at Indianapolis. He's in prime condition.*
> *I would recommend that you give the matter attention.*
> *With all good wishes, I am,*
> *Sincerely yours.*
> *[signed] James M. Cox.*

Cox followed this up with a telephone call, to which Herrmann replied on December 17, indicating that he would talk to Hendricks to ascertain the manager's interest in Dana. One week later Hermann again wrote the governor, saying that if the player's leg was in good condition, Hendricks would be very much interested. He asked Cox to talk to Fillingim to see under what conditions he could obtain his release, pointing out that if the title to his services belonged to another club, Cincinnati had no right to negotiate directly with the pitcher.

Dana then contacted the Beaumont club and was informed that his release could be purchased for $2,500. Finally on January 11, 1926, Herrmann wrote to Cox that he had looked over the records and discovered that the player was 33 years old and had a record of seven wins and 15 losses last year for Beaumont. "This record, of course, does not impress me very much," the president wrote. The frugal Garry Herrmann was not about to invest $2,500 in a 33-year-old minor league pitcher with a losing record. Needless to say, Fillingim never pitched for Cincinnati.

From 1926 through 1928 Fillingim remained in the Texas League, first with Beaumont and finally with San Antonio. He had a winning record in two out of the three years.

Fillingim's major league record:

Year	Club	W	L	Pct.	IP	H	BB	SO	ERA	WR	PTS
1915	Phi AL	0	5	.000	39	42	32	17	3.43	-1465	-7
1918	Bos NL	7	6	.538	113	99	28	29	2.23	1612	38

Year	Club	W	L	Pct.	IP	H	BB	SO	ERA	WR	PTS
1919	Bos NL	6	13	.316	186	185	39	50	3.38	-2071	12
1920	Bos NL	12	21	.364	272	292	79	66	3.11	-1881	21
1921	Bos NL	15	10	.600	240	249	56	54	3.45	2500	58
1922	Bos NL	5	9	.357	117	143	37	25	4.54	280	23
1923	Bos NL	1	9	.100	100	141	36	27	5.20	-2680	-9
1925	Phi NL	1	0	1.000	9	19	6	2	10.38	559	7
Total — 8 years		47	73	.392	1076	1170	313	270	3.56	-3146	143

We cannot agree with the writer for United Press International who dubbed Dana "one of the greatest spit-ball pitchers the Major Leagues have ever known."[4] The record shows he was a good pitcher, but not a great one, although he could rise to great heights on occasion. The fact that he usually pitched for second division teams impacted his record negatively, but even so his overall winning percentage was lower than that of the clubs for which he toiled.

Dana married Ava Eugenia Fort of Fort Davis, Alabama, on March 3, 1926, and spent the remainder of his life in the Heart of Dixie. He died in Tuskegee on February 3, 1961, not quite three months past his 69th birthday. The cause of death was listed as myocardial infarction with arteriosclerotic heart disease and bronchial asthma as contributing conditions. Services were conducted by the Corbitts Funeral Home. He was buried in Tuskegee City Cemetery.

After his death, his widow spoke out in favor of reinstating the spitball. "My husband Dana had the finest spitball pitch ever thrown and it ought to be returned to the game today," she said. "They've taken all the advantage away from the pitcher and given it to the batter." Thinking of Cleveland pitcher Herb Score, who was struck in the eye by a line drive, ending his 1957 season and nearly ending his career, she added: "Any man on the mound stands there like in a dart game. Except a baseball weighs more than a dart."[5]

Ava died December 4, 1997, in Houston, Texas, at the age of 94.

17

Marvin Goodwin

During spring training at Charlottesville, Virginia, on March 20, 1916, manager Clark Griffith of the Washington Nationals received a visit from E. A. Shannon of Gordonsville, a small city on the Orange-Louisa county line, just east of Charlottesville. Shannon, the coach of one of the top semipro teams in the state, suggested that Griff give a trial to one of his pitchers. He said the Gordonsville native had tremendous speed, a puzzling spitball, and great control. Having heard the same thing before about rookies who could not cut the mustard in the big leagues, Griff was a bit skeptical. However, he agreed to take a look at the youngster. The next morning, a blond-haired athlete named Marvin Goodwin appeared in Charlottesville. No sooner had Griffith watched Goodwin work than he became convinced that the young man had the makings of a major league pitcher. Marvin showed John Henry, who caught him, enough stuff to make the veteran backstop enthusiastic. Henry declared Goodwin's spitball to be the best he ever saw a rookie possess.[1] Unlike some spitball pitchers, the young Virginian had mastered the moist delivery at an early age.

Based on recommendations from Shannon and Henry and on his own observations, Griffith decided to offer Goodwin a contract. "That youngster Goodwin, if I am not mistaken, is going to make a major league pitcher," the manager said. "All he needs is someone to show him how to pitch. He is green, but has the right motion. He showed me enough stuff today to warrant closer watching. The fact that he has speed and perfect control impressed me. Why, he put the ball every place I told him. I am seriously thinking of signing him."[2]

Marvin Mardo Goodwin was born in Gordonsville, Virginia, on January 16, 1891. Of English and French ancestry, Marvin was a son of Susie May Boughan and P. M. Goodwin. In addition to Marvin, his parents had at least three other children — Mary, Allan, and Peyton. Marvin attended a Baptist elementary school in Gordonsville, graduated from Gordonsville High School, and attended college for two years in New Haven, Connecticut.

When Griffith offered him a contract to play in organized baseball, Goodwin was already 25 years old. He was an established star with his hometown semipro team and had a good position as a telegraph operator with the Chesapeake and Ohio Railroad. He had also worked as a brakeman with the C & O. He was not anxious to give up his job unless it was for one with brighter prospects. The Old Fox informed him that he had a great opportunity to make more money by playing professional baseball. To encourage the young man, the railroad agreed to let Goodwin off for several months to try his luck.

On March 27, 1916, Goodwin signed a contract with Washington, which optioned him to the Richmond club of the International League. Under the option agreement, Goodwin remained the property of the Washington club. Goodwin was the first player to be optioned by Griffith, who believed that the youngster had a very good chance of becoming a major league pitcher. As a reporter for the *Washington Post* explained it, a rookie very seldom develops in the big league. It is the minors that fit him for the majors.[3]

Goodwin did not last long in Richmond. Manager Billy Smith, claiming to be overstocked with pitchers, returned him to Washington on April 21. Griffith said he still had confidence that Goodwin in time would make a good pitcher and that he intended to place him with some other club where he would be given the opportunity to play regularly.[4]

That club turned out to be Martinsburg of the Class D Blue Ridge League. Goodwin got plenty of work, winning 19 games and losing 12. He led the league in wins, innings pitched, games, complete games, and shutouts. Most remarkable perhaps was the fact that he started 31 games and completed all 31 of them. Not once was he removed for a relief pitcher. Of his 31 starts, nearly one-third (10) resulted in shutouts. By way of comparison, the brilliant young left-hander of the Boston Red Sox, Babe Ruth, led the American League that year with nine shutouts in 41 starts.

Toward the end of the 1916 season, Goodwin was recalled to Washington and made his major league debut on September 7, 1916. He appeared in three games for the Nationals, all in relief, and pitched a total of five and two-thirds innings, during which he gave up two earned runs.

In 1917 Goodwin started the season with the Milwaukee Brewers of the American Association. By July he had won eight games against nine losses, but had a sparkling 1.91 earned run average. On July 19, a newspaper reported his acquisition by the St. Louis Cardinals with these words:

> With Uncle Sam having first call on the draft nowadays and baseball's future uncertain because of the war, wise magnates hesitate about going very deep in purchasing new talent, but occasionally a situation arises where one has to plunge to get what one wants. That was the case with Marvin Goodwin, star pitcher of the Milwaukee team. The St. Louis Cardinals outbid six other teams for him. They gave, according to report, $6,000 in cash and a quartet of players valued at an equal amount. Though there has been some disagreement over the transfer of these players, it is not regarded as serious and Goodwin is expected to report to the Cardinals this week. Goodwin is a young right-hander who has made a good record in his first year in high-class company. He had a brief trial with Washington in 1916, but not enough to show what he could do.... Branch Rickey says he is the best young pitcher developed this year.[5]

After his callup to the show, Goodwin won six games and lost four for the Cardinals that season. Soon after Marvin's arrival in St. Louis, a newspaper published the following assessment:

> Pitcher Marvin Goodwin, the highest priced piece of baseball furniture purchased by any club this season, has shown enough since joining the St. Louis Cardinals to prove his worth. He is

not strong on strikeouts and he does not have the blazing speed of an Alexander or a Johnson, but he pitched smart ball, has shown coolness and gameness under fire and Cardinal management and fans are well satisfied with him. He hasn't had much of the breaks of luck so far, but he is of the sort who will make them for himself in time.[6]

Goodie very quickly established that he wanted to finish what he started. Years later a sportswriter penned this story: "Once Marvin Goodwin, a pitcher for the St. Louis National League club, stormed across the old playground of the Cardinals so red in the face that he looked like a Harvard banner. He had been sent to the showers. As it was a very hot afternoon that appeared to be a comforting change for Goodwin, but it was not. He shouted loud as he went back to the clubhouse: 'How in … can a pitcher ever expect to be good enough to make good in this league if that … nut on the bench sends you out of the game the minute the other side gets two hits in succession?'"[7]

Before the calendar year 1917 was over Goodwin had joined the United States Army Air Corps. During the war he served as a flight instructor. On December 6, 1917, the *Sporting News* reported his enlistment with these words:

Pitcher Marvin Goodwin of the St. Louis Cardinals, just entering upon what had every indication of being a brilliant major league career, has sacrificed all that means to a young man and with the statement that he couldn't feel right by holding back when his country called, had joined the army's aviation department. His loss will be a severe one to the Cardinal owners, but they unite in bidding him good luck and congratulations. Goodwin was the most expensive player purchased last year, the Cardinals paying Milwaukee $15,000 in cash and player value for him. In his short career as a Cardinal he pitched good ball and was considered well worth all he cost. Goodwin expects to take a six week training course and then join the American flyers going to France. May he do his full duty and yet be spared to return and play ball is the wish of every fan.[8]

On February 21, 1918, a St. Louis newspaper published a cartoon of an airplane pilot throwing a baseball out of the cockpit and hitting a German soldier on the ground, a photograph of Goodwin in his army uniform, and this note about the young man:

Marvin Goodwin, St. Louis Cardinal pitcher, who gave up prospects of a major league baseball career to take a chance with Old Uncle Sam, was in St. Louis the other day on his way from a ground school in the East to San Antonio, where he will get his second course in flying as a member of the Army aviation corps. It so happens that the Cardinals, his old team, train at San Antonio and so Goodwin will be with them, though not of them. If steadiness, gameness and devotion to purpose are the things that go to make up a successful aviator then Goodwin should make his mark in the clouds. He showed all these qualities in his brief career as a Cardinal. He was sent right to the firing line when he reported as a minor leaguer and he performed like a seasoned veteran. Over night he became a popular favorite with the fans of the Mound City and the news that he had quit the team for the Big Game caused a pull in their hearts. Their best wishes go with him. They know he has the stuff heroes are made of and that he is just what Uncle Sam needs, and they will watch and pray that when his duty has been well done and the war won, he will come back to them, spared to again take his place in the old pitcher's box none the worse for wear.[9]

After his return from the service, Goodwin pitched for the Cardinals in 1919 and 1920 and split the 1921 and 1922 seasons between the Cards and their farm club, Houston of the Texas League. He was with Houston full time in 1923 and 1924. On May 29,

1924, he replaced Hunter Hill as manager of the Buffs. The *Sporting News* commented on his appointment: "Goodwin is a smart baseball man and decidedly popular. There is no finer fellow or more square shooter anywhere."[10]

In 1925 Goodwin had one of his most successful seasons in his entire baseball career. As manager he guided the Buffs to a second-place finish in the Texas League. As a pitcher he won 21 games and lost only nine, the only 20-win season in his professional career. Shortly before the end of the season he was sold to the Cincinnati Reds, on the condition that he stick with the Reds at least 30 days the following season before the deal would become final.

Goodwin's minor league record:

Year	Club	W	L	Pct.	IP	H	BB	SO	ERA
1916	Martinsburg	19	12	.594	271	188	55	165	n.a.
1917	Milwaukee	8	9	.471	170	133	47	78	1.91
1921	Houston	7	3	.700	83	77	16	43	3.90
1922	Houston	8	12	.400	179	177	32	75	2.77
1923	Houston	19	13	.594	286	268	83	92	3.30
1924	Houston	17	17	.500	296	310	70	100	4.14
1925	Houston	21	9	.700	269	289	59	106	3.55
Total — 7 years		99	75	.569	1554	1442	362	659	n.a.

League affiliations: Martinsburg, Blue Ridge; Milwaukee, American Association; Houston, Texas League.

Goodwin never achieved the big league stardom that some had predicted for him. Although he appeared in major league games in seven seasons, he spent the entire season in the majors only twice. His best year was 1919, when he won 11 games and lost nine for the St. Louis Cardinals. Arthur Daley told how Goodwin was victimized by a sign stealer one day when the Phillies were in St. Louis. Fred Luderus was hitting the spitballer hard and often. The Phillies had a reputation for stealing signs, so catcher Verne Clemons concealed his signs adroitly from any enemy spy. Big Fred figured out a system. As soon as the catcher crouched to give Goodwin the sign, Luderus stooped over and picked up a handful of dirt to rub on his hands, a natural thing to do. While he was bent over, he took a quick peek out of the corner of his eye at the number of fingers Clemons was sticking out. After Fred's fourth hit of the afternoon, Branch Rickey, the Cardinal manager, walked past Fred, shaking his head and muttering under his breath. "How are we ever going to get you out?" "Oh, well," Luderus replied, "That's just the way it goes."[11] However, not many hitters got four hits in one game off Marvin that season.

The last game Goodwin pitched in organized baseball came on the final day of the season in 1925. The newly crowned National League champion Pittsburgh Pirates came to Cincinnati and closed out the season with a doubleheader on October 4. Marvin pitched a complete game in the opener, but lost 4–2. Once again a batter collected four hits in one game off the spitballer. George Grantham went 4 for 4 for the Corsairs. There is no record of his stealing any signs.

Ernie Helm quoted Dusty Boggess as saying: "The former Cincinnati great. Marvin Goodwin, was another fine spitter. He took the slime off the bottom of his chin as he prepared to pitch. He had such a mouthful of slippery ellum at times that the corners of the mouth were sore."[12] We are not certain that Boggess should be considered an authority on Goodwin. It seems a bit odd that he would identify Marvin as a former Cincinnati great when Goodie never won a game for the Reds.

Marvin's major league record:

Year	Club	W	L	Pct.	IP	H	BB	SO	ERA	WR	PTS
1916	Was AL	0	0	—	6	5	3	1	3.18	0	0
1917	StL NL	6	4	.600	85	70	19	38	2.21	650	29
1919	StL NL	11	9	.550	179	163	33	48	2.51	3620	57
1920	StL NL	3	8	.273	116	153	28	23	4.95	-2530	0
1921	StL NL	1	2	.333	36	47	9	7	3.72	-699	1
1922	StL NL	0	0	—	4	3	3	0	2.25	0	0
1925	Cin NL	0	2	.000	21	26	5	4	4.79	-1060	-5
Total — 7 years		21	25	.457	447	467	100	121	3.30	-19	82

After his great season in Houston, at the age of 34 Goodwin was going to get another chance at the fame and fortune that had thus far eluded him. His brilliant performance in Houston was evidence that he still had the ability to pitch outstanding baseball. He must have been optimistic about the future in the autumn of 1925.

Then tragedy struck only two weeks after Goodwin pitched his final game for the Reds. Following his wartime service, Marvin had remained in the Army Air Service Reserve. On October 18, First Lt. Marvin Goodwin, an excellent flyer, took a plane up at Ellington Field, Texas. At an altitude of 200 feet it went into a tailspin and crashed. Early reports said that only the pilot's superb handling of the plane saved his life and that of his mechanic, Staff Sgt. W.H. McGrath, who suffered only slight injuries. Goodwin lay badly injured in a Houston hospital, but it was not known immediately that the crash would prove fatal.[13]

However, he was so badly mangled that he lived less than three days. Both his arms and his legs were broken in several places, and he received terrible internal injuries. He died at Baptist Hospital in Houston at 5:05 a.m. on October 21 at the age of 34. The official death certificate listed the cause of death as fracture at the base of the skull with multiple fractures of the limbs as contributing factors. The *Sporting News* paid tribute: "Marvin was a gentleman and an athlete of whom baseball can be proud.... Lieutenant Goodwin sacrificed his life in behalf of his country. No person can do more."[14]

After his untimely death, Goodwin was at the center of what has been called one of the most ghoulish squabbles ever between two clubs over a player transaction.[15] St. Louis Cardinals executive Branch Rickey demanded that the Reds make full payment of money and promised players for the pitcher. Cincinnati claimed that as Goodwin had not lasted the stipulated 30 days into the 1926 season, the sale had been voided. As the two clubs were unable to reach an amicable agreement, Commissioner Landis had to intervene. He ruled that the Cardinals were not entitled to anything in exchange for the dead pitcher.

Among the grandfathered spitballers, Marvin was the only one never to be married. At the time of his death he was residing with his brother Allan in Houston. He had been a member of a Masonic lodge in Houston and was a Shriner. After his death, Masons from his lodge brought his body back to his hometown of Gordonsville, Virginia, where the Settegast-Kopf Company arranged for his burial. He was interred in the Maple Wood Cemetery in Gordonsville.

Appendix: Rankings

Faber System

In Table 1 the spitball grandfathers are ranked according to their accumulated points in the Faber System of rating ballplayers. As one would expect, Red Faber and Burleigh Grimes head the list. These hurlers were the best exempted spitballers in the American and National League, respectively, and the first two of their ilk to be inducted into the National Baseball Hall of Fame.

What might surprise some fans is that the third Hall of Famer, Stan Coveleskie, did not make the top three. He ranks fifth, behind Jack Quinn, who had nine more years to rack up points than did the Big Pole, and also behind the always underrated Urban Shocker.

TABLE 1. FABER SYSTEM POINTS

	Pitcher	Dates	Years	W	L	Pct.	WR	PTS
1.	Red Faber	1914–33	20	254	213	.544	26938	874
2.	Burleigh Grimes	1916–34	19	270	212	.560	21356	848
3.	Jack Quinn	1909–33	23	247	218	.531	23478	760
4.	Urban Shocker	1916–28	13	187	117	.615	31510	683
5.	Stan Coveleskie	1912–28	14	215	142	.602	17093	658
6.	Bill Doak	1912–29	16	169	157	.518	13428	577
7.	Ray Caldwell	1910–21	12	134	120	.528	13448	486
8.	Clarence Mitchell	1911–32	18	125	139	.473	684	454
9.	Dutch Leonard	1913–25	11	139	113	.552	-728	431
10.	Ray Fisher	1910–20	10	100	94	.515	7344	373
11.	Dick Rudolph	1910–27	13	121	109	.526	7411	366
12.	Allen Sothoron	1914–26	11	91	99	.479	2845	291
13.	Phil Douglas	1912–22	9	94	93	.503	-6264	271
14.	Allan Russell	1915–25	11	70	76	.479	-940	263
15.	Doc Ayers	1913–21	9	64	78	.451	-9025	173
16.	Dana Fillingim	1915–25	8	47	73	.392	-3146	143
17.	Marv Goodwin	1916–25	7	21	25	.457	-19	82

Best Ten Years

In the book *Baseball Ratings*, Charles F. Faber made the assumption that ten years are enough to establish the quality of a baseball player. If he continues to excel after ten seasons, his stature can be enhanced, but a poor season after ten good ones should not diminish his standing. Therefore, he computed his ratings on a player's ten best years. Rankings in Table 2 are based on this formulation. For the pitchers having fewer than ten seasons, the entire career is used. Grimes, Faber, Shocker, and Coveleskie occupy the first four places in this ranking, but Quinn drops to sixth place, behind Bill Doak. Spittin' Bill ranked sixth in Table 1, so the same six hurlers comprise the top half dozen in both lists, but in a slightly different order.

TABLE 2. BEST TEN YEARS

	Pitcher	Dates	Years	W	L	Pct.	WR	PTS
1.	Burleigh Grimes	1918–31	10	201	118	.630	35529	694
2.	Red Faber	1914–28	10	175	117	.600	34295	637
3.	Urban Shocker	1917–27	10	177	108	.619	30285	634
4.	Stan Coveleskie	1916–26	10	193	125	.607	17192	581
5.	Bill Doak	1914–27	10	139	106	.567	26059	549
6.	Jack Quinn	1909–28	10	155	115	.574	20034	540
7.	Ray Caldwell	1911–21	10	128	108	.542	17329	450
8.	Dutch Leonard	1913–25	10	136	111	.551	389	416
9.	Clarence Mitchell	1916–31	10	88	78	.530	13071	403
10.	Ray Fisher	1910–20	10	100	94	.515	7344	373
11.	Dick Rudolph	1911–23	10	121	92	.568	8710	359
12.	Allen Sothoron	1914–26	10	90	96	.489	4367	293
13.	Phil Douglas	1912–22	9	94	93	.503	-6264	271
14.	Allan Russell	1915–24	10	68	72	.486	-940	263
15.	Doc Ayers	1913–21	9	64	78	.457	-9025	173
16.	Dana Fillingim	1915–25	8	47	73	.392	-3146	143
17.	Marv Goodwin	1916–25	7	21	25	.457	-19	82

Points per Year

In the Faber System a pitcher accumulates points for each year he pitches. This gives an advantage to pitchers with long careers, as indeed it should. A man who is a great hurler for fifteen years surely deserves to be ranked ahead of one who had a career of only five years, for example. But what about fairness to a pitcher who loses the possibility of a long career due to illness, military service, or as in the cases of Urban Shocker and Marvin Goodwin, premature death. Computing the average points per year recognizes this reality. The problem with this calculation is that a pitcher called up in late September, just before the end of the season, would have no opportunity to accumulate many points and should not be charged with a full year. In order to compensate for this injustice, seasons in which the hurler tossed fewer than 154 innings are counted as partial years. The number of innings pitched in partial seasons are combined and divided by 154 to give the number of "effective years" pitched. Table 3 ranks the spitball grandfathers according to points per effective year. The same names appear near the top of this list as in Tables 1 and 2 — Shocker, Coveleskie, Grimes, Faber, and Doak. The spitballer conspicuous by his absence from the top five is Jack Quinn, who fell all the way to tenth place in this calculation. Perhaps the reason that Quinn has not been inducted into the Hall of Fame is that electors view his modest ranking on this measure as not being worthy of recognition. If that is so, what is the reason Urban Shocker, who heads this list, has not been enshrined?

TABLE 3. POINTS PER YEAR

Pitcher	Dates	Years	W	L	Pct.	WR	PTS
1. Urban Shocker	1916–28	11	17	11	.615	2865	62.09
2. Stan Coveleskie	1912–28	12	19	12	.602	1424	54.83
3. Burleigh Grimes	1916–34	17	16	12	.560	1256	49.88
4. Red Faber	1914–33	18	14	12	.544	1497	48.56
5. Bill Doak	1912–29	13	13	12	.525	1033	44.38
6. Ray Caldwell	1910–21	11	12	11	.528	1223	44.18
7. Dutch Leonard	1913–25	10	14	11	.552	-73	43.10
8. Ray Fisher	1910–20	9	11	10	.515	816	41.44
9. Dick Rudolph	1910–27	8	15	14	.526	926	40.67
10. Jack Quinn	1909–33	19	13	11	.531	1236	40.00
11. Allen Sothoron	1914–26	8	11	12	.479	356	36.38
12. Clarence Mitchell	1911–32	13	10	11	.473	526	34.92
13. Phil Douglas	1912–22	8	12	12	.503	-783	33.88
14. Allan Russell	1915–25	9	8	8	.479	-104	29.22
15. Dana Fillingim	1915–25	5	9	15	.392	-629	28.60
16. Marv Goodwin	1916–25	3	7	8	.457	-6	27.33
17. Doc Ayers	1913–21	7	9	11	.451	-1289	24.71

Leaders by Category

In Table 4 the top five pitchers in various categories are listed. Red Faber's name appears in all twelve areas. Coveleskie is named in 11 of the 12 lists. Grimes, Quinn, and Shocker each rank in the top five in eight categories. Most of the areas are self-explanatory. Two separate rankings of ERA leaders are given because of the dramatic increase in run production that occurred with the rule changes and the introduction of a livelier ball. Coveleskie leads both lists, but he allowed an average of nearly one more earned run per game after 1920 than he did in the earlier Deadball Era. The same thing is true of Faber, who ranks third in both lists. Wins in Organized Baseball refers to regular season victories in major league and recognized minor league games. World Series rankings are based on number of wins, with winning percentage and earned run average as the first and second tie-breakers, respectively.

TABLE 4. LEADERS IN VARIOUS CATEGORIES

Lifetime Points		Best Ten Years		Average per Year	
1. Faber	883	Grimes	694	Shocker	62.05
2. Grimes	842	Faber	637	Coveleskie	54.83
3. Quinn	765	Shocker	634	Grimes	49.88
4. Shocker	684	Coveleskie	581	Faber	48.56
5. Coveleskie	664	Doak	549	Doak	44.38

Weighted Rating		Wins		Percentage	
1. Shocker	31587	Grimes	270	Shocker	.615
2. Faber	28375	Faber	254	Coveleskie	.602
3. Quinn	23176	Quinn	247	Grimes	.560
4. Grimes	20204	Coveleskie	215	Leonard	.552
5. Coveleskie	18425	Shocker	187	Faber	.544

Pre-1921 ERA		Post-1920 ERA		Saves	
1. Coveleskie	2.39	Coveleskie	3.34	Quinn	57
2. Leonard	2.45	Shocker	3.40	Russell	42
3. Faber	2.55	Faber	3.52	Faber	28
4. Shocker	2.56	Quinn	3.54	Shocker	25
5. Doak	2.61	Douglas	3.55	Coveleskie	21

Strikeouts		Organized Ball Wins		World Series Record		
1. Grimes	1512	Grimes	352	Faber	3–1	2.33
2. Faber	1471	Quinn	349	Coveleskie	3–2	1.74
3. Quinn	1329	Coveleskie	342	Quinn	3–4	4.29
4. Leonard	1160	Faber	332	Rudolph	2–0	0.50
5. Doak	1014	Caldwell	293	Leonard	2–0	1.00

Spitballers and Their Cohorts

How do the exempted spitballers stack up against their contemporaries? Very well indeed. Red Faber was the third best pitcher of the times, ranking behind only the great Walter Johnson and Grover Cleveland Alexander. Burleigh Grimes and Jack Quinn also rank in the top ten slabsters of the era. Six of the spitball grandfathers rank among the top 25 pitchers of the period, based upon their records during the 1909–34 seasons, which is the career span of the spitballers who were granted exemption from the ban. The data in Table 4 do not reflect the entire lifetime records of some of the pitchers, just the years in which their careers overlapped those of the spitballers. The exempted spitball pitchers are listed in ***bold italics*** type.

Table 5. 25 Best Pitchers 1909–34

	Pitcher	Dates	Years	W	L	Pct.	WR	Pts.
1.	Walter Johnson	1909–27	19	394	255	.607	92929	1419
2.	Grover Alexander	1911–30	20	373	208	.642	83454	1337
3.	**Red Faber**	**1914–31**	**20**	**254**	**213**	**.544**	**26938**	**874**
4.	Herb Pennock	1912–34	22	241	162	.598	24519	866
5.	**Burleigh Grimes**	**1916–34**	**19**	**270**	**212**	**.560**	**21356**	**848**
6.	Eppa Rixey	1912–33	21	266	251	.515	8070	803
7.	**Jack Quinn**	**1909–33**	**23**	**247**	**218**	**.531**	**23478**	**760**
8.	Sad Sam Jones	1914–33	20	213	198	.518	8809	731
9.	Dazzy Vance	1915–34	15	194	138	.584	33864	716
10.	Lefty Grove	1925–34	10	203	86	.702	35578	707
11.	Babe Adams	1909–26	17	194	137	.586	19797	705
12.	Eddie Rommel	1920–32	13	171	119	.590	32175	695
13.	**Urban Shocker**	**1916–28**	**13**	**187**	**117**	**.615**	**31510**	**683**
14.	George Uhle	1919–34	16	200	165	.548	18792	683
15.	Art Nehf	1915–29	15	184	120	.605	21640	679
16.	Wilbur Cooper	1912–26	15	216	178	.548	21502	676
17.	**Stan Coveleskie**	**1912–28**	**14**	**215**	**142**	**.602**	**17093**	**658**
18.	Jesse Haines	1918–34	16	194	145	.572	11125	657
19.	Waite Hoyt	1918–34	17	215	154	.583	7223	653
20.	Carl Mays	1915–29	15	208	126	.623	15087	652
21.	Slim Sallee	1909–31	13	169	135	.556	22849	630
22.	Lee Meadows	1915–29	15	188	180	.515	16756	608
23.	Hippo Vaughn	1909–21	12	176	137	.562	23680	602
24.	Ted Lyons	1923–34	12	161	157	.510	25885	578
25.	**Bill Doak**	**1912–29**	**16**	**169**	**157**	**.518**	**13428**	**577**

Miscellaneous Data

Table 6 provides data about the height and weight of the exempted spitball pitchers, the ages at which they pitched, and their batting and fielding exploits. The height of ballplayers remains fairly constant during their professional careers, but the weight can vary considerably from year to year. The data given in Table 6 reflect the approximate normal playing weight of the pitchers. Dick Rudolph had the slightest build of the spitballers, being both the shortest and the lightest. Phil Douglas was the tallest, while Jack Quinn was the heaviest. Although several of the pitchers participated in semipro or outlaw leagues at ages younger or older than those indicated, Dick Rudolph at 16 was probably the youngest to pitch in Organized Baseball. Jack Quinn was the oldest, both in the Major Leagues at 50 and in Organized Ball at 52. These observations are made in full awareness that the true ages of some of the players are in dispute.

The data bear out the reputation of Clarence Mitchell and Ray Caldwell as the best hitters among the exempted spitballers. Mitchell edged out Caldwell for highest batting average .252 to .248. Ray led in home runs with eight to seven for the Nebraskan. Jack Quinn also hit eight big league roundtrippers. Dana Fillingim led in fielding with a commendable .983 average. Mitchell ranked third in fielding percentage, the only grandfather to rank in the top five in all three categories—fielding, batting average, and home runs.

TABLE 6. MISCELLANEOUS DATA

Pitcher	Height	Weight	Organized Ball	Major Leagues	BA	HR	FA
Ayers	6–1	185	20–32	22–30	.171	0	.915
Caldwell	6–2	190	22–45	22–33	.248	8	.958
Coveleskie	5–11	175	19–39	23–39	.159	1	.972
Doak	6–0½	165	19–38	21–38	.127	1	.960
Douglas	6–3	190	19–32	22–32	.160	2	.948
Faber	6–1½	180	20–45	25–45	.134	3	.946
Fillingim	5–10	175	18–34	21–31	.209	2	.983
Fisher	5–11	185	20–32	22–32	.179	2	.946
Goodwin	5–11	170	25–34	25–34	.186	0	.925
Grimes	5–10	180	18–42	23–41	.248	2	.954
Leonard	5–10½	185	19–33	20–33	.173	0	.945
Mitchell	5–11½	190	19–49	20–41	.252	7	.972
Quinn	6–0	200	23–52	25–50	.184	8	.969
Rudolph	5–9½	160	16–40	22–40	.188	2	.970
Russell	5–11	165	18–35	22–32	.157	0	.925
Shocker	5–10	170	22–37	25–37	.208	1	.980
Sothoron	5–11	185	18–33	21–33	.206	0	.871

Age Range applies to Organized Ball and Major Leagues columns.

Chapter Notes

Preface

1. Charles F. Faber, *Baseball Ratings: The All-Time Best Players at Each Position* (Jefferson, NC: McFarland, 1995).
2. Ted C. Oliver, *Kings of the Mound*, 2nd ed. (Los Angeles: n.p., 1947).
3. Bill James, *The Bill James Historical Baseball Abstract* (New York: Willard Books, 1988), p. 471.

Introduction

1. *New York Times,* November 11, 1961.
2. *Atlanta Constitution,* April 25, 1990.
3. *New York Times,* April 21, 1957.
4. *New York Daily News,* May 19, 2003.
5. *Chicago Tribune,* February 24, 1918.
6. Steve Steinberg, *Baseball in St. Louis. 1900–1925* (Charleston, SC: Arcadia, 2004), p. 88.
7. John Thorn, *The Relief Pitcher: Baseball's New Hero* (New York: E. P. Dutton, 1979), p. 48.
8. *Washington Post,* February 22, 1918.
9. "The Vanishing Spit Ball," *Baseball Magazine* 29 (September 1922): 456.
10. *Washington Post,* August 8, 1931.
11. Billy Evans, "The Tough Break," *Harper's Weekly* 58 (June 13, 1914).
12. *Washington Post,* February 13, 1916.
13. Urban Faber, *New York World,* December 15, 1929, cited by Steve L. Steinberg, "The Spitball and the End of the Deadball Era," *National Pastime* 23 (2003).
14. Data compiled from *Total Baseball,* cited by Steinberg, *op. cit.,* p. 11.
15. Babe Ruth, quoted by George S. May, "Major League Baseball Players from Iowa," *Palimpsest,* April 1955: 155.
16. "Vanishing Spit Ball," *op. cit.*: 456.
17. *Ibid.*
18. *Washington Post,* March 1, 1920.
19. *Sporting News,* November 23, 1920.
20. *Ibid.*
21. *Ibid.*
22. *Sporting News,* February 3, 1921.
23. "Vanishing Spit Ball," *op cit.*: 455.
24. *Sporting News,* December 16, 1920.
25. *Ibid.*
26. *Atlanta Constitution,* February 27, 1920.
27. The grandfather clause is a provision exempting persons already engaged in an activity from rules or legislation affecting that activity. It was a device enacted by seven southern states between 1895 and 1910 to deny suffrage to African-Americans, by providing that those who had enjoyed the right to vote before 1867 or their lineal descendants would be exempt from educational, property, or tax requirements for voting. In other words, if their grandfathers had voted in the 1860s, whites could vote, but as no former slaves were allowed to vote at that time their black grandsons would not be eligible without meeting the new requirements, a nearly impossible task.
28. *Washington Post,* August 8, 1931.
29. Bill James and Rob Neyer, *The Neyer/James Guide to Pitching* (New York: Simon and Schuster, 2004), p. 58.
30. "Vanishing Spit Ball," *op. cit.*: 455–456.
31. Eugene Murdock, *Baseball Between the Wars: Memories of the Game by the Men Who Played It* (Westport, CT: Meckler, 1992), p. 47.
32. Spalding *Official Baseball Guide of 1935,* quoted by Gene Karst and Martin J. Jones, Jr., *Who's Who in Professional Baseball* (New Rochelle, NY: Arlington House, 1973), p. 250.
33. *New York Herald-Tribune,* March 29, 1957.
34. *Ibid.*
35. *Sporting News,* December 6, 1926.
36. *New York Times,* November 27, 1961.
37. *Ibid.*
38. *Sporting News,* November 29, 1961.
39. *New York Times,* November 29, 1961.
40. *Sporting News,* December 6, 1961.
41. *Ibid.*
42. *Ibid.*
43. *Ibid.*
44. Arthur Daley, *New York Times,* November 27, 1961.
45. Naiph J. Daher, *Baseball Magazine* (July 1931).

Chapter 1

1. *Washington Post,* October 16, 1917.
2. George S. May, "Major League Baseball Players from Iowa," *Palimpsest* 36 (1955):154.
3. Some sources give his middle name as Clarence.

4. James T. Farrell, *"My Baseball Diary: A Famed American Author Recalls the Wonderful World of Baseball, Yesterday and Today* (New York: Barnes, 1957).
5. "The Vanishing Spitball," *Baseball Magazine* (September 1922).
6. *Sporting News,* February 3, 1921.
7. Eugene Murdock, *op. cit.*, p.195.
8. *Ibid.*
9. *New York Times,* April 19, 1964.
10. Brian E. Cooper, quoted by Bill Steinbacher-Kemp, *Illinois-Indiana-Iowa League.* www.threeeye.com. May 18, 2004.
11. James E. Elfers, *The Tour to End All Tours: The Story of Major League Baseball's 1913–1914 World Tour* (Lincoln: University of Nebraska Press, 2003), p. 96.
12. *Ibid.*, p. 101.
13. *Chicago Tribune,* April 18, 1914.
14. *Ibid.*, June 2, 1914.
15. Cooper, *op. cit.*
16. *Los Angeles Times,* February 8, 1955.
17. *Ibid.*, March 3, 1946.
18. John Thorn and John Holway, *Pitcher* (New York: Prentice Hall Press, 1987), p. 45.
19. *Chicago Tribune,* May 13, 1915.
20. Glenn Stout and Richard A. Johnson, *Red Sox Century* (Boston: Houghton Mifflin, 2000).
21. Warren N. Wilbert and William C. Hageman, *The 1917 White Sox: Their World Championship Season* (Jefferson, NC: McFarland, 2004), p. 74.
22. Jack McCarthy, *Boston Herald-American,* February 4, 1977, cited by Leo Trachtenberg, *The Wonder Team: The True Story of the Incomparable 1927 New York Yankees* (Bowling Green, OH: Bowling Green State University Popular Press, 1995), p. 84.
23. *Ibid.*, pp. 146–147.
24. Farrell, *op. cit.*, pp. 58–61.
25. *Ibid.*, p. 185.
26. Bruce Nash and Allan Zullo, *The Baseball Hall of Shame 3* (New York: Pocket Books, 1987), p. 95.
27. Wilbert and Hageman, *op. cit.*, p. 196.
28. Tom Meany, *Baseball's Greatest Teams* (New York: Barnes, 1949).
29. Pete Palmer and Gary Gillette, eds., *The Baseball Encyclopedia* (New York: Barnes and Noble, 2004), p. 1613.
30. Jonathan Fraser Light, *The Cultural History of Baseball* (Jefferson, NC: McFarland, 1997), p. 799.
31. *Los Angeles Times,* June 7, 1918.
32. *Washington Post,* June 16, 1918.
33. Richard Lindberg, *The White Sox Encyclopedia* (Philadelphia: Temple University Press, 1997), p. 25.
34. Richard Lindberg, *Stealing First in a Two-Team Town* (Champaign, IL: Sagamore Publishing, 1994), p. 104. Cited by Wilbert and Hageman, *op. cit.*, p. 74.
35. Farrell, *op. cit.*, p. 201.
36. *Washington Post,* February 5, 1964.
37. Farrell, *op. cit.*, p. 201.
38. Palmer and Gillette, *op. cit.*, p. 1667.
39. Oliver, *op. cit.*, p. 108.
40. Faber, *op. cit.*
41. Thorn and Holway, *op. cit.*, p. 284.
42. W. R. Hoefer, "Urban Faber," *Baseball Magazine* 29 (September 1922): 452.
43. *Ibid.*
44. Farrell, *op. cit.*, p. 201.
45. Wilbert and Hageman, *op. cit.*, p. 134

46. John C. Skipper, *A Biographical Dictionary of the Baseball Hall of Fame* (Jefferson, NC: McFarland, 2000), p. 96.
47. Joseph J. Dittmar, *The Baseball Records Registry: The Best and Worst Single-Day Performances and the Stories behind Them* (Jefferson, NC: McFarland, 1997), pp. 222–223.
48. "The Pitching Wisdom of Red Faber," *Baseball Magazine* 48 (May 1932): 539.
49. *Ibid.*
50. *Ibid.*
51. Farrell, *op. cit.*
52. John Lardner, "Against the Clock," *Newsweek* 51 (February 3, 1958): 84.
53. Jerry E. Clark, *Anson to Zuber: Iowa Boys in the Major Leagues* (Omaha: Making History, 1992), p. 202.
54. Steve Steinberg, personal interview by Charles F. Faber, May 19, 2004.
55. Martin Appel and Burt Goldblatt, *Baseball's Best: The Hall of Fame Gallery* (New York: McGraw-Hill, 1977), p. 148.
56. Urban C. Faber II, personal interview by Charles F. Faber, June 5, 2004.

Chapter 2

1. F. C. Lane, "The Ace of National League Hurlers," *Baseball Magazine* (October 1929).
2. "Burleigh Grimes," www.thebaseballpage.com, April 20, 2004.
3. Lee Allen and Tom Meany, *Kings of the Diamond: The Immortals in Baseball's Hall of Fame* (New York: Putnam, 1965), p. 72.
4. *New York Times,* December 10, 1985.
5. Steve Gelman, *The Greatest Dodgers of Them All* (New York: Penguin Books, 1992), p. 60.
6. Allen and Meany, *op. cit.*, p. 71.
7. Ruth, *op. cit.*, p.77.
8. Anthony J. Connor, *Baseball for the Love of It* (New York: Macmillan, 1982), p. 54.
9. *Sporting News,* October 10, 1964.
10. Gelman, *op. cit.*, p. 78.
11. Headlines in the *New York Times* of January 10, 1918, were as follows: ROBINS GIVE PIRATES TWO PLAYERS FOR THREE IN BIG DEAL. MAMAUX OBTAINED BY ROBINS IN DEAL. TWO OTHER MEN INCLUDED. Burleigh Grimes, Another Twirler, and Chuck Ward an Infielder Will Also Play with Dodgers.
12. Gelman, *op. cit.*, p. 81.
13. Robert Objoski, *Baseball's Strangest Moments* (New York: Sterling, 1988), p. 107.
14. *Ibid.*
15. Gelman, *op. cit.*, p. 61.
16. Jack Kavanagh and Norman Macht, *Uncle Robbie* (Cleveland: Society for American Baseball Research, 1999), p. 134.
17. Meany (1949), *op. cit.*, pp. 75–76.
18. *Ibid.*, p. 76.
19. *Ibid.*
20. Kavanagh and Macht, *op. cit.*, pp. 159–160.
21. Dittmar, *op. cit.*, pp. 196–198.
22. *New York Times,* January 11, 1927.
23. *Sporting News,* February 3, 1921.
24. Lane, *op. cit.*
25. *Ibid.*

26. *Ibid.*
27. *Chicago Tribune,* March 23, 1930.
28. *Ibid.*
29. *Washington Post,* September 30, 1930.
30. *Los Angeles Times,* September 30, 1930.
31. *New York Times,* December 22, 1933.
32. *Ibid.*
33. *New York Times,* December 10, 1931.
34. *Los Angeles Times,* May 19, 1932.
35. Tom Meany, *Baseball's Greatest Pitchers* (New York: Barnes, 1951), p. 84.
36. Robert Obojski, *op. cit.,* p. 72.
37. *Los Angeles Times,* September 30, 1930.
38. John Rice, personal interview by Charles F. Faber, July 1, 2004.
39. Evelyn Trinkle, personal interview by Charles F. Faber, July 2, 2004.
40. Loma Hurst, personal correspondence to Charles F. Faber, June 20, 2004.
41. Ross, *op. cit.*
42. Light, *op. cit.,* p. 128.
43. *Milwaukee Journal Sentinel,* August 17, 2003.

Chapter 3

1. *Los Angeles Times,* April 19, 1946.
2. F. C. Lane, "The Oldest Veteran in the Major Leagues," *Baseball Magazine,* September 1930: 443.
3. *Sporting News,* April 25, 1946.
4. *New York Times,* May 21, 1936.
5. *New York Times,* February 12, 1931.
6. *Sporting News,* September 9, 1963.
7. Kieran (1931), *op. cit.*
8. Jim Zbick, "Jack Quinn: Ageless Wonder," www.tnonline.com (May 17, 2003).
9. www.fortunecity.com/vicorian/mill/1215/wmorris.htm (June 11, 2004).
10. William C. Kashatus, *Diamonds in the Coalfields: 21 Remarkable Baseball Players, Managers, and Umpires from Northeast Pennsylvania* (Jefferson, NC: McFarland, 2002), p. 11.
11. *Ibid.*
12. *New York Times,* July 29, 1931.
13. Kashatus, *op. cit.,* pp. 1–2.
14. Kashatus, *op. cit.,* p. 35.
15. Kashatus, *op. cit.,* pp. 8–9.
16. Kashatus, *op. cit.,* p. 11.
17. Lane, *op. cit.*
18. Zdick, *op. cit.*
19. Lane, *op. cit.*
20. Zdick, *op. cit.*
21. *New York Times,* May 12, 1912.
22. *Chicago Tribune,* April 14, 1914.
23. *New York Times,* December 13, 1918.
24. *Sporting News,* February 3, 1921.
25. *Washington Post,* March 1, 1920.
26. George Herman Ruth, *Babe Ruth's Own Book of Baseball,* Bison Book Edition (Lincoln: University of Nebraska Press, 1992), p. 55–56.
27. Kashatus, *op. cit.,* p. 105.
28. *Washington Post,* November 13, 1930.
29. *Los Angeles Times,* January 9, 1934. The same newspaper reported in its January 24 edition that the vote was 5–1, with the Seals listed on the affirmative side in this account.

30. Clifford Bloodgood, "The Vanishing Spit Ball Pitchers," *Baseball Magazine* 39 (June 1927): 318, 326.
31. "The Oldest Veteran," *op. cit.*
32. *Washington Post,* January 31, 1930.
33. *Ibid.*
34. Lardner, *op. cit.*
35. Kashatus, *op. cit.,* p. 122.

Chapter 4

1. F. C. Lane, "Urban Shocker One of the Great Pitchers of 1920," *Baseball Magazine* (January 1921): 381–382.
2. *New York Times,* March 17, 1916.
3. *Ibid.,* August 13, 1916.
4. Glenn Stout and Richard A. Johnson, *Yankees Century: 100 Years of New York Yankees Baseball* (Boston: Houghton Mifflin, 2002), p. 71.
5. *Sporting News,* February 3, 1921.
6. Murdock, *op. cit.,* p. 47.
7. Godin, *op. cit.,* p. 26.
8. *USA Today Baseball Weekly,* March 11–17, 1999.
9. Mel Allen, "How about That!" *Sport* 9 (October 1950): 9.
10. *Sporting News,* May 29, 1922.
11. Thorn and Holway, *op. cit,* pp. 43–44.
12. Roger Godin, *The 1922 St. Louis Browns: The Best of the American League's Worst* (Jefferson, NC: McFarland, 1991), p. 83.
13. *Ibid.,* pp. 83–84.
14. The 1920 United States Census for Detroit listed Urban Shocker, age 29, baseball player, and his wife, Minerva, age 28, vaudeville actress.
15. *Chicago Tribune,* December 4, 1923.
16. *Sporting News,* September 27, 1923.
17. *Ibid.,* January 3, 1924.
18. Steve L. Steinberg, "Urban Shocker: Free Agency in 1923?" *National Pastime* 20 (2000): 123.
19. Frank Graham, *The New York Yankees: An Informal History* (New York: Putnam, 1943), pp. 103–104.
20. *New York Times,* October 4, 1926.
21. Red Smith, *Red Smith on Baseball: The Game's Greatest Writer on the Game's Greatest Years* (Chicago: Ivan R. Dee, 2000), p. 315.
22. Ruth, *op. cit.,* p. 38.
23. *New York Times,* October 2. 1927.
24. *Washington Post,* October 2, 1927.
25. *Chicago Tribune,* October 4, 1927.
26. *New York Times,* October 10, 1927.
27. Bloodgood, *op. cit..* p. 326.
28. Leo Trachtenberg, *The Wonder Team: The True Story of the Incomparable 1927 New York Yankees* (Bowling Green, OH: Bowling Green State University Popular Press, 1995), p. 92.
29. *Chicago Daily Tribune,* February 17, 1928.
30. Trachtenberg, *op. cit.*
31. *New York Journal-American,* February 15, 1957, cited by Trachtenberg, *ibid.*
32. *Chicago Daily Tribune,* September 10, 1928.
33. Ruth, *op. cit.,* pp. 45–46.
34. Shatzkin, *op. cit.,* p.997.
35. *Sporting News,* January 8, 1931.
36. James, *op. cit.,* p. 236.

Chapter 5

1. Martin Appel and Burt Goldblatt, *Baseball's Best: The Hall of Fame Gallery* (New York: McGraw-Hill, 1977), p. 110.
2. Kashatus, *op. cit.*, p. 31.
3. Raymond J. Nemec, personal correspondence to Charles F. Faber, 2004.
4. Peter Filichia, *Professional Baseball Franchises: From the Abbeville Athletics to the Zanesville Indians* (New York: Facts on File, 1993).
5. Kashatus, *op. cit.*, p. 44.
6. *Ibid.*
7. Lawrence E. Ritter, *The Glory of Their Times: The Story of the Early Days of Baseball Told by the Men Who Played It* (New York: Quill, 1985), pp. 122–123.
8. *Ibid.*, p. 123.
9. "A Good Word for the Spit Ball," *Baseball Magazine* (March 1920).
10. *Ibid.*
11. *Los Angeles Times,* July 8, 1928.
12. *Los Angeles Times,* April 18, 1916.
13. Dave Anderson, "Harry and Stanley," *The National Pastime* 20 (2000): 40.
14. "Stan Coveleskie, www.baseballlibrary.com. July 4, 2004.
15. *New York Times,* October 6, 1920.
16. *Ibid.*
17. *Ibid.*, October 10, 1920.
18. *Ibid.*
19. *Los Angeles Times,* October 13, 1920.
20. *Washington Post,* October 14, 1920.
21. *Ibid.,* October 13, 1920.
22. Palmer and Gillette, *op cit.*
23. *Chicago Tribune,* October 21, 1920.
24. *Sporting News,* February 3, 1921.
25. *Sporting News,* January 27, 1921.
26. Harry Grayson, *They Played the Game: The Story of Baseball Greats* (New York: Barnes, 1944), p. 92.
27. *Ibid.*
28. Dittmar, *op. cit.*, pp. 176–178.
29. *New York Times,* November 27, 1961.
30. *Washington Post,* December 12, 1924.
31. *Ibid.*, January 3, 1925.
32. *Ibid.*, January 14, 1925.
33. *Ibid.*, September 29, 1925.
34. Eric Weiss, "Hall of Fame Pitching Match-ups," paper presented at SABR National Convention, Cincinnati, OH, July 16, 2004.
35. Thorn and Holway, *op. cit.*, p. 55.
36. *Washington Post,* May 15, 1927.
37. *Ibid.,* June 18, 1927.
38. *New York Times,* December 22, 1927.
39. *Los Angeles Times,* July 8, 1928.
40. "The Name Behind Stanley Coveleski Regional Stadium," www.silverhawks.com/mediaguide, 2003.

Chapter 6

1. Stephen Boren, "Bill Doak's Three No-Hitters," *Baseball Research Journal* 31 (2002): 62.
2. Stephen Steinberg in Tom Simon, ed., *Deadball Stars of the National League* (Washington: Brassey's, 2004), p. 358.
3. *Ibid.*
4. C. P. Stack, "Doak, of the Cardinals," *Baseball Magazine* 14 (November 1914): 86.
5. Cited by James and Neyer, *op. cit.*, p. 186.
6. *Sporting News,* February 3, 1921.
7. *New York Times,* November 11, 1961.
8. Stack, *op. cit.*, p. 85.
9. *Los Angeles Times,* March 27, 1932.
10. *Washington Post,* February 9, 1922.
11. *New York Times,* March 8, 1925.
12. Bloodgood, *op. cit.*, p. 326.
13. *Ibid.*, March 17, 1928.
14. *Washington Post,* January 11, 1932.
15. *Washington Post,* June 21, 1936.
16. Steinberg, *op. cit.*
17. *Ibid.*

Chapter 7

1. Bill Stern, *Bill Stern's Favorite Baseball Stories,* Garden City, NY: Doubleday, 1949), p. 113.
2. Russell J. Schneider, *The Cleveland Indians Encyclopedia*, 2nd ed. (Champaign, IL: Sports Publishing L. L. C., 2001), p.141.
3. Some sources list his birthplace as Croydon, Pennsylvania.
4. *Washington Post,* August 4, 1912.
5. *New York Times,* September 10, 1910.
6. *Ibid.*, March 1, 1911.
7. *Ibid.*, June 15, 1913.
8. *Washington Post,* July 1912.
9. *New York Times,* August 1, 1913.
10. *Washington Post,* August 13, 1913.
11. *New York Times,* March 9, 1914.
12. *New York Times,* March 21, 1914.
13. *Encyclopedia Britannica*, 11th ed., Vol. 8 (Cambridge: University Press, 1911), p. 601.
14. *New York Times,* November 27, 1914; December 3, 1915.
15. *Washington Post,* March 12, 1915.
16. *New York Times,* June 5, 1915.
17. John J. Ward, "Ray Caldwell, the Hard Luck Pitcher," *Baseball Magazine,* September 1916.
18. *Ibid.*
19. *Ibid.*
20. *Sporting News,* February 3, 1921.
21. *Washington Post,* November 29, 1916.
22. *Ibid.*, December 19, 1916.
23. *Ibid.*, December 31, 1916.
24. *Ibid.*, February 25, 1917.
25. *New York Times,* August 18, 1918; August 20, 1918.
26. *Ibid.*, December 19, 1918.
27. Cited in James and Neyer, *op. cit.*, p. 155.
28. Gutman, *op. cit.*, p. 162.
29. *New York Times,* October 8, 1920.
30. *Ibid.*
31. *New York Times,* September 26, 1921.
32. *Washington Post,* April 19, 1933.
33. *Sporting News,* May 3, 1961; June 7, 1961.

Chapter 8

1. Andrea Paul, "The Life and Times of Clarence Mitchell," *NEBRASKAland,* August 1993: 38.
2. *Ibid.*
3. Dittmar, *op. cit.,* pp. 82–85.
4. Paul, *op. cit.,* p. 40.
5. Jerry E. Clark, *Nebraska Diamonds: A Brief History of Baseball Major Leaguers from the Cornhusker State* (Omaha: Making History, 1991), p. 17.
6. *Ibid.,* p. 41.
7. *Ibid.,* p. 41.
8. *New York Times,* June 13, 1918.
9. *New York Times,* February 16, 1923.
10. *Washington Post,* February 16, 1923.
11. *Chicago Tribune,* March 31, 1923.
12. Paul, *op. cit.,* p. 44.
13. *New York Times,* June 7, 1928.
14. *Los Angeles Times,* September 30, 1928.
15. Paul, *op. cit.,* p. 44.
16. *Washington Post,* October 10, 1928.
17. *Chicago Tribune,* March 3, 1937.
18. Paul, *op. cit.,* pp. 42, 44–45.
19. Dittmar, *op. cit.,* pp. 224–225.
20. *Ibid.,* p. 45.
21. *Ibid.*
22. Clark, *op cit.,* p. 18.
23. *Ibid.,* p. 74.

Chapter 9

1. *Los Angeles Times,* October 12, 1915.
2. *Chicago Tribune,* April 25, 1915.
3. Stout and Johnson, *op. cit.,* p. 96.
4. Ruth, *op. cit.,* p. 36.
5. *Los Angeles Times,* October 12, 1915.
6. *Washington Post,* March 21, 1952.
7. *New York Times,* October 12, 1916.
8. *Ibid.*
9. *New York Times,* July 11, 1917.
10. *Los Angeles Times,* May 21, 1919.
11. Gutman, *op. cit.,* p. 187.
12. *Ibid.,* p. 188.
13. Light, *op. cit.,* p. 290.

Chapter 10

1. John Leidy, Jr., correspondence to Charles F. Faber, May 17, 2004.
2. *Ibid.*
3. *Ibid.*
4. *Ibid.,* May 16, 2004.
5. *Ibid.*
6. *Ibid.,* May 17, 2004.
7. Dittmar, *op. cit.,* pp. 159–160.
8. *Sporting News,* February 3, 1921.
9. Leidy, May 17, 2004.
10. *Ibid.,* November 13, 2004.
11. *Ibid.,* May 18, 2004.
12. *Ibid.*
13. *Ibid.,* November 13, 2004.
14. *Ibid.,* May 20, 2004.
15. *Ibid.*
16. Shatzkin, *op. cit.,* p. 338

Chapter 11

1. *Deadball Stars, op. cit.,* p. 327.
2. *New York Times,* February 19, 1911.
3. F.C. Lane, "Dick Rudolph, Pennant Winner," *Baseball Magazine* 14 (February 1915): 40.
4. Harold Kaese, *The Boston Braves* (New York: Putnam, 1948), p. 143.
5. *Ibid.,* p. 162.
6. Lane, *op. cit.,* pp. 38–39.
7. *Ibid.,* p. 39.
8. Cited by James and Neyer, *op. cit.,* p. 366.
9. F.C. Lane, "Should the Spitball be Abolished?" *Baseball Magazine* 23 (June 1919): 70.
10. F.C. Lane, "When the Pitcher Meets the Batter in a Battle of Wits," *Baseball Magazine* 15 (Aug. 1915): 66.

Chapter 12

1. There is some dispute about Sothoron's college experience. John Spalding wrote that he had attended Albion College; some writers opined that he played for Albright College. We are accepting the findings of Rick Benner, the nation's foremost researcher on the matter whose extensive research found that Sothoron had played only for Juniata. Rick Benner, personal correspondence to Charles F. Faber, September 2004.
2. *Los Angeles Times,* June 5, 1916.
3. John E. Spalding, *Pacific Coast League Stars, Vol. 2: Ninety Who Made it in the Majors, 1903–1957* (San Jose, CA: Spalding, 1997), pp. 33–34.
4. *Washington Post,* September 18, 1914.
5. www.BaseballLibrary.com, July 3, 2004.
6. *Washington Post,* January 7, 1924.
7. Ty Cobb, *Memoirs of Twenty Years in Baseball,* p. 69.
8. *Los Angeles Times,* September 24, 1933.
9. *Washington Post,* July 20, 1933.
10. Lee, *op. cit.,* p. 375.

Chapter 13

1. Tom Clark, *One Last Round for the Shuffler* (New York; Truck Books, 1979).
2. *Ibid.,* p. 13.
3. *Ibid.,* p. 14.
4. *Ibid.,* p. 22.
5. *Ibid.,* p. 11.
6. *Chicago Tribune,* August 31, 1912.
7. *New York Times,* September 10, 1918.
8. John Lardner, "The Snake Pit and the Letter," *Newsweek* 41 (June 15, 1953): 91.
9. Tom Clark, *op. cit.,* pp. 79–80.
10. Gutman, *op. cit.,* p. 145.
11. Stant and Johnson, *Yankee Century* (Boston: Houghton Mifflin, 2002), p. 181.
12. *Washington Post,* August 5, 1922.
13. *Ibid.,* August 9, 1922.
14. See for example, Lardner, Light, Gutman, Shatzin, and various Web sites, such as http://www.BaseballLibrary.com.
15. *Chicago Tribune,* August 17, 1922; *New York*

Times, August 17, 1922; *Los Angeles Times,* August 17, 1922.
  16. *New York Times,* August 17, 1922.
  17. *Chicago Tribune,* August 17, 1922.
  18. *Sporting News,* August 24, 1922.
  19. *Los Angeles Times,* August 19, 1922.
  20. *Washington Post,* August 22, 1922.
  21. *New York Times,* August 29, 1922.
  22. *The Sporting News,* August 24, 1922.
  23. *Ibid.*
  24. *Washington Post,* October 12, 1922.
  25. *New York Times,* October 13, 1922.
  26. *Washington Post,* August 5, 1923.
  27. Gutman, *op. cit,* pp. 147–148.
  28. *Ibid.,* p. 148.
  29. Tom Clark, *op. cit.,* p. 253.

Chapter 14

  1. Ruth, *op. cit.,* p. 76.
  2. *New York Times,* September 18, 1915.
  3. *New York Press,* September 18, 1915.
  4. Norman Macht, personal correspondence to Charles F. Faber, August 4, 2004.
  5. Thorn, *op. cit.,* p. 447.
  6. *Sporting News,* February 3, 1921.
  7. James, *op. cit.,* p. 201.

Chapter 15

  1. Tom Hufford, personal correspondence to Charles F. Faber, July 19, 2004. Other sources (e.g. Baseball-reference.com) state that Doc attended Roanoke College from 1909 to 1913.
  2. *Washington Post,* February 23, 1917.
  3. *Washington Post,* March 31, 1913.
  4. *Chicago Tribune,* May 10, 1914.
  5. *Washington Post,* March 22, 1914.
  6. *Ibid,* March 3, 1943.
  7. Billy Evans, "An Unusual Performance," *Harper's Weekly* 58 (May 23, 1914): 25.

  8. J. C. Kofoed, "Major Leaguers Who Were Downright Unlucky," *Baseball Monthly* 32 (February 1924): 403.
  9. *Sporting News,* May 12, 1921.
  10. *Washington Post,* February 23, 1917.
  11. *Ibid.,* April 26, 1917.
  12. Hufford, *op. cit.*
  13. *Ibid.*
  14. *Ibid.*

Chapter 16

  1. *New York World-Telegram,* September 12, 1933.
  2. *Atlanta Constitution,* February 27, 1920.
  3. *Sporting News,* February 2, 1921.
  4. *Washington Post, Times Herald,* August 19, 1962.
  5. *Ibid.*

Chapter 17

  1. *Washington Post,* March 22, 1916.
  2. *Ibid.*
  3. *Ibid.,* March 27, 1916.
  4. *Ibid.,* April 22, 1916.
  5. Marvin Goodwin file, National Baseball Hall of Fame, Cooperstown, N.Y.
  6. *Ibid.*
  7. *Ibid.*
  8. *Sporting News,* December 6, 1917.
  9. Goodwin file, *op. cit.*
  10. *Sporting News,* May 29, 1924.
  11. *New York Times,* May 20, 1951.
  12. Dusty Bogess as told to Ernie Helm, *Kill the Ump!* (San Antonio: Lone Star Brewing), 1966. p. 55.
  13. *Chicago Tribune,* October 19, 1925.
  14. *Sporting News,* November 5, 1925.
  15. Donald Dewey and Nicholas Acocella, *The Biographical History of Baseball* (New York: Carroll and Graf, 1995), p. 175.

Bibliography

Allen, Lee, and Tom Meany. *Kings of the Diamond: The Immortals in Baseball's Hall of Fame.* New York: G.P. Putnam's Sons, 1965.

Allen, Mel. "How about That," *Sport* 9 (October 1950).

Anderson, Dave. "Harry and Stanley." *National Pastime* (2000): 39–41.

Appel, Martin, and Burt Goldblatt. *Baseball's Best: The Hall of Fame Gallery.* New York: McGraw-Hill, 1977.

Bloodgood, Clifford. "The Vanishing Spitball Pitchers." *Baseball Magazine* 39 (June 1927): 318–319.

Boren, Stephen. "Bill Doak's Three No-Hitters." *Baseball Research Journal* 31 (2002): 62–63.

Bradley, Hugh. "Stars in the Sunset." *Baseball Magazine* 58 (February 1937): 387–388, 432.

Browning, Reed. *Baseball's Greatest Season: 1924.* Amherst: University of Massachusetts Press, 2003.

"Burleigh Grimes." www.thebaseballpage.com. April 20, 2004.

Clark, Jerry E. *Anson to Zuber: Iowa Boys in the Major Leagues.* Omaha: Making History, 1992.

_____. *Nebraska Diamonds: A Brief History of Baseball Major Leaguers from the Cornhusker State.* Omaha: Making History, 1991.

Clark, Tom. *One Last Round for the Shuffler.* New York: Truck Books and Pomerica Press, 1979.

Connor, Anthony J. *Baseball for the Love of It.* New York: Macmillan, 1982.

Daher, Naiph J. "The Spitter Hits the Trail." *Baseball Magazine* (July 1931).

Daniel, W. Harrison, and Scott P. Mayer. *Baseball and Richmond: A History of the Professional Game, 1889–2000.* Jefferson, NC: McFarland, 2003.

Dewey, Donald, and Nicholas Acocella. *The Biographical History of Baseball.* New York: Carroll and Graf, 1995.

Dittmar, Joseph J. *Baseball Record Registry: The Best and Worst Single-Day Performances and the Stories Behind Them.* Jefferson, NC: McFarland, 1997.

Elfers, James E. *The Tour to End All Tours: The Story of Major League Baseball's 1913–1914 World Tour.* Lincoln: University of Nebraska Press, 2003.

Evans, Billy. "The Tough Break." *Harper's Weekly* 58 (June 13, 1914).

Faber, Charles F. *Baseball Ratings: The All-Time Best Players at Each Position.* Jefferson, NC: McFarland, 1995.

Farrell, James T. *My Baseball Diary: A Famed American Author Recalls the Wonderful World of Baseball, Yesterday and Today.* New York: Barnes, 1957.

Filichia, Peter. *Professional Baseball Franchises: From the Abbeville Athletics to the Zanesville Indians.* New York: Facts on File, 1993.

Gelman, Steve. *The Greatest Dodgers of Them All.* New York: Putnam, 1968.

Godin, Roger A. *The 1922 St. Louis Browns: Best of the American League's Worst.* Jefferson, NC: McFarland, 1991

Graham, Frank. *The New York Yankees: An Informal History.* New York: Putnam, 1943

Grayson, Harry. *They Played the Game: The Story of Baseball Greats.* New York: Barnes, 1944.

Gutman, Dan. *Baseball Babylon.* New York: Penguin Books, 1992.

Honig, Donald. *Baseball America.* New York: Macmillan, 1985.

James, Bill, and Rob Neyer. *The Neyer/James Guide to Pitchers.* New York: Simon and Schuster, 2004.

Johnson, Lloyd, and Miles Wolff, eds. *The Encyclopedia of Minor League Baseball.* Durham, NC: Baseball America, 1993.

Jordan, David M. *The Athletics of Philadelphia: Connie Mack's White Elephants, 1901–1954.* Jefferson, NC: McFarland, 1999.

Kaese, Harold. *The Boston Braves.* New York: Putnam, 1948.

Karst, Gene, and Martin J. Jones, Jr. *Who's Who in Professional Baseball.* New York: Arlington House, 1973.

Kashatus, William C. *Diamonds in the Coalfields: 21 Remarkable Baseball Players, Managers, and Umpires from Northeast Pennsylvania*. Jefferson, NC: McFarland, 2002.

Kavanagh, Jack, and Norman Macht. *Uncle Robbie*. Cleveland: Society for American Baseball Research, 1999.

Kofoed, J.C. "Major Leaguers Who Were Downright Unlucky." *Baseball Magazine* 32 (February 1924): 403–405.

Lane, F.C. "The Ace of National League Hurlers." *Baseball Magazine* (October 1929).

____. "Dick Rudolph: Pennant Winner." *Baseball Magazine* 14 (May 1915): 37–41.

____. "The Oldest Veteran in the Major Leagues." *Baseball Magazine* (September 1930).

____. "Should the Spit Ball Be Abolished?" *Baseball Magazine* 23 (June 1919): 67–70, 118.

____. "Urban Shocker, One of the Great Pitchers of 1920." *Baseball Magazine* (January 1921).

____. "When Pitcher Meets Batter in a Battle of Wits." *Baseball Magazine* 15 (August 1915): 58–67.

Lardner, John. "Against the Clock." *Newsweek* 51 (February 3, 1958).

____. "The Snake Pit and the Letter." *Newsweek* 51 (June 15, 1953).

Lee, Bill. *The Baseball Necrology: The Post-Baseball Lives and Deaths of Over 7,600 Major League Players and Others*. Jefferson, NC: McFarland, 2003.

Lieb, Frederick G. *The St. Louis Cardinals: The Story of a Great Baseball Club*. New York: Putnam, 1945.

Light, Jonathan Fraser. *The Cultural History of Baseball*. Jefferson, NC: McFarland, 1997.

Lindberg, Richard. *Stealing First in a Two-Team Town*. Champaign, IL: Sagamore, 1994.

____. *The White Sox Encyclopedia*. Philadelphia: Temple University Press, 1997.

May, George S. "Major League Baseball Players from Iowa." *Palimpsest* 36 (1955): 133–164.

Meany, Tom. *Baseball's Greatest Pitchers*. New York: Barnes, 1951.

____. *Baseball's Greatest Teams*. New York: Barnes, 1949.

Murdock, Eugene. *Baseball between the Wars: Memories of the Game by the Men Who Played It*. Westport, CT: Meckler, 1992.

Nash, Bruce, and Allan Zullo. *The Baseball Hall of Shame 3*. New York: Pocket Books, 1987.

Obojski, Robert. *Baseball's Strangest Moments*. New York: Sterling, 1988.

____. *Bush League: A History of Minor League Baseball*. New York: Macmillan, 1975

Oliver, Ted C. *Kings of the Mound*. 2nd ed. Los Angeles: The Author, 1947.

O'Neal, Bill. *The American Association: A Baseball History, 1902–91*. Austin: Eakin Press, 1991.

____. *The International League: A Baseball History, 1884–1991*. Austin: Eakin Press, 1992.

____. *The Pacific Coast League, 1903–1998*. Austin: Eakin Press, 1990.

Palmer, Pete, and Gary Gillette, eds. *The Baseball Encyclopedia*. New York: Barnes and Noble, 2004.

Paul, Andrea. "The Life and Times of Clarence Mitchell." *NEBRASKAland* (August 1993).

Porter, David L., ed. *Biographical Dictionary of American Sports*. Westport, CT: Greenwood Press, 1987.

Rapoport, Ron. "Should They Legalize the Spitball?" *Baseball Digest* 12 (December 1972): 39–44.

Reidenbaugh, Lowell. *Baseball's Hall of Fame: Where the Legends Live Forever*. New York: Arlington House, 1986.

Ritter, Lawrence E. *The Glory of Their Times: The Story of the Early Days of Baseball Told by the Men who Played It*. New York: Quill, 1985.

Ruth, George Herman. *Babe Ruth's Own Book of Baseball*. Lincoln: University of Nebraska Press, 1992.

Schneider, Russell J. *The Cleveland Indians Encyclopedia*, 2nd ed. Champaign, IL: Sports Publishing, 2001.

Shatzkin, Mike, ed. *The Ballplayers: Baseball's Ultimate Biographical Reference*. New York: Arbor House and William Morrow, 1990.

Simon, Tom, ed. *Deadball Stars of the National League*. Washington: Brassey's, 2004.

Skipper, John C. *A Biographical Dictionary of the Baseball Hall of Fame*. Jefferson, NC: McFarland, 2000.

Smith, Ira. *Baseball's Famous Pitchers*. New York: Barnes, 1954.

Smith, Red. *Red Smith on Baseball: The Game's Greatest Writer on the Game's Greatest Years*. Chicago: Dee, 2000.

Snelling, Dennis. *The Pacific Coast League: A Statistical History, 1903–1957*. Jefferson, NC: McFarland, 1995.

Spalding, John E. *Pacific Coast League Stars, Vol. II: Ninety Who Made it to the Majors 1903–1957*. San Jose: Spalding, 1997.

Stack, C.P. "Doak, of the Cardinals." *Baseball Magazine* 14 (November 1914): 85–86.

Steinbacher-Kemp, Bill. *Illinois-Indiana-Iowa League*. http://www.three-eye.com, 2004.

Steinberg, Steve L. *Baseball in St. Louis, 1900–1925*. Charleston, SC: Arcadia, 2004.

____. "The Spitball and the End of the Deadball Era." *National Pastime* 23 (2003): 7–17.

____. "Urban Shocker: Free Agency in 1923?" *National Pastime* 20 (2000): 121–123.

Stern, Bill. *Bill Stern's Favorite Baseball Stories*. Garden City, NY: Doubleday, 1949.

Stockton, J. Roy. *The Gashouse Gang and a Couple of Other Guys*. New York: Barnes, 1945.

Stout, Glenn, and Richard A. Johnson. *Red Sox Century*. Boston: Houghton Mifflin, 2000.
_____. *Yankees Century*. Boston: Houghton Mifflin, 2002.
Thorn, John, and John B. Holway. *The Pitcher*. New York: Prentice Hall, 1987.
Ward, John J. "Ray Caldwell, the Hard Luck Pitcher." *Baseball Magazine* 17 (September 1916): 33–36.
Wilbert, Warren H., and William C. Hageman. *The 1917 White Sox: Their Championship Season*. Jefferson, NC: McFarland, 2004.
Wright, Marshall D. *The American Association: Year-by-Year Statistics for the Baseball Minor League*. Jefferson, NC: McFarland, 1997.
_____. *The International League: Year-by-Year Statistics, 1884–1953*. Jefferson, NC: McFarland, 1998.
_____. *The Southern Association in Baseball, 1885–1961*. Jefferson, NC: McFarland, 2002.
Zbick, Jim. "Jack Quinn: Ageless Wonder." www.tnonline.com. May 17, 2003.
Zingg, Paul J., and Mark D. Medeiros. *Runs, Hits, and an Era: The Pacific Coast League 1903–58*. Urbana: University of Illinois Press, 1994.

Newspapers

Atlanta Constitution
Chicago Tribune
Los Angeles Times
Milwaukee Journal Sentinel
New York Daily News
New York Herald-Tribune
New York Press
New York Times
New York World
Sporting News
Washington Post

Index

Accidental deaths 6, 19, 77, 153, 184
Adams, Babe 191
Alcohol use 64, 66, 98, 100–101, 105–106, 150, 152, 154–157
Aldridge, Vic 44
Alexander, Grover 43, 65, 69, 72, 75, 116–117, 119, 122, 137, 142, 182, 190–191
Allen, Lee 38, 54
Allen, Mel 69
Ayers, Doc 5, 12, 167–173, 187–189, 192
Ayers, Elizabeth Dunlap 173
Ayers, Jefferson 167
Ayers, Mildred 173
Ayers, Yancey, Jr. 173

Baer, Bugs 145
Bagby, Jim 39, 77, 82, 106
Baker, Frank 69, 169
Baker, Newton 27
Ballou, Win 165
Bancroft, Dave 90
Bancroft, Frank 113
Barnhart, Clyde 149
Barrow, Ed 87
Barry, Jack 25, 169–170
Baseball gloves 93, 95
Bassler, Johnny 107
Beck, Fred 138
Bedient, Hugh 121
Bender, Chief 120, 140
Benton, Larry 61
Benton, Rube 26
Benz, Joe 27
Bezdek, Hugo 38
Bishop, Max 47
Blackburne, Lena 22
Blankenship, Ted 71
Bloodgood, Clifford 63, 73, 94
Blue, Lu 107
Bluege, Ossie 165
Boeckel, Tony 176
Boggess, Dusty 184
Boone, Dan 102
Boren, Steve 113
Bottomley, Jim 117
Braden, Kittie 112
Braden, Samuel 112
Branham, W.H. 63

Breadon, Sam 116
Brecheen, Harry 77, 83
Brickell, Fred 52
Brown, Buster 139
Brown, Three Finger 64
Burg, Pete 138
Burkett, Jesse 151, 155–158
Burnham, Walter 138
Bush, Donie 22, 31, 58
Bush, Joe 23, 60, 71, 190
Butler, John 43, 49

Cadore, Leon 39
Cady, Forest 23
Caldwell, Estelle 110
Caldwell, James 110
Caldwell, Ray 5, 12, 39, 66, 77, 98–110, 125, 187–188, 191–192
Callahan, Nixey 21–22, 153
Campbell, Colin 3
Carlson, Hal 5
Carlton, Steve 29
Carrigan, Rough 122–124
Casey, Hugh 61
Caswell, Henry 135
Chance, Frank 22, 100–101
Chapman, Ray 6, 19, 77, 153
Cheney, Larry 37–38
Chesbro, Jack 4, 7, 13
Cicotte, Eddie 5, 11, 25–26, 28
Clabaugh, Moose 43
Clark, Jerry 34, 119
Clark, Tom 156
Clarke, Fred 19
Clemons, Verne 183
Cobb, Ty 20, 29–30, 102–103, 120, 123, 126–128, 172
Cochrane, Mickey 46
Coffey, Jack 113
Cole, Bert 107
Coleman, Bob 19
Collins, Eddie 22, 25–28, 163, 169
Collins, Ray 122
Collins, Rip 60
Collins, Shano 25, 28, 163
Combs, Earle 176
Comiskey, Charles 20, 24, 27–28, 32, 59, 152
Comiskey, Lou 30
Coolidge, Calvin 87
Coolidge, Grace 87

Coombs, Jack 41
Cooper, Wilbur 191
Corum, Bill 74
Coveleskie, Frances 89
Coveleskie, Frank 78
Coveleskie, Harry 78, 80, 88
Coveleskie, Jacob 78
Coveleskie, John 78
Coveleskie, Stan 5, 6, 9, 11–13, 34, 39, 64, 77–89, 94, 106, 187–192
Coveleskie, William 89
Covington, Ella 166
Covington, Sam 175
Cox, Dick 43
Cox, James 83, 178
Crawford, Sam 22
Cronin, Joe 14
Cruisenberry, Jim 23
Crum, Cal 175
Cullop, Nick 66, 131
Cunningham, George 80
Cutshaw, George 37–38, 123
Cuyler, Kiki 61, 86, 149
Cy Young award, ex post facto 29, 41, 44–45, 86

Daher, Naiph 15
Daley, Arthur 15, 85, 183
Daniel, Dan 174
Daubert, Jake 37, 41
Dauss, George 22
Deadball Era 2, 4, 8, 131, 154
Dean, Dizzy 47, 64, 75, 108, 118
DeBerry, Hank 42–43
Dick, Lucy 105
Dickerman, Leo 93
Dittmar, Joe 85
Doak, Bertha Shattenbrand 97
Doak, Bill 3, 5–6, 9–10, 12, 63, 90–97, 187–192
Doak, Jesse Porter 87
Doak, Robert 90, 96
Doak, William E. (father of Bill) 90
Doak, William E. (son of Bill) 97
Doctoring the baseball 4, 8, 68–69, 133, 147
Donovan, Bill 104
Douglas, Eunice 152
Douglas, Jacqueline Hodges 160
Douglas, John A. 151

203

Douglas, Louise Wepf 152, 159–160
Douglas, Mary Louise 152
Douglas, Phil 5, 10, 12–13, 152–160, 187–189, 191–192
Doyle, Larry 38, 138
Drebinger, John 46, 73, 92
Dreyfuss, Barney 4–5, 45–46
Drysdale, Don 64
Duboc, Jean 58
Dugan, Joe 24, 98
Dylan, Bob 89

Earnshaw, George 46–47
Easterly, Ted 143
Ebbets, Charles 41, 114, 154
Ellerbe, Frank 70
Embarrassing moments 26, 129
Emery balls 4, 8, 147
Engel, Joe 169
Erickson, Eric 172
Evans, Billy 7, 10, 20, 66, 69, 84, 92, 103, 133, 155, 163, 176–177
Evers, Johnny 22

Faber, Charles F. 29, 188
Faber, Frances Knudtzon 34
Faber, Irene Walsh 30, 34
Faber, Margaret 17
Faber, Nicholas 17, 34
Faber, Red 5–7, 9, 12–15, 17–33, 50–51, 66, 68, 71, 77, 83, 86–88, 142, 187–192
Faber, Urban II 34
Faber System 1–2, 29, 39, 41, 44, 68, 93, 102, 122, 187–191
Farrell, James T. 28, 32
Feller, Bob 34, 125
Felsch, Happy 26, 28, 133, 163
Ferguson, Alex 44
Filichia, Peter 78
Fillingim, Ava Fort 179
Fillingim, Dana 5, 12, 174–179, 187–189, 192
Fillingim, Henry Vann 174
Fillingim, Terah Fort 174
Fines 66, 70–72, 99, 101, 104, 153, 156, 168
Fisher, Albert 129
Fisher, Alice Seeley 130
Fisher, Anthony 129
Fisher, Emerett New 129
Fisher, Ray 5, 7, 12, 99, 105, 129–136, 187–189, 192
Fitzgerald, J.V. 173
Flagstead, Ira 85
Fleming, David P. 63
Fletcher, Art 116
Fonseca, Lew 22
Ford, Gerald 135–136
Ford, Russell 147
Ford, Whitey 64
Foster, Eddie 170
Foster, Rube 122–123
Fournier, Jack 43, 90, 93
Foxx, Jimmie 46–47
Frankhouse, Fred 46
Frazee, Harry 60
Freak deliveries see doctoring the baseball; emery balls; mud balls; raised seams; shine balls; spitballs

Frick, Ford 14, 135
Frisch, Frank 39
Fullerton, Hugh 116

Gaffney, James E. 58
Gallagher, Joe 14
Gallia, Bert 5, 11
Gandil, Chick 25, 28, 133, 170
Gardner, Larry 25, 77
Gaston, Milt 71
Gazella, Mike 76
Gedeon, Joe 66, 131
Gehrig, Lou 72, 76
Gehring, Hank 36
Gehringer, Charlie 30
Gelman, Steve 38
George V, King of England 21
Giard, Joe 71
Gibson, Bob 96, 119
Giles, Warren 14
Gilhooey, Frank 105, 125
Gillette, Gary 27, 41, 44–45, 82, 86
Gleason, Kid 21–22
Godin, Roger 70
Goebel, Al 174
Goodwin, Allan 180, 185
Goodwin, Marvin 5, 12, 180–185, 187–189, 192
Goodwin, Mary 180
Goodwin, P.M. 180
Goodwin, Peyton 180
Goodwin, Susie May Boughan 180
Gowdy, Hank 165
Grantham, George 42, 149, 183
Grayson, Harry 84
Griffith, Clark 4–5, 86, 114, 161, 168–170, 172, 180–181
Griffith, Tommy 106
Grimes, Burleigh 5–7, 9–15, 20, 34–52, 64, 81–82, 88, 93, 110, 112, 114, 117, 187–192
Grimes, Cecil 35
Grimes, Florence van Patten 51
Grimes, Inez Martin 52
Grimes, Laura 51
Grimes, Lillian 52
Grimes, Ruth Tuttle 35
Grimes, Zerita Brickell 52
Grimm, Charlie 32, 52
Groom, Bob 146
Grove, Lefty 46–47, 191
Gutman, Dan 128

Hagerman, Rip 22
Haines, Jesse 72, 75, 191
Hall of Fame see Iowa Sports Hall of Fame; Loras College Athletic Hall of Fame; National Baseball Hall of Fame; Nebraska Sports Hall of Fame; Polish-American Hall of Fame
Hallahan, Bill 47
Hamlin, Luke 150
Harder, Mel 119
Harding, Warren G. 83
Harmon, Tom 135
Harper, George 44
Harridge, Will 135
Harris, Bucky 165
Harrison, James B. 44

Hart, Bill 176
Hartley, Grover 123
Hartnett, Gabby 42, 61
Hatten, Clyde 150
Hayworth, Ray 20
Heathcote, Cliff 131
Heilmann, Harry 85, 128
Helm, Ernie 184
Hendricks, Jack 121, 178
Hendrix, Claude 5, 11
Hendryx, Tim 66
Henline, Walter 44
Henry, John 170
Herman, Babe 32
Herrmann, Garry 123, 134, 136, 139, 178
Herzog, Buck 153
Heving, Joe 150
Heydler, John 4
Hill, Hunter 183
Hillenbrand, George 69
Hinchman, Bill 37
Hinckley, David 4
Hoefer, W.R. 29–30
Hogg, Brad 5, 11, 176
Holke, Walter 26, 176
Holway, John 29, 80–81, 85, 87, 122
Hooper, Harry 25, 154
Hornsby, Rogers 44, 90, 131, 149–150
Horstman, Oscar 145
Houk, Ralph 14
Hoyt, Waite 68, 72–73, 75–76, 141, 191
Hubbard, Cal 15
Hubbell, Carl 116
Hufford, Tom 173
Huggins, Miller 69, 71–72, 74, 91, 163

Illnesses 47, 65, 72–75, 88, 109–110, 119, 131, 150, 156, 158–160
Ineligible list 134–136, 153, 158, 160, 168
Injuries 19, 23, 44–46, 48, 63, 66, 68–69, 87, 103–104, 114, 126, 160, 163, 170, 177, 179, 184
Iowa Sports Hall of Fame 35
Irwin, Arthur 99, 130

Jackson, Joe 26, 28, 133, 135
Jackson, Travis 165
James, Bill (author) 2, 75, 164
James, Bill (pitcher) 137, 140–142
Jamieson, Charlie 77
Jennings, Hughie 112
Jim Creighton award 29, 45, 80–81, 122
Johnson, Ban 4, 57–59, 102, 128, 168
Johnson, Richard A. 156
Johnson, Walter 6, 24, 27, 29, 69, 86, 102, 142, 165, 182, 190–191
Johnston, Doc 77
Johnston, Jimmie 106, 123, 176
Jones, Percy 46
Jones, Sam 60, 191
Joss, Addie 125
Judd, Ralph 117

Index

Kashatus, William C. 54, 56, 78
Kauff, Benny 26
Kavenaugh, Marty 22
Keating, Ray 5
Keener, Sid 75
Kelley, Joe 138
Keltner, Ken 150
Kerr, Dickie 28, 133
Kieran, John 53–54
Kilduff, Pete 40–41–110
Killefer, Bill 150
Klem, Bill 4, 26
Kluszewski, Ted 89
Kofoed, J.C. 170
Konetchy, Ed 81, 114
Koufax, Sandy 64, 90, 142
Kowaleweski *see* Coveleskie
Kuhn, Bowie 135–136

Laabs, Chet 150
Lambert, Ross 63
Landis, Kenesaw M. 25, 50, 70–71, 74, 128, 134, 136, 158–160, 184
Lane, Bill 63
Lane, F.C. 40, 65, 142
Lannin, Joe 123
Laporte, Frank 99
Lapp, Jack 102
Lardner, John 33–34, 64, 156
Lazzeri, Tony 49, 72
League leaders 21, 23–24, 27, 29–30, 33, 39, 41, 43–45, 48, 59–60, 65–66, 68–70, 72, 74, 77, 80–81, 85–86, 88, 92–93, 96, 101–102, 109, 121–122, 125–126, 129–132, 137, 139–140, 143, 146–147, 150, 152, 154–156, 162, 164, 168–170, 181
Le Bourveau, Bevo 90
Lee, Bill 150
Legal difficulties 58, 70–71, 101, 105, 158–159, 184–185
Leidy, Janet Fisher 130
Leidy, John, Jr. 131, 135–136
Leonard, Cuyler 120
Leonard, David 120
Leonard, Dutch *see* Leonard, Emil; Leonard, Hubert
Leonard, Ella 120
Leonard, Elmer 120
Leonard, Emil "Dutch" 120
Leonard, Hubert "Dutch" 5, 12, 25, 105, 120–128, 187–192
Leonard, Ralph 120
Leonard, Sibyl Hitt 124–125
Lewis, Duffy 25, 105, 122, 125
Lieb, Fred 158
Lightning 98
Lindberg, Richard 28
Loras College Athletic Hall of Fame 35
Love, Slim 105, 125
Luderlus, Fred 36, 183
Lynn, Byrd 28
Lyons, Ted 22, 33, 86, 165, 191

Mack, Connie 4–5–, 47, 61, 78, 102, 140, 142
Mails, Duster 39, 77, 82
Maisel, Fritz 66, 131

Mamaux, Al 38
Mann, Les 157–159, 176
Maranville, Rabbit 177
Marberry, Fred 62, 161, 164–165
Marcum, Johnny 149
Marichal, Juan 64
Marquard, Rube 38–39, 123
Martin, Pepper 47
Mathewson, Christy 21, 69, 82, 92, 113, 137, 140, 142
Mayer, Erskine 122
Mays, Carl 6, 13, 23, 69, 122–123, 153–155, 163, 168, 191
McAleer, James 121
McAllister, Jack 80
McBride, George 170
McCaffery, J.J. 66
McCormick, Bill 176
McDonald, Hank 61
McGinnity, Joe 64
McGrath, W.H. 184
McGraw, Bob 27, 163
McGraw, John 13, 17, 20, 44, 78, 138–139, 151, 154–159
McInnis, Stuffy 169
McKechnie, Bill 117
McQuillen, Hugh 101
Meadows, Lee 5, 191
Meany, Tom 49
Medwick, Joe 108
Meine, Heinie 48
Merkle, Fred 123
Merritt, Herm 107
Milan, Clyde 108
Miller, Bing 47
Miller, Doc 138
Miller, Hack 177
Miller, Otto 110
Millken, Stanley 104
Mitchell, Clarence 5, 12, 15, 39, 43, 64, 111–119, 126, 187–189, 191–192
Mitchell, Clarence, Jr. 117
Mitchell, Fred 129
Mitchell, Marion 117
Mitchell, Wallace 112, 117
Mitchell, Willie 103
Moistening agents 3–4, 20, 36, 45, 57, 79, 112, 130, 133, 152, 184
Moore, Johnny 62
Moore, Randy 61
Moore, Wilcy 73
Moran, Pat 133–134
Moriarty, George 22, 80, 87–88
Most Valuable Player of World Series 27, 82
Mostil, Johnny 30
Mowrey, Mike 124
Mud balls 4
Murdock, Eugene 20, 68
Mueller, Heinie 37
Musial, Stan 89
Myers, Hi 106, 123

National Baseball Hall of Fame 19, 33–34, 51, 64, 75, 88
Navin, Frank 128
Nebraska Sports Hall of Fame 119
Nehf, Art 191
Neis, Bernie 176

Nelson, Gaylord 89
Nelson, Willie 89
Nemec, Raymond J. 78, 137
Neyer, Rob 13
Niekro, Joe 88
Niekro, Phil 88
Nixon, Richard 51
No-hitters 19, 66, 90, 123, 125
Nunamaker, Les 66, 102–103, 131

O'Day, Hank 4
O'Doul, Lefty 85
Oldring, Rube 102
Oliver, Ted C. 2, 29
O'Loughlin, Silk 58, 102–103
Olson, Ivy 37, 106, 176
O'Neal, Skinny 177–178
O'Neil, Mickey 176
O'Neill, Steve 77, 85, 98
Orth, Al 57

Palmer, Pete 27, 41, 82, 86
Paul, Andrea 111–112, 116
Peckinpaugh, Roger 60, 86
Peel, Homer 108
Pegler, Westbrook 96
Pennock, Herb 64, 73, 75, 140, 191
Perfect game 19
Perritt, Pol 26
Perry, Gaylord 13, 88
Perry, Jim 88
Picinich, Val 164
Pick, Charlie 66, 176
Picus, Anna Czarik 54
Picus, John Quinn *see* Quinn, Jack
Picus, Michael 54
Piercy, Bill 60, 146
Pipgras, George 73
Pipp, Wally 68–69
Plank, Eddie 66, 131, 140
Polish-American Hall of Fame 88–89
Potter, Nelson 14
Povich, Shirley 12, 169
Powell, Ray 176
Pratt, Del 66, 105, 131
Prediger, Marion Rudolph 140, 144
Price, Jim 138
Proctor, Donald 135–136
Prouty, Pat 30

Quinn, Georgenia Lambert 64
Quinn, Jack 4–7, 10, 13–14, 53–64, 87, 89, 105, 119, 187–192

Raised seams on baseball 68, 147
Rariden, Bill 26, 138
Rath, Morrie 133
Reese, Bonesetter 87
Relief pitchers 31, 61, 134, 161, 164–165
Rhyne, Hal 149
Rice, Grantland 46–47, 50, 102
Rickey, Branch 14, 92, 134, 146–147, 158, 181, 183–184
Risberg, Swede 25, 28, 133
Rixey, Eppa 86, 191
Roberts, Robin 69
Robertson, Dave 26, 154–155
Robertson, Gene 76

Robinson, Wilbert 38, 41, 43, 82, 94, 176
Rommel, Eddie 29, 191
Roosevelt, Franklin D. 178
Rose, Pete 135
Ross, Daniel 51
Rowland, Clarence 22, 25, 27, 33
Rudolph, Alice 144
Rudolph, Dick 5, 12, 137–144, 187–192
Ruel, Muddy 164
Ruether, Dutch 73
Ruffing, Red 117, 141
Ruppert, Jacob 163
Russell, Allan 5, 12, 161–166, 187–190, 192
Russell, Clarence 161
Russell, Myrtle 166
Russell, Myrtle Rebecca 166
Russell, Reb 22, 25–26
Ruth, Babe 4, 9, 25, 37, 49, 60, 72, 84, 103, 122–123, 154, 162, 181
Ryan, Rosy 5, 165

Salaries 19, 28, 41, 44–45, 50, 57–58, 71, 74, 94, 104, 124, 126, 131, 133, 134, 139, 143, 159, 168
Sallee, Slim 9, 25, 133, 191
Sanborn, I.E. 4, 21, 153
Sanders, Roy 5, 11
Saves 32, 61–62, 81, 163–164
Scandals 11, 25, 28, 30–31, 127–128, 133
Schalk, Ray 22, 25, 28, 31, 22
Schang, Wally 154
Schneider, Pete 131
Schumacher, Hal 118
Score, Herb 179
Scott, Everett 25, 60, 122
Scott, Jack 44
Scott, Jim 23
Severeid, Hank 123
Sewell, Joe 77, 84–85, 106, 110
Shanks, Howard 164
Shannon, E.A. 180
Shattenbrand, Leopold 90
Shawkey, Bob 60, 72, 106, 140
Shealy, Al 74, 88
Shellenback, Frank 12, 13
Sherdel, Bill 5, 46
Sherman, James S. 57
Shine balls 4, 9, 11
Shivetts, Anna 89
Shockcor, Anna Spies 65
Shockcor, Urbain *see* Shocker, Urban
Shockcor, William 65
Shocker, Urban 5, 6, 10–13, 20, 65–76, 94, 131, 187–192
Shook, Hazel Doak 97
Shore, Ernie 105, 122–123, 125
Short, Ed 14

Simmons, Al 46–47, 89
Sisler, George 69
Skipper, John C. 31
Smith, Billy 181
Smith, Bob 176
Smith, Carr 85–86
Smith, Elmer 39, 41, 77, 82
Smith, George 115–116
Smith, Mrs. J.O. 97
Smith, Red 14
Smith, Sherry 39, 81–82, 176
Sothoron, Allen 11–12, 62, 105, 145–150, 187–189, 192
Sothoron, Bernard 145
Sothoron, Dorothy Clemens 150
Sothoron, Harriett 150
Sothoron, Ida 145
Southworth, Billy 72
Speaker, Tris 4, 24, 77, 84–85, 98, 106–107, 120, 122, 127–128, 168
Speece, Byron 85
Spitball pitchers: early 4, 13; exempted 1920 5; grandfathered 1921 12–13; illegal 13, 15; not exempted 5, 11; rankings 187–192
Spitballs: criticism of 6–8, 13, 79; definition 3; early efforts to ban 4; how thrown 3, 37, 79–80, 133; 1920 rule 4; 1921 rule 12; recent efforts to reinstate 13–15
Stack, C.P. 92
Stallings, George 140
Stanage, Oscar 22, 58
Standaert, Jerry 43
Stant, Glenn 156
Steinberg, Steve 5, 90, 96
Stengel, Casey 37–38, 49
Stephenson, Riggs 32
Stern, Bill 98
Street, Gabby 46–47, 58
Strunk, Amos 169
Suicide attempt 30
Sullivan, John 176
Suspensions 50, 58, 70, 99, 103–105, 107
Sweeney, Bill 138

Taylor, John I. 120
Taylor, Zack 42–43
Teachout, Bud 47
Tener, John K. 6
Terry, Bill 44–45, 118, 165
Tesreau, Jeff 13
Thomas, Miles 76
Thomas, Tommy 31
Thompson, Fresco 44
Thorn, John 5, 29, 44–45, 80–81, 85, 87, 122
Thurston, Hollis 71
Tiant, Luis 80
Tipple, Dan 191

Toney, Fred 5
Trachtenberg, Leo 73
Trull, Ethel Rudolph 144
Tuero, Oscar 5
Tyler, Lefty 137, 140, 154

Uhle, George 192

Vance, Dazzy 34, 42–43, 118, 191
Vaughan, Irving 70, 73
Vaughn, Hippo 58, 101, 191
Veach, Bobby 22, 165
Veeck, Bill 4, 8
Vidmer, Richards 116
Vincent, Fay 160

Wagner, Honus 37
Walker, Curt 90
Walsh, Ed 4, 6–7, 13, 84, 112, 152, 174
Walters, Al 105, 125
Wambsganss, Bill 39, 77, 82, 110
Ward, Arch 33
Ward, Chuck 38
Ward, John J. 91, 103
Warner, Jack 126
Weaver, Buck 22, 25–26, 28, 135
Webb, Earl 32
Weis, Al 42–43
West, Fred 127
Wheat, Zach 37, 43, 106, 123–124, 176
Wheatley, Cliff 176–177
Williams, Cy 90
Williams, Jesse 112
Williams, Lefty 12, 26, 28
Williams, Robert 50
Wilson, Hack 47
Wingo, Ivy 133
Witt, Whitey 69
Wolverton, Harry 58, 100
Wood, Joe 23, 122, 127
World Series 65, 72–74, 77, 81–83, 86, 88, 106, 108, 111, 114–117, 119–120, 122–124, 126, 133, 140, 144–145, 149, 154–155, 165
World tour 20–21, 27
World War I 27, 38–39, 68, 114, 125, 131, 154, 163, 170, 175, 182
Worth, Muriel *see* Leonard, Sybil Hitt
Wright, Marshall 138

York, Rudy 150
Young, Cy 29, 125
Young, Nick 168

Zachary, Tom 165
Zbick, Jim 54, 57
Zeider, Rollie 129
Zimmerman, Heinie 26

www.ingramcontent.com/pod-product-compliance
Lightning Source LLC
Chambersburg PA
CBHW081159230426
43666CB00016B/2863